WITHDRAWN

D1598919

WITHDRAWN

The Poems of
HENRY KING
BISHOP OF CHICHESTER

The [Poems] of
HENRY KING

EDITED BY

MARGARET CRUM

OXFORD

AT THE CLARENDON PRESS

1965

Oxford University Press, Amen House, London E.C.4

GLASGOW NEW YORK TORONTO MELBOURNE WELLINGTON
BOMBAY CALCUTTA MADRAS KARACHI LAHORE DACCA
CAPE TOWN SALISBURY NAIROBI IBADAN
KUALA LUMPUR HONG KONG

PRINTED IN GREAT BRITAIN
AT THE UNIVERSITY PRESS, OXFORD
BY VIVIAN RIDLER
PRINTER TO THE UNIVERSITY

PREFACE

THIS edition was undertaken because of suggestions contained in Dr. Percy Simpson's article in the *Bodleian Quarterly Record* for March 1929, 'The Bodleian Manuscripts of Henry King'. He described 'Hannah's manuscript', which had then newly come to light, and had been acquired for the Bodleian in 1928; he showed its connexion with Henry King himself, and its relation to the Malone manuscript of King's poems already in the Bodleian; he also printed, from other Bodleian manuscripts, poems which Lawrence Mason, in a doctoral dissertation of 1913, had attributed to Henry King, and others which he saw belonged with them; and he suggested the possibility that more were to be found in a related collection in the British Museum (Harleian MSS. 6917–18).

By the generosity of Sir Geoffrey Keynes, who had lately (in 1952) added the Phillipps manuscript to his collection at Hampstead, I was able to work with all three of King's surviving collections, an opportunity which earlier editors had not possessed. It was found that Mason's attributions were based on his confusion of the hand of Henry King with that of his brother John, and that the canon was in fact smaller, and not larger, than had been thought. But if there was nothing to add, the three manuscript collections, taken together, seemed to throw enough light on the text of the authentic poems to justify a new edition, in which a text very close to Henry King's own original copies could be provided; and from which John's poems should be excluded.

The manuscripts also suggested a chronological arrangement. In the following pages the occasional poems are printed first in chronological order, followed by the undated poems in what the manuscripts suggest to be approximately the order of their composition.

Sir Edmund Gosse, in the excitement of his discovery of Donne, claimed for him the credit for Henry King's poems as well as his own. In the light of the manuscripts, and a perhaps closer acquaintance now with the character of King's writing, it is not possible to agree when Gosse says: 'We need not question that the Dean [Donne] saw, and even possibly touched up, the majority of [King's] poems'; nor should Gosse's judgement of King as 'the earliest of Donne's disciples in poetry' be repeated.

I have received much kindness in preparing this edition, and thank those who gave it. In the earliest stages Dr. Helen Gardner, with Miss Helen Darbishire, Dr. G. K. A. Bell, then Bishop of Chichester, and Professor F. P. Wilson, gave encouragement and advice; Mr. Philip Robinson, as well as Sir Geoffrey Keynes, generously deposited a manuscript for me to use in the Bodleian; Mrs. Vivian Ridler, Miss Anne Whiteman, and Mr. Paul Morgan have read different parts of the introduction, and (so far as I was capable) I have gratefully carried out their suggestions, and those of Miss Jonquil Bevan and of the Rev. Michael Gallagher, S. J., who looked at some of the page proofs; my brother Michael transcribed and played to me Dr. John Wilson's settings of King's songs; the librarians of Trinity College and of St. John's College, Cambridge, showed me manuscripts in their keeping; and the governing bodies of those colleges have given their permission to quote from their manuscripts. It will be clear that I am indebted to the earlier editors of King's poems—Archdeacon John Hannah (1843); Lawrence Mason (1914); Saintsbury in *Minor Poets of the Caroline Period*, iii (1921), and John Sparrow (1925)—and to the writers of other books mentioned in the course of this one. Though I had enjoyed conversation with Mr. Ronald Berman, his book, *Henry King and the Seventeenth Century*, appeared when mine was virtually finished; it is not from want of respect that his views are unmentioned here. Whatever deficiencies are found in this edition would have been greater if I had not, while I was occupied with it, been working in the Department of Western Manuscripts at the Bodleian. The debt to the care and skill of those concerned at the Clarendon Press is everywhere apparent.

M. C. C.

Islip April 1965

CONTENTS

CONTENTS

CONTENTS

CONTENTS

CONTENTS

ABBREVIATIONS

Manuscripts of King's poems

H	Bodl. MS. Eng. poet. e. 30.
M	Bodl. MS. Malone 22.
P	Phillipps MS. 9325, owned by Sir Geoffrey Keynes.
MSS.	*H*, *M*, and *P*.

Other abbreviations for manuscripts are explained as they are used, except for these three, which occur often:

Add.	British Museum Add. MS. 25707.
Harl.	British Museum Harl. MSS. 6917–18.
TM	Thomas Manne's notebook, owned by Mr. Philip Robinson.
misc. MSS.	numerous miscellaneous manuscript copies.

Printed books

1657, 1664	*Poems, Elegies, Paradoxes and Sonnets,* 1657, and second issue, 1664.
misc. pr.	miscellaneous early printed copies.
Hannah	*Poems and Psalms by Henry King,* edited by the Rev. J. Hannah, B.A., Fellow of Lincoln College, 1843.
Mason	*The English Poems of Henry King,* edited by Lawrence Mason, Ph.D., 1914.
Sparrow	*The Poems of Bishop Henry King,* edited by John Sparrow, Nonesuch Press, 1925.

INTRODUCTION

LIFE OF HENRY KING

THE family to which Henry King belonged was eminent in the Church and in some favour at Court for just over a century, under the later Tudors and the earlier Stuarts. Robert King, the last Abbot of Osney, became the first Bishop of Oxford in 1542. His nephew Philip, who in his minority was a page to Henry VIII, inherited Bishop Robert's estates, and lived at Worminghall in Buckinghamshire. Here his twelve children were born, and Henry, his grandson. On Henry's father, Philip's fourth son, John King, the family's reputation mainly rested. By the third generation after his, their name was no longer heard.

Fuller gave the following account of John King in the *Church-History of Britain*, 1656:[1]

He was Chaplain to Queen ELIZABETH, and as he was appointed by Her Councel to preach the first *Sermon* at Court when Her Body lay Inhearsed in the Chappel of *White-Hall*, so was he designed for the first *Sermon* to Her Successour King JAMES at *Charter-House* when He entred *London*, then sworn his first *Chaplain*; Who commonly called him *the King of Preachers*. And Sir *Edward Coke* would say of him, *He was the best Speaker in Starre-Chamber in his time*. Soon after he was made Dean of *Christ-Church, Oxon*; and chosen one of the four Preachers in the Conference at *Hampton-Court*. Then advanced to the Bishoprick of *London*: Where he let the world see his high Place of Government, did not cause him to forget his Office in the Pulpit; shewing by his example, That *a Bishop might Govern and Preach too*. In which service he was so frequent, that unlesse hindred by want of health, he omitted no Sunday whereon he did not visit some Pulpit in *London*, or neer it.

The Papists raised an aspersion, as false, as foule, upon him; That, *at his death he was reconciled to the Church of* Rome, sufficiently confuted by those eye- and ear-witnesses, present at his pious

[1] x. 91.

departure. . . .[1] Something, Bp. *King* endevoured in the repairing of S. *Paul's*; but alas! a private mans estate may be invisibly buried under the rubbish of the least Chappel therein. By order in his *Will* he provided, that nothing should be written on his plain Grave-stone, save only RESURGAM: and still he is alive, both in his memory, and happy posterity.

Izaak Walton's generous character of him was 'an Angel of our once glorious Church, and now no common Star in heaven'.[2]

Henry, who was in Fuller's mind when he spoke of John King's 'happy posterity', was his eldest son, and was thought[3] to 'beare a lively image both of his person and vertues'. He was born 'in the same . . . chamber . . . wherein his father had received his first breath', and baptized at Worminghall, 16 January 1591/2.[4] By 1594 John King was 'farre from the native place both of [his] birth and breede', in York, preaching 'to the most intelligent auditory of the place' forty-eight 'Lectures upon Jonas'.[5] He was domestic chaplain to the archbishop, John Piers, whose funeral sermon he preached in the Minster on 17 November 1594.[6] His wife was with him in York, and their next son, John, was born there in 1595. Three younger sons were born in the south: Robert in Berkshire about 1598, and William and Philip in London, about 1601 and 1603; there were also four daughters. Strong affection bound this family, and for all of them but one there is evidence that in later years there existed some special tie with the eldest brother.

In 1597 the York sermons were published with an 'Epistle Dedicatorie' to the Lord Keeper, Sir Thomas Egerton, in which King speaks of himself as the keeper's chaplain, 'being yet to begin my first houres attendance'. This was, as Walton said, 'the time of Mr. *Donnes* being his Lordships Secretary',[7] and

---

[1] This refers to Henry King's *Sermon . . . touching the supposed Apostasie of . . . John King*, 1621.   [2] *The Life of John Donne*, 1658, sig. A5ᵛ.

[3] By Henry Mason, one of the Bishop's chaplains. 'Epistle Dedicatory', to Henry King, of *Christian Humiliation, or A Treatise of Fasting*, 1625.

[4] Wood, *Athenae Oxonienses*, ed. Bliss, 1813–20, iii. 839, and *Hannah*, p. i, from Worminghall Register of Baptisms.

[5] *Lectures upon Ionas delivered at Yorke . . . 1594*, 1597.

[6] Printed 1597, op. cit., pp. 661–83.   [7] *Life of Donne*, p. 44.

the beginning of that friendship between Donne and John King which he calls 'a marriage of souls'.[1] Henry King was in his earliest childhood when he first saw Donne; and to this time also belongs the recollection mentioned by him in a letter printed at the beginning of Walton's life of Hooker: 'though I dare not say that I knew Mr. *Hooker*; yet, as our Ecclesiastical History reports to the honour of *Ignatius*, that he lived in the time of S. *John*, and had seen him in his Childhood; so I also joy that in my Minority I have often seen Mr. *Hooker* with my Father.'[2] Other friends in this revered circle were Dr. John Spenser, the Cranmers, who were connexions of Spenser's by marriage, and the family of Archbishop Sandys. When Dr. Spenser died in 1614 he left his manuscript of the *Ecclesiastical Polity* to John King. Henry's Latin elegy on his death is in the Bodleian Library;[3] it is a fair copy heavily bordered with black ink, and at the corners are pin-holes, suggesting that this paper was actually fastened to the hearse.

In 1603/4 John King was, according to Hannah, 'one of the only two Clergymen below the rank of Bishops and Deans, who were called to attend at the Hampton Court Conference . . . on the Ecclesiastical side'.[4] In October 1604 the king granted the petition of Christ Church, Oxford, that he should be their dean,[5] and the family settled in Oxford. When James I, with the queen and Prince Henry, visited the University in 1605 John King preached a sermon in English, and took part in disputations at St. Mary's. It was in 1606 that he was appointed to be one of four preachers to address the Scottish clergy at Hampton Court.[6] He was Vice-Chancellor of Oxford University from 1607 until he became Bishop of London in 1611.

The last ten years of his life were quiet and prosperous. By

---

[1] Op. cit., Epistle Dedicatory, sig. A5.

[2] *The Life of Mr. Richard Hooker*, 1665, sig. A3ᵛ. Henry King was not quite nine years old when Hooker died.　　　　[3] MS. Rawl. D. 912, fol. 305.

[4] *Hannah*, p. v; S. R. Gardiner, *History of England, 1603–1642*, i, 1887, p. 153.

[5] The petition, signed by thirty-two members of the college, is Bodl. MS. Wood F. 28, fol. 209; printed *Hannah*, pp. xc–xci.

[6] *Hannah*, p. v. Hannah cites Spotswood's *History of the Church of Scotland*, 1655, p. 497.

one incident his almost untried integrity was illustrated. This was his opposition, alone with George Abbot, to the king's will concerning the divorce of the Earl of Essex in 1613. Fuller says he afterwards spoke of the trial to Bishop Overall 'to this effect, *I should never have been so earnest against the Divorce, save that because perswaded in my conscience of falshood in some of the depositions of the Witnesses on the Ladies behalf*'.[1] Abbot was present at the lady's wedding to the Earl of Somerset: John King was not.[2] It was to this uncompromising man, Walton says,[3] as to 'his dear friend', that Donne went when he decided to take orders: 'That Reverend man did receive the news with much gladnesse, and after some expressions of joy, and a perswasion to be constant in his pious purpose, he proceeded with all convenient speed to ordain him both *Deacon* and *Priest*.'

Towards the end of Bishop John King's life there was a renewed effort to restore the fabric of St. Paul's; the steeple was nearing ruin 'by the corroding quality of the Coale smoake, especially in moist weather, whereunto it had been so long subject'.[4] James I came in state on 26 March 1620 to hear the bishop preach 'on a Text given him by his Majesty as pertinent to the business in hand, *viz.* on *Psalme* 102. *ver.* 13 & 14',[5] and afterwards 'repaired to the Bishops Palace, with his . . . Nobles and the whole train of his servants attending him; where they were magnificently entertained with severall set Banquets'. John King undertook to contribute £100 a year to the restoration. Henry was a commissioner. Fuller's hint at disastrous generosity in this cause is contradicted by a letter of John Chamberlain's at the time of the bishop's death: he 'left a goode state (they say) to the value of twelve or fifteen thousand pound'.[6]

His intention had been that all his five sons should be ordained.

[1] *Church-History of Britain*, 1655, x. 67–68.
[2] *The Letters of John Chamberlain*, ed. N. E. McClure, 1939, i. 496.
[3] *Life of Donne*, pp. 43–44. Donne's ordination was 23 January 1614/15; see *John Donne, Complete Poetry and Selected Prose*, ed. John Hayward, 1929, pp. 465–6.
[4] *The History of St. Paul's Cathedral*, by W. Dugdale, 1658, sigs. Mm1ᵛ–Nn1ᵛ; cf. p. 19 below.
[5] 'Both preached and published by his Majesties commandement'. See also Chamberlain's *Letters*, ii. 297.   [6] *Letters*, ii. 360.

Henry, in the sermon alluded to by Fuller, 'touching the sup-posed Apostasie of ... John King', said of him that 'as a Torch hee consumed himselfe to light others; and, when Himselfe should faile, provided, so farre as in him lay, for a succession in his Blood, to set *hand* to the same *plough*; having dedicated (in his desire) all his Sonnes (in act Two) to the Ministery of this Church, and by no meanes willing to heare of any other course (though otherwise invited by Gracious offers for some of them in particular) to be undertaken by them, save that function alone'.[1]

Henry and his next brother had been sent to Westminster School, where they were both King's Scholars. Wood says that Henry was 'educated partly in grammar learning' at Thame Free School;[2] possibly he was left behind as an infant in Bucking-hamshire when his parents went to York, and began his schooling at Thame. Westminster differed from other schools in starting Greek earlier, in order to gain time for Hebrew in the top form,[3] a difference which probably commended it to John King as giving the best preparation for divine studies.

Much time was spent, here as in other schools, in the study of classical poetry and rhetoric, and in making epistles, themes, declamations, orations, and epigrams, in Greek and Latin, prose and verse.[4] An old Westminster had told Archbishop Laud by 1630 that the boys in the top forms were sometimes set to turn 'Latin and Greek verse into English verse';[5] and perhaps it is not a chance coincidence that so many seventeenth-century poets— of various stature—were Westminster boys: among them are Dryden, Jonson, Cowley, George Herbert (Henry King's exact contemporary), Randolph, Alabaster, Strode, Corbet, William Cartwright, Giles Fletcher, Martin Lluellyn, and Jasper Mayne.

---

[1] *A Sermon . . .*, 1621, pp. 62–63.

[2] *Athenae Oxonienses*, iii. 839, and Bodl. MS. Wood D. 11, fol. 172ᵛ.

[3] *William Shakspere's Small Latine and Lesse Greeke*, by T. W. Baldwin, 1944, i. 384.

[4] *Annals of Westminster School*, by J. Sargeaunt, 1898, chapters iii, 'The Early Curriculum', and iv; *Educational Charters and Documents, 598–1909*, by A. F. Leach, 1911, pp. 508–17.

[5] Laud's account of routine at Westminster, 1630, printed by Baldwin, op. cit. i. 360. C. Hoole, in *A New Discovery of the old Art of Teaching Schoole*, 1660 (quoted by Baldwin, ii. 395), speaks of English versification as an innovation needing to be justified.

The dates of the brothers' arrival at Westminster are not known, but they will have missed Camden, who retired from the headmastership in 1598, and were probably too young to come into contact with Lancelot Andrewes, Dean of Westminster from 1601 to 1605. When in the summer of 1606 the University of Oxford prepared a book of verses to be presented to the queen's brother, King Christian of Denmark, on his visit to England, four epigrammatic lines in Latin by Henry, and two by John (then aged about eleven), were copied amongst those of their father's colleagues.[1] There was probably little doubt of their election to Christ Church, which happened in 1608. Wood says that Henry was 'put under the tuition of a noted tutor', and John 'under . . . a good tutor'.[2]

The relationship between Henry and John was more like that of twins than of brothers divided in age by three years. They took their degrees together, B.A. 19 June 1611, M.A. 7 July 1614, and later on B.D. and D.D. 19 May 1625. They commemorated their companionship in the names of their own sons, each calling his first John, another Henry. The character of their English verse reflects this condition of their early life: Henry is slow, giving an impression of ample time to consider, to explore, and to define; John is facile, imitative, not unduly critical, and can have seen little difficulty in keeping pace with him.

Henry's departure from Christ Church is mentioned in the college disbursement books: 'Mr. King abiit July 10 1616.' By the patronage of his father he had become prebendary of St. Pancras at St. Paul's on 24 January 1615/16. John Chamberlain wrote to Sir Dudley Carleton on 21 December 1616,[3] with much incorrect detail: 'By the death of Dr. Pasfield[4] one of the principall prebends or masters of Powles (as they call them) that place is bestowed on the bishop of Londons eldest sonne, a youth of two and twenty yeares old, who is well provided alredy of

---

[1] 'Charites Oxonienses', British Museum MS. Royal 12 A. LXIV. I owe this reference to Mr. Geoffrey Bill. The boys' verses are on fol. 44.

[2] *Athenae Oxonienses*, iii. 839, and ii. 632.

[3] *Letters*, ii. 44.

[4] Pasfield was really succeeded by the Bishop's chaplain, Richard Cluet.

spirituall livings, besides a younge wife worth fowre or five thousand pound at least daughter to Robin Barkley (yf you knew him) and brought up with her aunt at Oxford.' Two days after Chamberlain's indignant letter John, though still only a deacon, was given the prebend of Kentish Town.

Henry's wife was Anne, elder daughter of Robert Berkeley of Boycourt in the parish of Ulcombe, Kent, grand-daughter of Sir Maurice Berkeley; their name was ancient and famous.[1] The 'aunt at Oxford' was one of Lady Berkeley's family, the Loughers of Tenby, Pembrokeshire; she was Anne Berkeley's great-aunt and godmother, the widow of the second Principal of Jesus College, Dr. Griffith Lloyd. Robert Berkeley's will, dated 22 May 1614, when Anne was about 14 years old, had left her his 'silver Bason and Ewer only[,] uppon perswasion that [his] good Aunte Lloyd will bestowe her in marriage accordinge to her promise as shee hathe heatherunto freely given her education'.[2] He died in the following September, and Mrs. Lloyd also died before Anne married, leaving the child most of her 'goods move-ables and imm[ov]eables', and ultimately the house, gardens, and orchards they had leased from Brasenose College.[3] The will was proved 11 July 1615. Disputes over both this will and Robert Berkeley's, on which sentences were given 13 June 1616, were perhaps connected with Anne's marriage to Henry King.

The writers of verses on her death a few years later show wonder at her unspectacular choice. Robert Gomersall said:

> Sure there were Velvet-cloakes that woo'd, & those
> That could weare Scarlet;[4]

---

[1] See *The Berkeley Manuscripts*, ed. Sir John Maclean, 1883–5, vols. i–ii, 'A rela-tion of the lives of the Lord Berkeleys of Berkeley Castle ... from ... 1066 ... until ... 1618', by John Smyth, steward of the hundred of Berkeley. In 1624 Smyth added Henry Kinge as Anne Berkeley's husband; in 1628 he mentioned their children John and Henry: op. cit. i. 267.

[2] Cope 129; proved 13 June 1616, after dispute. Robert Berkeley's memorial verses, which are on the south wall of the nave of Canterbury Cathedral, were printed in *Parnassus Biceps*, 1656, p. 95; and John Smyth quoted them in his 'Lives of the Lord Berkeleys'.

[3] Rudd 67; sentence after dispute, 13 June 1616, Cope 55.

[4] *Poems*, 1633, p. 2.

and her brother-in-law John:

> Her Consort was, as was her soule, Divine;
> what greater Titles wooed her might repine,
> she would devote herselfe to bee his bride
> whose calling wean'd her from all pompe and pride.[1]

What she herself was to Henry King is intimated in his 'Exequy', but there is no detail there, and only faint suggestions of her character are given by lesser elegists. Thomas Goffe remembered her relations with Bishop John King, claiming his welcome for her as sharer of his tomb, 'Who once too nere thy soul could never rest.'[2] Respect and warmth of affection emerge from amongst some fantastic lines by the younger John King:

> Thy gift, thy Candlestick I prize
> first cause twas thine,
> . . . this saw
> thy secret gestures, with what awe
> thy Chamber thou a Church didst make,
> which holines from thee did take.[3]

They lived in the parish of St. Gregory by St. Paul's, the church of which was on the south side of the cathedral, near the west end. (It was burnt in the fire of 1666.) This was probably the 'new dwelling house near St. Paul's Church Yard' which Bishop John King mentioned in his will,[4] provided by him for their use. By his patronage Henry became Archdeacon of Colchester,[5] 10 April 1617, and sinecure rector of Fulham, 18 November 1618. An ill-natured comment on the young man's first sermon was made by John Chamberlain, 8 November 1617:[6]

On Wensday the fifth of this present younge Kinge the bishop of

---

[1] British Museum MS. Harl. 6917, fol. 91ᵛ; cf. Appendix II (i).

[2] Bodl. MS. Rawl. D. 398, fols. 172–3. John King copied an 'Elegie' and an 'Epitaph' together, and subscribed them 'Tho: Goff'; it was common practice for a poet to append a brief epitaph to an elegy, and Goffe probably wrote both; but cf. *Bodleian Quarterly Record*, v, 1926–9, pp. 331–2. Thomas Goffe was a year behind Henry and John King at Westminster and at Christ Church.

[3] MS. Harl. 6917, fol. 90ᵛ; see Appendix II (i).

[4] An abstract of this will was printed in *Hannah*, pp. cvii–cviii.

[5] In 1635 he was one of three archdeacons of the diocese of London who 'made no return at all' to the Bishop, 'so that he can certify nothing but what has come to his knowledge without their help'. *Works of Laud*, Library of Anglo-Catholic Theology, v, 1853, 332. [6] *Letters*, ii. 114.

Londons eldest sonne of the age of 23 yeares preacht at Paules-crosse. Yt was thought a bold part of them both that so younge a man shold play his first prises in such a place and such a time, beeing as he professed the *primitiæ* of his vocation, and the first sermon that ever he made, but this world (as they say) is made for the presumptuous: he did reasonablie well but nothing extra-ordinarie, nor neere his father, beeing rather slow of utterance *orator parum vehemens*.

When towards the end of the year 1621, after the Bishop's death, the report 'that he was reconciled to the Church of Rome' 'like a Snow-ball by rolling [was] growne greater', Henry King undertook his defence modestly enough: 'I have at last ad-ventured to speake: Not that I hold my selfe fit or able for this taske at any time, much lesse now; but onely for that I hoped what I should say might win more beliefe, as having been an eare-witnesse, and which is more . . . an eye-witnes of all his last passages, and could beare record against his Accusers fals-hood, as Saint *John* did of the truth, *Quod vidimus, quod audi-vimus, &c.*'[1] Henry King's poetry on the occasion is in the passage on the moment of his father's death: 'which, as if reserved by Gods favour, was that very day his Saviour dyde on, *Good Friday*: and that time of the day when our whole Church was exercised in prayer, according to the custome of that Day (neere eleven of the clocke in the fore-noone) as if he had stayed to take the helpe and advantage of good mens devotion to set him forward'.[2]

When the Bishop died, Henry and Anne had two children, John (his godson) aged a year and a half, and Anne five weeks.[3] An earlier John had died in infancy (one of the best of his uncle John King's poems was written on his death).[4] The Parish Register of St. Gregory by St. Paul's gives the baptisms of all

---

[1] *A Sermon*, 1621, p. 51. When the sermon was published Henry added a note denying a rumour that he and the younger John had deserted the reformed Church. The Roman Catholic story was elaborated in *The Bishop of London his legacy*, 1623/4 (cf. A. F. Allison and D. M. Rogers, *Catalogue of Catholic Books . . . 1558–1640*, 1956, nos. 555–6).   [2] Op. cit., p. 69.

[3] Funeral Certificate, quoted by Hannah, p. xiii.

[4] See Appendix II (i). Printed as Henry's in *Mason*, p. 173, in *Saintsbury*, p. 269, and in *Sparrow*, p. 152.

the other children: the second John, 9 December 1619; Anne, 3 April 1621; Henry, 4 April 1622; and Philip, 6 October 1623. Anne died before her second birthday, and was buried 3 January 1622/3. The mother died the following year and was buried 5 January 1623/4.[1]

On his wife's death Henry King wrote the poem 'An Exequy' for which he is remembered. Much of his earlier writing may seem to deserve attention rather as preparing the way for the 'Exequy' than as poetry in its own right. 'The Anniverse', for the sixth year after it, suggests that he wrote little during that interval, for of King's earlier poems only one is likely to have grown from the state of mind he describes, that 'Desert . . . Sprung out of my lone thoughts, which know no path But what my own misfortune beaten hath'; the exception is the enigmatic piece 'On two Children dying of one Disease, and buryed in one Grave', enigmatic because the misfortune can have been King's in fear only. Of the three boys who survived their mother, Philip died a child and was buried 25 January 1627/8. John and Henry both grew up, and died after the Restoration. The existence of this poem may be seen as a warning against taking literally every situation so described.[2]

If there was an arid period after the 'Exequy', it came to an end soon after 'The Anniverse'. 'By Occasion of the young Prince his happy Birth, May 29 1630', though it takes the form of apology for lateness, is unlikely to have been delayed for very long; the elegy on Donne's death was written soon after its occasion, 31 March 1631; and the elegy on Gustavus Adolphus, who died in November 1632, was printed in *The Swedish Intelligencer* in 1633. Other poetry, on less solemn themes, seems to belong to the same years.

Even before Anne's death, King's poetry was seldom the immediate outcome of happy feeling. The happiness there must have been is reflected only in the fullness of his apprehension of

[1] Dr. Percy Simpson found that the register was kept at St. Martin's, Ludgate. He extracted the King entries, and printed them in the *Bodleian Quarterly Record*, v, 1926–9, p. 333. Henry King is called 'Residentiary' in the register.

[2] See Appendix I, p. 247.

transience and loss. The pessimistic 'Sic Vita' and 'Midd-night Meditation' were among the favourites of his contemporaries, and what was expected of him may appear from Bodleian MS. Don. d. 58, where Bacon's paraphrase of an epigram from the Planudean Anthology attributed to Posidippus, 'The world's a bubble', was headed 'Dr. King before his death'.[1] His later poems, whether because of a natural bent or because in some measure the mood of the 'Exequy' persisted, show that if his contemporaries expected the best writing to come from his most serious frame of mind, they were right.

Henry King was sometimes at Oxford after his wife's death. His brother John had returned to Christ Church, and was the University's Public Orator from 1622 till 1625, when he resigned the place to his youngest brother, Philip.[2] Henry and John became Canons of Christ Church, Henry on 3 March 1623/4, John on 28 August in the same year. In 1625 they took the degrees of B.D. and D.D., as 'accumulators and compounders'; the reason they gave for being unwilling to wait for the usual time to elapse between B.D. and D.D. was that Henry as Archdeacon of Colchester, and John as 'Clericus' appointed by the Chapter of Christ Church, were to attend the next Convocation, 'et pro dignitate loci hoc gradu adornari cupia[n]t.'[3] On Act Sunday they preached at St. Mary's, Henry in the morning on 'David's Enlargement', and John in the afternoon on 'David's Strait'. They printed their sermons together, with the text on the title-page, 'Behold how good, and how pleasant it is, for brethren to dwell together in unitie.' Henry is described on the title-page as 'one of his Majesties Chaplaines in Ordinary'.[4]

In 1621 Donne had become Dean of St. Paul's; his presence may

[1] Fol. 8ᵛ. Sir Herbert Grierson discussed this poem in *M.L.R.* vi, 1911, p. 145. The confusion may have arisen because King made use, in 'An Elegy Occasioned by Sicknesse', of Bacon's last line, 'Not to be born, or being born to die'.

[2] *Acta Convocat. Univ. Oxon.*, Arch. N. 23, fol. 212. The witnesses of his declaration were Samuel Fell and Thomas Manne, mentioned below as Henry King's copyist, p. 48.

[3] Ibid., fol. 204ᵛ. Latin verses on John's Vesper Questions, in his own hand, are in Bodl. MS. Rawl. D. 317, fols. 166–7.

[4] Henry King appears in the Oxford volume on James I's death, *Parentalia*, 1625, as 'servus et sacellanus'.

have induced Henry King to stay in London rather than join his brother at Christ Church. Walton said that Donne's love for Bishop John King was 'doubled upon his Heire':[1] Henry was, in his own words, 'by [Donne's] favour no stranger to [his] temporal estate',[2] and, in Walton's, was 'trusted . . . with the very secrets of his soul'.[3] It was while Donne was ill in 1623 that King offered to contrive that he should benefit from a transaction concerning cathedral property. King, from a memory perhaps intensified by the sense of his shame and of his privilege in Donne's rebuke, was able to reconstruct what was said on this occasion for Walton, who added the story, with other information derived from Henry King, to the second edition of the *Life*:[4] Donne,

after a short pause, and raising himself upon his bed, . . . made this reply. 'My most dear friend, I most humbly thank you for your many favours, and this in particular: But, in my present condition, I shall not accept of your proposall; for doubtlesse there is such a Sinne as *Sacriledge*, if there were not, it could not have a name in Scripture. . . . Our times abound with men that are busie and litigious about trifles and Church-Ceremonies; and yet so far from scrupling *Sacriledge*, that they make not so much as a quære what it is: But, I thank God I have, and dare not now upon my sick bed, when Almighty God hath made me uselesse to the service of the Church, make any advantages out of it. But if he shall again restore me to such a degree of health, as again to serve at his *Altar*, I shall then gladly take the reward which the bountifull Benefactours of this Church have designed me; for God knowes my Children and relations will need it. In which number my mother (whose Credulity and Charity has contracted a very plentifull to a very narrow estate) must not be forgotten: But Dr. *King*, if I recover not, that little . . . must, if you deny me not so Charitable a favour, fall into your hands as my most *faithfull friend* and Executor; of whose Care and Justice, I make no more doubt then of Gods blessing on that which I have conscienciously collected for them.' . . . The reply to this was onely a promise to observe his request.

[1] *Life of Donne*, 1658, sig. A5ᵛ. [2] Op. cit., p. 68.
[3] Op. cit., sig. A6. [4] Op. cit., pp. 69–72.

Donne was presented to the vicarage of St. Dunstan's in the West in March 1623/4, and found Izaak Walton living in his parish. The beginning of Henry King's friendship with Walton was at this time, for his letter to Walton about Hooker, printed in *The Life of Mr. Richard Hooker*, 1665, is dated 13 November 1664, and speaks of 'a Familiarity of almost Forty years continuance'. In Walton's writings is revealed the quality of the friendship that existed between Donne and the King family, and the happy intimacy to which he was himself admitted.[1]

Henry King's eldest sister Elizabeth, with her husband and growing family, were living with him in the house at St. Paul's. Elizabeth's husband was Edward Holt, son and heir of Sir Thomas Holt, Bart., of Aston, Warwickshire. Sir Thomas, apparently in anger at their marriage, would do nothing for them, and Henry King had taken them into his own house, where their son Robert, afterwards second Baronet, was born;[2] he lent the family a sum of money which seems, from his will, to have been more than £2,000. Probably Elizabeth looked after Henry's motherless children with her own sons and daughters. To Robert Holt, thirty years later, Walton dedicated his revised *Life of John Donne*, 1658, saying: 'you have . . . a . . . title to what was Dr. *Donne*'s, by that dear affection & friendship that was betwixt him and your parents, by which he entailed a love upon your self, even in your infancy, which was encreased by the early testimonies of your growing merits, and by them continued, till D. *Donne* put on immortality; and so this mortall was turned into a love that cannot die. And Sir, 'twas pity he was lost to you in your minority, before you had attained a judgement to put a true value upon the living beauties and elegancies of his conversation.'[3]

In 1630 Donne fell ill, and began to make his preparations for

[1] Among presentation copies of Walton's works which have survived are two inscribed to members of the King family: in a copy of the life of Hooker he wrote, 'ffor doc:̃ Phill. King ffrom his old ffrend Izaak: Walton'; and the *Compleat Angler*, 1661, was given to Henry King's daughter-in-law Anne (for whom see p. 21). N. *&* Q. cxlvii, 1924, p. 200. See also p. 23 below.

[2] *Hannah*, p. cxi.

[3] *Life of Donne*, 'The Epistle Dedicatory', sigs. A6–7.

death. Henry King was closely involved. As he reminded
Walton,

three days before his death [Donne] delivered into my hands
those excellent Sermons of his now made publick: professing be-
fore Dr. *Winniff*, Dr. *Montford*, and I think your self then present
at his bed-side, that it was by my restless importunity that he had
prepared them for the Press; together with which (as his best
Legacy) he gave me all his Sermon-Notes, and his other Papers,
containing an Extract of near Fifteen hundred Authors.[1]

The shrouded portrait, 'drawn at his just height', was given to
Henry King, who 'caused him to be thus carved in one entire
piece of white Marble, as it now stands in the Cathedrall Church
of S. *Pauls*'.[2] Donne bequeathed to King a 'medal of gold of the
synod of Dort . . . as also the two pictures of Padre Paolo and
Fulgentino which hang in the parlour at my house at Paul's',[3]
and one of the '*Helitropian* Stones . . . set in gold' with the em-
blem of 'Christ extended upon an Anchor'[4] was for him.

The sermons and papers 'were got out of [Henry King's]
hands', and though Walton was 'the Messenger for them', they
were lost both to him and to King.[5] It is thought that the
younger John Donne had them, and that they were in the
Cabinet which he said in his will[6] was to be returned with 'all
those Papers which are of Authors Analysed by my Father;
many of which he [King] hath already received with his
Common-Place-Book'. Before they were taken away, one of the
sermons, the last, was printed, with an engraving from the
shrouded portrait and (at the end) King's elegy on Donne's
death. This was *Deaths Duell*, 1632, and King must have been
concerned in it.[7] Grierson thought that he might also have

---

[1] *The Life of Mr. Richard Hooker*, 1665, 'Letter writ . . . by Dr. King', sig. A2ᵛ.
[2] *Life of Donne*, p. 113. A hundred marks were sent to Donne's executors by
the physician Dr. Fox, 'towards the making of his Monument'.
[3] Donne's will, printed in *Life and Letters of John Donne*, by E. Gosse, 1899,
Appendix B. The pictures were a present from Sir Henry Wotton: see his *Life
and Letters*, by L. Pearsall Smith, 1907, ii. 478–9 (Appendix III).
[4] *Life of Donne*, p. 80.   [5] *Life of Hooker*, loc. cit.
[6] Printed broadsheet, 23 February 1662.
[7] Mrs. Percy Simpson gave me information about *Deaths Duell*.

'assisted' John Marriot, the publisher of the edition of Donne's *Poems* of 1633,[1] but there is no evidence that he did. In 1657 Marriot's son Richard expected that Henry King would look on the publication of his own poems 'with some disdain';[2] so that it is scarcely possible that he had helped the Marriot family to bring to light those of his friend.

On 2 January 1638/9 Henry King's brother John died.[3] When alterations were being made in Christ Church Cathedral he and Henry had caused Bishop Robert King's tomb to be moved to the South aisle, and a picture of him to be painted in a window;[4] and John was buried near by.

The landmarks of King's life are a succession of losses; but the names with which his is found associated in the decade after Donne's death suggest no desolate solitude. There were, besides Walton, among Donne's close friends Henry Wotton and Brian Duppa, both friends also of King's. When Duppa chose contributors for *Jonsonus Virbius*,[5] King was among them, and it is likely that of those who were gathered as mourners for Ben Jonson many were King's friends or acquaintance in London or at Oxford. With Waller and Godolphin he was associated a second time in Gauden's collection on Lady Anne Rich in 1638,[6] and again in the same year (with Lord Falkland, Thomas Carew, and Dudley Digges as well) in the commendatory poems printed in George Sandys's *Paraphrase upon the Divine Poems*.

Fuller speaks of King's having studied music,[7] and a 'cabonett organ'[8] was among the few possessions he retained through the Civil War. Much later, in 1665, his name appears amongst the

[1] *Poems of John Donne*, ed. H. J. C. Grierson, 1912, ii, pp. lxvi and 255.

[2] *Poems*, *Elegies*, *Paradoxes and Sonnets*, 1657, 'The Publishers to the Author', sig. A3^{v}.

[3] Martin Lluellyn wrote verses on his death, Bodl. MS. Rawl. D. 1092, fol. 267. Apparently he did not think them good enough for inclusion in the collection *Men Miracles*, 1646.

[4] 'The said window was pulled down when the presbyterians and independants governed, an. 1651, by one of the family of Kings . . . who preserved it safe till the restauration, an. 1660, was soon after set up again, where it yet continues', Wood, *Athenae Oxonienses*, ii. 775; and it is still there.

[5] Printed 1638.

[6] Bodl. MS. Eng. misc. e. 262.

[7] Cf. p. 27 below.

[8] Cf. p. 20 below.

'strangers' who contributed towards the expense of refurnishing the Music School at Oxford, which had suffered during the interregnum.[1] But there is no record of contact with musicians, unless the settings of all his earlier 'Sonnets' by John Wilson may be taken as a sign of friendship between them. These settings are included among Wilson's collected songs in Bodl. MS. Mus. b. 1: they show the care for which he was renowned, that the musical phrase should hold the poetic rhythm without distortion; and the predominantly melancholy tone of King's words is reflected in harmony and melody, a turn of mood or stroke of wit (in which often lies the point of these 'sonnets') being similarly reflected in melodic break or harmonic change. About the time when Wilson became one of the King's Musicians in Ordinary, May 1635, he set to music Henry King's 'Penitentiall Hymne', of which the words are in royal anthem books, though the music has disappeared.[2]

He was attracted by explorers, Sandys, Henry Blount, and James Howell. To Henry Blount he confessed an occasional restlessness:

> . . . since I had the witt to understand
> The Termes of Native or of Forraine land;
> I have had strong and oft desires to tread
> Some of those Voyages which I have read.[3]

These impulses had been shared by his brother Robert, who had neglected his father's wish, abandoned theology, and 'changing his Course . . . went to the Wars in Holland then to some Service by Sea lastly he engaged in a Voyage to the Amazons in the West Indies, which proving successless to his Fortune and Health gave him a lingring preparation to his last Voyage of his Life'.[4] Robert lived until 1654.

[1] Sir John Hawkins, *General History of Music*, 1776, iv. 375.

[2] 30 May: *The King's Musick*, H. C. de Lafontaine, 1909, p. 91; cf. note to 'A Penitentiall Hymne'. Hannah thought the manuscript of King's poems here called *H* had belonged to Wilson (*Hannah*, p. 171); but Dr. Percy Simpson showed that this was not so (*B.Q.R.* v, 1926–9, p. 326).

[3] 'To . . . Sir Henry Blount', p. 83, 5–8.

[4] Memorial inscription formerly at Langley, Bucks. Printed by Hannah from seventeenth-century transcripts, pp. xciv–xcv.

Henry's life was more nearly in accordance with Bishop John King's purpose. He became an esteemed preacher, and his *Exposition on The Lords Prayer*, first printed in 1628, reached a second edition in 1634. Abraham Wright, who was concerned with the technique of preaching, chose him as a model: in a note made in the summer of 1643 he exhorts himself: 'Speake not too Confidently and yet not at all fearfully for this will spoile the cause; but after a modest and mowrnfull tone, especially the last part and this is Dr. Kings way, which faile not to follow and to leave your owne bold way, and this imitate when you walke alone and that often.'[1] Thomas Pestell, another poet among the king's chaplains, praised Henry King both as preacher and as poet, calling him 'The Double Second to two Phenixes': to 'His father first, our King of preists', and to Donne, 'The late Copernicus in Poëtrie, / That rappt the whole Earth round, & gave it sence / Of Love, to move by his Intelligence'.[2] Some of his poems found their way into manuscript collections. James Howell wrote on the gift or loan of one of these, 3 February 1637:[3]

To Mr. Thomas W. at his Chambers in the Temple.
　Sir,
You have much streigthtned [*sic*] that knot of love which hath been so long tied between us, by those choice Manuscripts you sent me lately, among which I find divers rare pieces; but that which afforded me most entertainment in those Miscellanies, was Dr. *Henry King's* Poems, wherein I find not only heat and strength, but also an exact concinnity and evenness of fancy: they are a choice race of Brothers, and it seems the same Genius diffuseth itself also among the Sisters. . . .

He goes on to speak of the youngest sister, Anne; some of her verses are printed below, p. 22. Howell's own poems, edited by Payne Fisher in 1663, were dedicated to 'the Right Reverend and Innately Noble Dr. Henry King'.

Promotion came to Henry King when troubles in Church and

---

[1] Bodl. MS. Eng. th. f. 27, fol. 74ᵛ. This note was written partly in code, on a draft of a sermon preached 6 July 1643.

[2] *Poems of Thomas Pestell*, ed. Hannah Buchan, 1940, p. 36.

[3] *The Familiar Letters of James Howell*, ed. Joseph Jacobs, 1890, pp. 406–7.

State were gathering towards the point of explosion. He was installed as Dean of Rochester on 6 February 1638/9, and Sir Henry Wotton, who was being urged by Walton to carry out an undertaking to write Donne's life, wrote of his hopes to see him there, to confer with him about the life and to introduce him to his own relations at Boughton Malherbe;[1] but Wotton died in December 1639, and King did not stay long in Kent. In October 1641 he was elected Bishop of Chichester, being (Fuller says) 'acceptable on the account of his own merit, and on the score of a *Pious*, and *popular Father*'.[2] He said himself that this was 'more then [he] ever expected',[3] and he was not the first choice: whoever that was had 'desire[d] to be spared'; the king admitted to having 'altered somewhat frome [his] former thoughts, to satisfie the tymes'.[4] John Walker afterwards said that Henry King was 'Esteemed to be Puritanically Affected, and was Promoted to this *Bishoprick* to please that Party',[5] a view which his life and poems confute; but he will not have been feared as a formidable adversary by the genuinely 'Puritanically Affected'. There was an ineffective protest made in the House of Commons, printed as *Mr. Rowse his Speech . . . the thirtieth of December, 1641, In opposition of the making of Doctor Winniff, Doctor Holsworth, Doctor King, Bishops . . . till a setled Government in Religion be established in this Kingdome*; but Henry King was consecrated, with Winniff, on 6 February 1641/2. The day before this a bill had been passed depriving the Bishops of their vote in the House of Lords, and an act for the abolition of episcopacy was passed within a year.

King went down to Chichester and lived in the Palace, apparently keeping another house at Petworth.[6] His sister

[1] *Reliquiæ Wottonianæ*, 1651, p. 512.

[2] *Church-History*, xi. 194.

[3] Preface to *The Psalmes of David . . . turned into Meter*, 1651, sig. A2ᵛ.

[4] Correspondence of Charles I and Sir Edward Nicholas, printed in Evelyn's *Memoirs*, ed. William Bray, 1818, II. ii. 31–32.

[5] *An Attempt towards . . . an Account of the . . . Sufferings of the Clergy*, 1714, ii. 11.

[6] He held the rectory of Petworth *in commendam*; his curate was Oliver Whitby. Mr. John Buxton tells me that a paten and flagon bearing King's arms belong still to Petworth church.

Dorothy, who had married Sir Richard Hubert, Groom Porter to Charles I, stayed with him during these uneasy months. Her daughter Dorothy was born in his house, and christened in the Bishop's chapel.[1]

In the autumn of 1642 Sir William Waller was sent to secure the south-eastern counties for Parliament, and was in Sussex by Christmas. The Royalists defended Chichester during a brief siege, and Waller came in on 28 December. Though a pamphlet called *Brave news of the Taking of the City of Chitchester* claimed that 'the Bishop, some Lords, and about fourscore Commanders' were taken prisoner, Henry King seems really to have escaped with his household.[2] Waller allowed his soldiers to plunder the Cathedral;[3] and he took possession of the Bishop's palace, where soon after William Chillingworth was imprisoned. Chillingworth had there (if Cheynell is to be believed) 'very courteous usage, and all accommodations which were requisite for a sicke man', and in his will left £10 to 'Mistresse *Mason*, who keepes the Bishops house'.[4]

A petition of Henry King's after the Restoration describes his personal loss: from April 1643 he was deprived of his whole estate, by William Cawley, who seized his bishopric rents, his goods, and his library; and by John Downes, who took his corn and household stuff from Petworth and demolished his chief house in Chichester. He had granted leases of property to his two sons; these had been detained from them by Downes.[5] When during the interregnum he was asked for information for Dugdale's use, concerning St. Paul's, his answer revealed that 'through the barbarous usuage of a wretched Committee at Chichester' he had been deprived even of his own 'Private Papers, which had bene the moniments of [his] course in study through

---

[1] Henry King's will, printed in *Hannah*, p. cxii.

[2] He was supposed by a writer in *Mercurius Aulicus*, 8 April 1643, to have been 'detained by the Rebels forces'; cf. *Oxford Books*, by F. Madan, 1912, ii. 235.

[3] An account of their conduct is in Bruno Ryves's *Mercurius Rusticus*, 1646, pp. 204–6.   [4] *Chillingworthi Novissima*, 1644, sig. B3.

[5] *Calendar of State Papers, Domestic Series, 1660–1661*, p. 290. The order for sequestration was passed in the House of Commons 27 June 1643; a petition of King's relating to the order was refused on 3 October.

all [his] life'.[1] His will, written in July 1653,[2] shows that he some-
how saved a few of his most precious possessions: the plate
which Queen Anne gave his father, his 'Cabonett organ made
by Craddocke',[3] and a number of books, including a 'great
french Bible' that had belonged to Donne; but most had to be
left behind, and 'contrary to the condition and contracte of the
Generall and Counsell of warre', was not restored to him.
Probably at this time the Earl of Northumberland (his neighbour
at Petworth) entered into a bond, in the name of his son John
King, to safeguard a sum of money for the family; the details
of this agreement were confided to Henry King's youngest sister
Anne, 'from whome during [his] misfortunes since the losse of
all [he] had at Chichester [he] received speciall signification of
her love'.

According to a Rector of Stopham, near Petworth, in the reign
of Queen Anne, Henry King 'was not suffered to enjoy himself
quietly at his freinds Houses; but escaping one night privatly
to the parish of Sheers near Guilford in Surry, he there liv'd
a retir'd life with one of his acquain[tan]ce, by whose Charity
he was maintain'd'.[4] The mathematician William Oughtred was
Rector of Albury, the next parish to Shere, and a friendship
grew up between his family and Elizabeth Holt's daughters,
who were still living with Henry King. Henry's son John went
daily to Oughtred 'for his willing and free helpes . . . in reading
to him the choicest bookes and learning', till he was found to
have seduced Oughtred's youngest daughter. The relationship
of the two families is described in painful detail in the unfinished
drafts of a petition by Oughtred relating to this wrong.[5] John
abandoned Miss Oughtred; he married someone with whom,

---

[1] *Life, Diary, and Correspondence of Sir William Dugdale*, ed. W. Hamper, 1827,
pp. 317–18.   [2] Printed in full, *Hannah*, pp. cviii–cxiv.

[3] In *The King's Musick*, by H. C. de Lafontaine, 1909, Thomas Craddock is
mentioned as having been the king's organ maker until 1660 (p. 121).

[4] Collections for Walker's *Sufferings of the Clergy*: letter from Thomas Newcomb
to Joshuah Reighnolds of Corpus Christi College, Oxford, Bodl. MS. J. Walker
c. 3, fol. 378ᵛ.

[5] Bodl. MS. Rawl. D. 1361, fols. 389–97. Mason drew attention to these papers,
'Life and Works of Henry King', in *Transactions of the Connecticut Academy of Arts
and Sciences*, xviii, 1913, pp. 241–2.

through his mother's family, there was a distant connexion, Anne, daughter of Sir William Russell of Strensham, Worcestershire.[1] The petition shows that by 20 February 1646/7 Henry King had gone to Blakesware in Hertfordshire, which belonged then to his brother John's elder son. From here he visited Walton's friends, the owners of the Otter-dogs in *The Compleat Angler*, the Sadlers of Standon. A letter of his written long after from London, to thank Lady Sadler for a present of venison, is in the library of Trinity College, Cambridge: in it he speaks of 'the many hospitable receptions afforded me at Stendon' during his 'sojourn in Hertfordshire some years past'.[2]

Izaak Walton ignored this unhappy interval. Some time about 1673, collecting materials for a life of John Hales, he wrote:[3]

After Doc^r King late B^p of Chich^r was sequesterd and plunderd. he, his 2 sons, a brother,[4] Sr Rich Hubert who married one of his sisters, and an other of the Bish sisters then the widow[5] of Mr Dutton of Sherborne (now wife to Sr Rich How) and 2 or 3 gent. of note (sons of the Church) made some Contrackt with the lady Salter to Cohabit in her howse: to wch end they got a steward and a Chaplin (which was their freind Mr Hales) and their they made a kinde of Collage as to praying the Church prayers. rec the Sacram^t and // and // [the details were never supplied].

Lady Salter was Brian Duppa's neice. She was a widow, her

---

[1] Memorial inscription in Chichester Cathedral. Her elder sister married Charles Cotton, whose poem, 'La Illustrissima. On my Fair and Dear Sister, Mrs. Anne King', is printed in his *Poems on Several Occasions*, 1689, pp. 68–73. Anne was not mentioned in the Visitation, 1634, *Harleian Society*, 90, 1938. For the Russells of Strensham and the Berkeleys, see I, *William Shakespeare*, by Leslie Hotson, 1937, pedigree facing p. 141, where Sir Henry Berkeley, who was half-brother to Robert Berkeley of Boycourt, Kent, appears in relationship with Russells and the Digges family.   [2] 14 August 1661. MS. R. 5. 5.

[3] Walton's notes are now partly in Bodl. MS. J. Walker c. 2, fols. 198–9, ending with a catch-word 'I have told'; and partly in Fulman's MS. 12, now MS. Corpus Christi College, Oxford, 306, on a leaf between fols. 88 and 89, beginning 'I have told'. The Walker part is marked 'To be Return'd to Mr. Archdeacon Davies', who inherited Fulman's manuscripts in 1688. Walker used what Davies sent him in his *Sufferings of the Clergy*. The Fulman part was printed by Hannah, and by John Butt in *Modern Language Review*, xxix, 1934, pp. 267–73.

[4] This was Dr. Philip King. Walton first named him after Sr *Richard How*, but crossed the words out and added the anonymous *brother* after *sons*.

[5] Anne was not yet a widow. John Dutton died 14 January 1656/7.

husband, Sir Walter Salter, having died in 1643. She lived at Richkings, 'a faire howse (then hers) about 3 miles from Eaton College', Walton says. The Huberts' house was in the next parish, Langley. Hales, according to Nathaniel Ingelo,[1] 'went to the Lady Salters sometime after Bpp King, and about a year after his ejection from the College [1648]'. He insisted on leaving when the declaration forbidding the harbouring of malignants was published, 24 November 1655.[2]

Walton's account of the community continues:

About the time [John Hales] was forc't from the lady Saltrs that ffamily or Collage broke up, or desolv'd, a littel before wch time, they were resolv'd to have Mr Ha. picture taken, and to that end, a picture maker had promis'd to atend at Richkings to take it, but faild of his time; and M^r Ha being gone thence dyed not long after. the not having his picture, was lamented very much, by the societie, in wch nomber the Bish^s sister (once Mrs Anne King now the lady How) undertooke boeth for theirs and her owne satisfaction to draw it, and did so, in black and white boeth exilently well to the Curiousnes . . . as well as to the likenes.[3]— but before she wood shew it to any that knew either him or her selfe, she writ underneth it, this which she ment to be an Apologie for her undertaking it

> Though by a sodaine and unfeard surprise,
> thou lately taken wast from thy friends eies:
> Even in that instant, when they had design'd
> to keipe thee, by thy picture still in minde:
> least thou like others lost in deths dark night
> shouldst stealing hence vanish quite out of sight;
> I did Contend with greater zeale then Art,
> This shadow of my phantie to impart:
> which all shood pardon, when they understand
> the lines were figur'd by a woman's hand,

[1] Ingelo wrote down what details they could remember at Eton and sent them to Walton's friend Richard Marriot. MS. CCC. 306, fols. 81–82.

[2] *A Bibliography of Royal Proclamations*, by Robert Steele, *Bibliotheca Lindesiana*, v, 1901, 3065.

[3] Jasper Mayne wrote a poem on Anne's 'Table Book of Pictures', praising her drawings. The poem is in a number of manuscript miscellanies. Fulman had a copy, MS. CCC. 309, fol. 60.

who had noe Copy to be guided by
but Hales imprinted in her memory.
> Thus ill Cut Brasses serve uppon a grave
> Which less resemblance of the persons have.

Y^u may take notice that she is a most generose and ingenious lady.—greate friendship 'twixt her and M^r Ha.

From Anne, Walton learned some intimate details of the last months of his friend's life. He left her a ring when he wrote his will in 1683.[1]

Henry King occupied some of his time in making a metrical paraphrase of the Psalms, 'having', as he said, 'now leisure from those greater employments, to which I was called more then I ever expected'.[2] A wish had been expressed for a new version in *The Bishop of Armaghes Direction Concerning the Lyturgy, and Episcopall Government*, 1642.[3] King wrote to Ussher from Langley, 30 October 1651, of his own attempt to provide one:

One *Sunday* at Church, hearing a Psalm sung, whose wretched expression quite marred the Pen-man's Matter, & my Devotion, I did at my return that Evening, try, whether from the Version of our Bible I could not easily, and with plainness, suiting the lowest Understandings, deliver it from that garb, which indeed made it ridiculous.[4]

The book was licensed 7 January 1650/1, and was printed that year with the title *The Psalmes of David, From the New Translation of the Bible Turned into Meter: To be Sung after the Old Tunes used in the Churches*. A second edition came out in 1654, and some of his versions were included in Playford's settings of the old tunes in *Psalms and Hymns in Solemn Musick of Foure Parts*, 1671. The verdict of John Holland in his study of *The Psalmists of Britain*, 1843 (ii, 51), was that 'it would not be easy to name a Version of the Psalms, which presents, on the whole, less to redeem it from the character of baldness and tameness'. Not many people

---

[1] A facsimile of Walton's will is in *The Compleat Angler*, ed. G. A. B. Dewar, 1902, between pp. xliv and xlv.
[2] Preface to *The Psalmes . . . Turned into Meter*, sig. A2^v.   [3] Sig. A3^v; cf. *D.N.B.*
[4] *The Life of . . . Ussher*, by Richard Parr, 1686, p. 567.

are in a position to argue against this harsh judgement; but the versions written for the old tunes seem not to deserve reprinting. King thought the stanzas would be improved by the change of their rhyme-scheme from alternating rhymes (*abab, cdcd,* &c.) to pairs (*aabb, ccdd,* &c.); but his idea, though it is at first sight, and in isolated instances, successful, gives only the briefest respite from monotony. It may at least fairly be claimed for King that to a great extent he avoided those distortions of grammar and emphasis common in poetry forced into too restrictive a form, and that in some passages his aim, of dignified plainness, has been fulfilled. I take an example from Psalm CIV:

> He from the hills his Christall springs
> Down running to the vallies brings:
> Which drink supply, and coolnes yield,
> To thirsting beasts throughout the field.
> By them the fowles of heaven rest,
> And singing in their branches nest.
> He waters from his clouds the Hills;
> The teeming earth with plenty fills.

From Psalm CXXI:

> Up to the Hills I lift mine eyes,
> From whence my help and comfort rise.
> My safety from the Lord doth spring,
> Who made the world, and every thing;

and from Psalm CXXVII:

> You vainly with the early light
> Arise, or sit up late at night,
> To find support, and dayly eat
> Your bread with sorrow earn'd and sweat;
> When God, who His beloved keepes,
> This plenty gives with quiet sleepes.

One version, for which he chose his own metre, and which gained the approval of Samuel Woodforde, has been reprinted here with King's other poems (p. 190).

At one time, in the summer of 1655, Henry King had hopes of more active service. The anxiety over the preservation of 'the Succession of the English Church' is described in his sermon on Brian Duppa:[1] Charles II, 'sensible of His *Bishops* Decay, Most whereof were Dead, & Those Few who remain not likely to last long, was pleas'd to commit this Trust principally to [Duppa's] Solicitation. In discharge whereof how industrious He was, some who yet live know, and none better than My self, who was His only associate in several travels undertaken to bring it to effect.' The safest plan was thought to be that two of the remaining bishops should go over to Charles's court, and there with Bishop Bramhall 'might Canonically Consecrate some of Those eminently deserving Divines who then attended Him; Thus Preserving the Order in a Few, untill God gave opportunity to fill up the other Vacancies'. Henry King was one of five bishops who were approached; and he was willing to accept the summons: 'I never declin'd any hazard when I might doe the King my Master or the Church Service. But great Age and greater Infirmity denying the concurrence of any One of the Rest (though otherwise most ready) that designe fell.' Edward Hyde received an account from Dr. Duncon, dated June 1655, of the interview with King: 'Chichester offered to come over with me, if I thought good, and would willingly wait upon his Majesty, if he were assured his service might be acceptable, &c. He doth often ordain Priests and Deacons, and hath ordained many excellent scholars since these calamitous times, by letters dimissory from other Bishops, if the See were full, or if empty, without them.'[2]

At the Restoration Henry King went back to Chichester. He assisted at the consecration of Bishops Sheldon, Henchman, Morley, and Sanderson in King Henry VII's Chapel in Westminster Abbey on 28 October 1660. When Richard Busby had to produce a certificate of loyalty to continue as Headmaster of Westminster School, Henry King signed it for him.[3] He was

[1] *A Sermon ... at the Funeral of ... Bryan Lord Bp. of Winchester*, 1662, pp. 42–43.
[2] *State Papers collected by Edward, Earl of Clarendon*, iii, 1786, Appendix, pp. c–ci.
[3] *C.S.P.D. 1660–1661*, p. 60.

called upon to preach at Whitehall on the first anniversary of Charles II's return,[1] and, according to a ballad, he also 'Preach't first the Memory / Of *Charles* King-Martyr, thirtieth *January*'.[2] When Duppa was ill in April 1661, King took his place at the Feast of St. George at Windsor 'by Particular Licence and Approbation of his Soveraign'.[3] A year later he made Duppa's funeral sermon, in which he described, as if he had been present, the king's visit to the bishop on his death-bed. Until he was within a few months of his own death he preached occasionally before the King.[4] His younger son Henry became a Gentleman in Ordinary of the Privy Chamber.[5] But nothing more was to happen.[6] He seems, like his brother Philip, for whom places had been found in the diocese of Chichester, to have 'lived . . . in a quiet and sedate repose'.[7] Wood says that he 'became esteemed by many persons of his neighbourhood and diocess', and was ' "the epitome of all honours, virtues and generous nobleness", and a person never to be forgotten by his tenants, and by the poor'.[8] He died 30 September 1669, and was buried in Chichester Cathedral.[9]

Fuller, writing in 1660, included Henry King among his Worthies, after Bishop John King:[10] 'We know the Scripture-Proverb used in Exprobation, *As is the mother so is the daughter*, both wicked, both wofull. But here it may be said by way of

---

[1] Printed at London, 1661.

[2] 'A Grateful Mention of Deceased Bishops', Bodl. Wood 276a, 541. The first sermon was really by another King, the Dean of Tuam; on 12 March 1664/5 Pepys 'read over' Henry King's, printed that year, and thought it 'but a mean sermon'. *Diary*, ed. H. B. Wheatley, iv, 1894, p. 370.

[3] *A Sermon . . . at the Funeral* of Duppa, 1662, p. 32.

[4] Evelyn mentions his sermon in Lent, 28 February 1669, *Diary*, ed. E. S. de Beer, 1955, iii. 524. Cf. King's letter to Sheldon, Bodl. MS. Tanner 44, fol. 80.

[5] Memorial inscription, Chichester Cathedral.

[6] R. S. Bosher in *The Making of the Restoration Settlement*, 1951, explains the neglect of King and the other bishops at the restoration as Hyde's response to their failure during the interregnum to consecrate others; p. 125 and n.

[7] Wood, *Fasti Oxonienses*, ed. Bliss, ii, 1820, 89.

[8] *Athenae Oxonienses*, iii. 841. Wood heard that 'being not removed to a better see, [he] became discontented, . . . and a favourer thereupon of the presbyterians in his diocese'.

[9] Memorial inscription, Chichester Cathedral, 'Prid. Kalend. Oct.'

[10] *The History of the Worthies of England*, 1662, sig. T3.

thankfullness to God, and honour to the persons, *As was the father so is the son,* both pious, both prosperous, till the calamity of the times involved the later.' Fuller goes on to speak of Henry's work, though with more regard to what might seem fitting than to the actual sequence of his activities:

David saith, that the good *Tree [Man] shall bring forth his fruit in due season*; so our Doctor varied his fruits according to the diversity of his age. Being brought up in *Christ-church in Oxford,* he delighted in the studies of *Musick* and *Poetry,* more elder he applyed himself to *Oratory* and *Philosophy,* and in his reduced age fixed on *Divinity,* which his Printed Sermons on the Lords-prayer;[1] and others which he preached, remaining fresh in the minds of his Auditors will report him to all posterity.

THE POEMS

Fuller's anxiety to dissociate Henry King's poetry from the time of his eminence in the Church was shared by his 'Publishers' in 1657. Their address 'to the author' contains a deprecating reference to his poems as '*Juvenilia,* most of them the issues of your youthful Muse'; and perhaps their arrangement was partly dictated by the same view of propriety as Fuller revealed in his account of the succession of interests: first 'Musick and Poetry'; then 'Oratory and Philosophy'; and at last 'Divinity'. First are songs, with verse of a social kind, such as inscriptions for presents to friends, and epigrams. Then come occasional poems on public events, though some which contained outspoken political comment were held back to appear only in a second issue after the Restoration. At the end are meditative and religious poems.

The occasional verse, which can be dated, shows that King was writing over a period of at least forty-five years, from the death of Prince Henry in 1612 until that of the Countess of Leinster, 1657; in an elegy on her death he took his leave of poetry. In the authoritative manuscripts the dated poems are not together, but are found associated in small groups with others of different kinds; though scattered, they are in chrono-

---

[1] *An Exposition on the Lords Prayer,* 1628; second edition 1634.

logical order. It looks as if in these groups poems written during successive periods of activity have been kept together, and as if it was only in the last ten years of his life that King wrote no poetry.

The arrangement of the poems in the manuscripts suggests a chronological sequence which breaks into three parts. The twenty poems forming the first part seem to have been fairly early gathered together,[1] and were arranged by kind according to a discernible plan; the 'Exequy' and the 'Epitaph on the Earl of Dorset', which belong to the early months of the year 1624, are the last dated poems in this section. The middle part consists of several smaller and less orderly groups, almost but not quite identical in each manuscript, including occasional poems belonging to the early sixteen-thirties. In the last part are those which were late additions, and to these must be added some that were not included in the manuscripts at all. The occasional poems here date from 1636 to 1657.

There are, in the general characters of these sections, stylistic differences of a kind compatible with a natural course of development: in the first there seems to be reflected a phase of conscientious experiment and effort, leading to a single moment of release from all impediment of expression in the 'Exequy'. The poems belonging to the next section, though they do not equal the 'Exequy', stand in little need of explanation or of excuse. At the last there is shown a readier skill, but the quality becomes markedly uneven; there are now sometimes deficiencies in matter or in expression such as would scarcely have been permitted in the more strenuous and more fastidious earlier years; and there are signs of excessive detachment in an occasional dryness and stiffness of argument and of imagery.

But there was, over the years, no essential change either in what King saw as a theme for poetry, or in how he thought it should be treated. The occasion was nearly always some situation or event of public or of private concern, to be argued out at length or crystallized into a song or a dirge. He has little to do with narrative writing, and still less with descriptive: the ele-

[1] See pp. 52 and 54–55 below.

ments of his situations are left to be inferred from his comment; and the external world is present only in imagery. But he never loses contact with the plain known facts of the case; speculation on abstract subjects hardly attracted him; he was not, in that sense, metaphysical. In manner, he gives an impression of extreme reserve, with rare moments of intimacy. In his poetry there is not that sense of immediacy, either in argument or in feeling, that is characteristic of the best of his contemporaries; he seldom creates the illusion of re-entering the experience which had moved him to write, nor does his argument impress as something alive and growing. He discloses the result of consideration in deliberate phrases, which ask for a slow and closely attentive reading.

The nature of King's poetry was probably very much affected by the training of Westminster, a discipline from which he showed at first no anxiety to break loose. Among the earliest collection of his poems are some which probably differ little from exercises he had written at school. T. W. Baldwin, in *Shakspere's Small Latine and Lesse Greeke*, recovered the details of what was done in English grammar schools in the sixteenth and at the beginning of the seventeenth century. Part of their aim was that it should be impossible to avoid familiarity with chosen classical texts; and this was achieved through exercises in translation, in paraphrase, and in imitation. King, paraphrasing Isaiah in 'The Woes of Esay' or imitating (at some distance) Horace and Martial in 'The Ill-favoured Choice', was doing in English verse the same kind of thing as he had practised at school in Latin and in Greek, and possibly (for a peculiarity of Westminster was the early introduction of exercise in writing English verse)[1] even in his own language. But composition was also attempted; they began with letters, for which Cicero was their model and their guide Erasmus, *De Conscribendis Epistolis*. King starts 'A Letter' with a repudiation of all this, 'I ne're was drest in Formes'; but an element now lost in the appeal of this poem was probably just

---

[1] T. W. Baldwin, *Shakspere's Small Latine and Lesse Greeke*, 1944, i. 360. See p. 5 above.

the conformity which, in his assertion of artless sincerity, he disclaimed. From letters they proceeded to themes. They began by stringing together a few *sententiae*, and went on to more elaborate constructions, working by established formulae which were inherited, ultimately, from Quintilian. 'An Essay on Death and a Prison' is a deliberative theme,[1] persuading that death is to be preferred to imprisonment. The argument is conducted through set phases: the *exordium* is the challenging definition of lines 1–3; the *narratio* (3–34) tells of the condition of the soul in death and in the imprisoned body; *confirmatio* follows (35–46); *confutatio* disposes of the hypothetical wish of one dead to 'be re-inspir'd with Life ... to gaine a Monarchy' (47–80); finally there is *conclusio*. From themes they went on, in the highest forms, to declamations, in which a thesis was to be upheld or opposed. Henry King glances, not over-solemnly, at the practice of declamation in his 'Defence' and 'answere to the Blackmore'. These (if judgement may be based on the frequency of copies in miscellaneous collections) were among his contemporaries' favourites.

If the lessons of Westminster determined the structure of some of King's poems, other aspects of his style were not less affected. He was not taught by Camden himself, but came soon enough after him to find his tradition persisting. It was Jonson who claimed with pride a debt in poetry to the teaching of Camden, 'to whom I owe All that I am in arts, all that I know';[2] he said his verses were 'wrott all . . . first in prose, for so his master Cambden had Learned him';[3] and though this is acceptable as an explanation only of some of his less characteristic verse, there are times when both he and King may well have done just that; and in such undistinguished passages a marked likeness between them emerges, in tone, in cadence, and in grammatical construction; they share also an obscurity which comes from a close compression, with frequent parentheses, and from

[1] T. W. Baldwin, op. cit. ii. 295–6, quoting R. Brinsley's *Ludus Literarius*, 1627.

[2] *Epigrammes*, xiv. 1–2.

[3] *Conversations*, ed. G. B. Harrison, 1923, p. 16. ·

unexpected word-order, rather than from any difficulty in their thought. They approach, in fact, the manner, though not the deliberate cacophony, of 'strong-lined' writers.[1] Lines of Jonson's might be grafted without incongruity, apart from the details of their circumstance, into poems of King's such as 'To his Freindes of Christchurch', his 'Letter', the congratulation of Sir Henry Blount 'upon his Voyage', or the presentation poems; and when his printers wanted to dispose of copies remaining unsold in 1700 it seemed worth trying to pass them off as 'Ben Johnson's'. For comparison with King's 'Letter' and the longer presentation poems may be suggested the end of Jonson's Epigram xliii, 'To Robert Earle of Salisburie',

> [I] dare not, to my thought, least hope allow
> Of adding to thy fame; thine may to me,
> When, in my booke, men reade but Cecill's name,
> And what I write thereof find farre, and free
> From servile flatterie (common Poets shame)
> As thou stand'st cleere of the necessitie.

Or this from the 'Epistle. To Katherine, Lady Aubigny',[2]

> This makes, that wisely you decline your life,
> Farre from the maze of custome, error, strife,
> And keepe an even, and unalter'd gaite;
> Not looking by, or backe (like those, that waite
> Times, and occasions, to start forth, and seeme)
> Which though the turning world may dis-esteeme,
> Because that studies spectacles, and showes,
>
>   .   .   .   .
>
>   . . . and therefore cannot see
> Right, the right way: yet must your comfort bee
> Your conscience, and not wonder, if none askes
> For truthes complexion, where they all weare maskes.

Jonson's address to Sir Henry Savile on his *Tacitus* is like King's to Sir Henry Blount in much more than manners:

> But when I read that speciall piece, restor'd,
> Where Nero falls, and Galba is ador'd,

---

[1] See F. P. Wilson, *Elizabethan and Jacobean*, 1945, pp. 41–41, and note on p. 134; and G. Williamson, 'Strong Lines', *English Studies*, 1936, xviii. 152–9.
[2] *The Forrest*, xiii. 59–70.

To thine owne proper I ascribe then more;
And gratulate the breach, I griev'd before:
Which Fate (it seemes) caus'd in the historie,
Onely to boast thy merit in supply.
O, wouldst thou adde like hand, to all the rest!
Or, better worke! were thy glad countrey blest,
To have her storie woven in thy thred;
Minervaes loome was never richer spred.[1]

When the content is sufficient (and neither Jonson nor King spoke without having found something to say) and the verse well managed, writing of this kind has merit of its own; but the ability to produce it was not exceptional,[2] and if this were their best, there would be little need to remember either of them as poets. The gifts which inform their more characteristic utterance are of other kinds than intellectual and metrical competence; and though there was not the slightest chance that Jonson's irrepressible energy and originality might fail to make their impact, Henry King's approach, at once more conservative and less confident, has made his distinctive quality harder to discern. But his most careful and perceptive critic, Miss Rosemond Tuve (with whom his contemporary James Howell seems remarkably to agree),[3] has found and described individual excellence in him, of which she seems most to be aware in relation to his treatment of imagery (with which her study of him was primarily concerned)[4] and also of sound.[5]

His metrical skill was apparent from the beginning. The susceptibility of a musical ear, heightened by his school's training in classical prosody, made possible to him a range of effects appropriate to many changes of mood and of purpose. The appearance of his pages is remarkably little varied: he wrote always

---

[1] *Epigrammes*, xcv. 7–16.
[2] Cf. Jonson's censure of Drummond's verses: 'they smelled too much of the schooles . . . for a child says he may writte after the fashion of the Greeks and latine verses in cunning.' *Conversations*, § 6.
[3] See p. 17 above.
[4] *Elizabethan and Metaphysical Imagery*, 1947.
[5] Speaking of the 'Exequy', she says 'the grave and lovely sweetness . . . is in great part a metrical achievement', p. 134.

in rhymed couplets, either of ten or of eight syllables, even (with two exceptions) in his songs; but monotony is never in question; and this is due to his control of movement, both pace, and length of phrase. A slow tempo was probably natural to him, but for some particular effect he could hasten: the letter 'To his un-constant Freind' bursts into a torrent of expostulation; in 'To his Freinds of Christchurch' he seems to clamour for news; though in both the impetus of the opening lines subsides as he turns to develop the argument. At the other extreme, there is the ponderous opening of 'An Elegy upon Prince Henryes Death'. The movement is delayed here in the first line by the number of stresses, six instead of five, and their placing; and by the use of words beginning and ending with consonants, sometimes with clusters of consonants, making it hard or even impossible to gather speed. In 'The Defense' (a poem which shares something of the combined gravity of manner and beauty of sound that belong to the 'Exequy', though it is on a much smaller scale) the number and placing of stresses is much varied. The couplet is here of eight syllables, so that a mechanical count in the open-ing four lines would make sixteen lightened syllables: but on half this number the meaning demands instead some degree of stress. This produces a slow and emphatic opening; and there is a sense of relief and of escape from tension in the easy music of the more regular beat later; the change of sound coincides with a change from the tone of expostulation to one of serene description. The metrical plan of 'The Defense' is unusual: it proceeds in distinctly paired verses, through phrases of increas-ing length: two couplets are followed by three, four, and finally five, an orderliness which gives the poem a kind of security and even finality.

A distinction, though not a rigid one, may be drawn in King's poetry between two main kinds: the elegiac, slowly moving through long phrases of irregular length; and the brisker and more predictable rhythm of the satiric. In the elegiac 'Woes of Esay' the sentences run through to a pause which most com-monly falls after the second stress, with an almost liturgical effect of the same solemn cadence often repeated. The phrasing of the short 'Elegy upon Prince Henryes Death', after its pent-up opening, is rather similar. In both, for an epigrammatic close, there are more sharply articulated couplets:

> Their vines shall barren be, Their Land yeild Tares;
> Their house shall have no dwellers; They no heires.
>
> 'Woes of Esay', 17–18.

> For all the woe ruine e're buryed
> Throngs in this narrow compass, Henry's dead.
>
> 'Elegy upon Prince Henryes Death',
first version, 17–18.

Other poems, like the satirical address 'To his Unconstant Freind', move entirely in this pointed and emphatic rhythm.

Henry King depended very much upon imagery, and here there is, as Miss Tuve showed, much variety of intention and of treatment. In the thirteenth chapter of *Elizabethan and Metaphysical Imagery* she chose to illustrate the 'effects of specific logical functions upon the poetic character of images' mainly from his work, finding both in the poems and in the sermons abundant examples of three distinct qualities: 'witty compression' characteristic of defining images;[1] the 'special concision and neat concreteness' belonging to passages using 'images which differentiate';[2] and 'acutely argued similitudes' whose

---

[1] Op. cit., p. 356; among her examples is this from 'An Elegy Occasioned by Sicknesse':

> I would informe the Soule before the Eyes:
> Make Man into his proper Opticks look,
> And *so become the Student and the Book.*

[2] Op. cit., p. 365; Miss Tuve gives (p. 369) examples of figures of difference used in complaint, in argument, and to cheer or hearten: in 'A Sermon of Deliverance' (1626), to cheer: 'And although *like a tempestuous Autumne,* [Death] shakes us *by heaps* into our Graves, our Extraction *will be more orderly*'; in an 'Elegy on Lady Anne Riche' (1638), he complains against Death:

> Think'st Thou 'tis just
> To sprinkle our fresh Blossomes with thy Dust?
> Till by abortive Funeralls *thou bring*
> *That to an Autumne, Nature mean't a Spring?*

And in his last Elegy (1657) he disputes:

> O wherefore since we *must in Order rise,*
> Should wee not *Fall in equal Obsequies?*
> But bear th'Assaults of an uneven Fate . . .

function was to 'bring proof or support a position'.[1] In the course of her discussion much light is thrown on King's art. She demonstrates the special skill with which he was able to assess the varying need for explanation: in some cases he prepared the way for an image by direct statement of the situation which was to be illustrated;[2] in others he made use of similitudes 'never openly stated' though unmistakably implied.[3] She praises his use of imagery 'with far-echoing suggestions, exquisitely controlled';[4] and perhaps here it is worth noting, as an example of this kind of tact, how in the 'Elegy upon S. W. R.' he has allowed a hint of the outward aspect of his subject—*wither'd, ag'd, white*— to grow from words which primarily belong to distinct images carrying the argument:

> I would pitty those
> Thy most industrious and freindly foes:
>
> .   .   .   .
>
> That thought by cutting off some wither'd dayes,
> (Which thou couldst spare them) to ecclipse thy praise,
> Yet gave it brighter foile, made thy ag'd fame
> Appeare more white and faire, then foule their shame;
> And did promote an Execution,
> Which (but for them) Nature and Age had done.

Miss Tuve's case, that the treatment of imagery was essentially functional, and was dictated by a well-defined concept of decorum, is irrefutable. King gives an impression of being, by natural bent and by training, both rational and decorous, and his manner of writing accords with contemporary literary theory as she has described it. There must sometimes have remained questions as to the share to be taken in a poem by imagery, and

---

[1] Op. cit., pp. 371, 372. An example comes from 'Silence. A Sonnet', where he proves the impossibility of 'bestowing' grief:

> Was ever Stomack that lack't meat
> Nourish't by what another eat?

[2] Op. cit., p. 176 and n. 27.

[3] Op. cit., p. 362: 'the basic similitude is unstated, as in the military figure which constitutes a comment upon an unseasonable death: "nor are wee *billeted in one Clime*".'   [4] Op. cit., p. 177.

how illustration was to be chosen and developed, which could finally have been decided only on grounds of individual preference, and on such decisions, to some extent, poetic character depends. Henry King's poems display varied aspects. His inclination was ordinarily towards a free use of imagery, so that even in such plain and informal pieces as the addresses to his 'Freinds at Christchurch', and to his sister Anne 'who chid [him] in verse for being angry', figurative speech came naturally and inevitably: 'is it true . . . Their Hobby-horse from ours hath borne the bell?' and

> Well is a Passion to the Markett brought
> When such a Treasure of Advise is bought
> With so much Drosse.

In more highly-wrought pieces the formation of images to convey his meaning is so rapid and free, and so apparently spontaneous, as to seem almost involuntary. Favourite pictures recur often: there is frequent reference to altars, shrines, and flames; ice, tempest and flood; quarries, rocks, and tombs; the relations of the heavenly bodies; and amongst human affairs, legal processes, journeys, and war. His interest and pleasure in imagery are reflected in the skill with which he draws from simple and limited sources apt and sometimes subtle parallels to the situations with which he is concerned.

The presence or absence of figures, and the variation in treatment of those that were admitted, was always in accordance with King's sense of what was appropriate. His rare approaches to plainness seem to indicate moments of intensest feeling, as in 'The Departure', 'But here I am quite lost; writing to you All that I pen or think is forct and new'; or in the account of what was visible to the lover of the 'ill favour'd' woman,

> A richer Beauty in her mind:
> Where somthing is so lasting Faire,
> As Time, or Age cannot empaire.

This plainness of statement in 'The Defence' is a strong element in its calculated contrast with 'The Ill-favour'd Choice', a poem (in King's own term elsewhere) 'larded' with crude simile; crudeness and excess there were the means to a particular effect. There was deliberate aim, similarly, in the quick strokes of verbal wit which give edge to the tone of satirical passages: in 'To his unconstant Freind' he has escaped the danger of lunacy from her 'changing Moon-like fitts'; and he will not run 'upon his Verses' feet' to the *lugentes campi* of lovers in Virgil's hell; again with play on words, but of a different kind, he mocks in 'A Letter' an undignified satisfaction in the notice of an armigerous acquaintance, 'If but the Passant Lord . . . afford The Nod Regardant'. King produces this kind of ingenuity without awkwardness, but seems not to have been drawn to it often. Very different in aim, in treatment, and in emotive quality is the majestic growth of the figure which opens 'An Elegy upon Prince Henryes death', where the picture is completed and the application made clear only at the end of six slow lines:

> Keep station Nature, and rest Heaven sure
> On thy Supporter's shoulders, least past cure
> Thou dash't in ruine fall, by a griefe's weight
> Will make thy bases shrink, and lay thy height
> Lowe as the Center! Heark, and feele it read
> Through the astonish't kingdom, Henry's dead.

His treatment, in three poems written at widely separate dates, of the single concept of love as fire, reflects the change which came over his poetry as he passed from the earliest careful attempts to the expressive verse of his middle years and the uneven writing of the last poems. These examples are from the 'sonnet' 'Tell me no more' (Saintsbury's favourite); an earlier 'sonnet' from the first collection, 'Tell me you stars'; and 'St. Valentine's Day', written apparently about 1647/8 and referring to his long mourning for the wife who died in 1624. The early poem ends, neatly but without subtlety, on the antithesis of two impossible outcomes of a situation:

> O! or give Hir my flame, to melt that snow
> Which, yet unthaw'd, does on hir Bosome grow:

> Or make mee Ice; and with Hir Christall chaines
> Bind up all Love within my frozen Veines.

An extra dimension seems to have been achieved in the middle-period sonnet. The function of the image in its close is to express and to reconcile the elements of a paradox: glory and destructive power are present together in the flame

> Which crownes my Heart, when e're it dyes,
> In that it falles Hir Sacrifice.

The dry argument of 'St. Valentine's Day', in contrast to this, may seem to reflect a loss of vitality: the poet's

> fading day
> Like to a dedicated Taper lay
> Within a Tomb, and long burnt out in vain
> Since nothing there saw better by the flame.

That his metrical gift was inborn, whilst the management of imagery was achieved through effort, may be argued from the corrections he made:[1] almost the only revisions concerned primarily with sound are those in 'An Epitaph on . . . the Earle of Dorset', where there is a deliberately introduced iteration of the word *one*; and 'By Occasion of the Young Prince his happy Birth', in which the word *long* was treated in the same way: usually his alterations reflect dissatisfaction with imagery. On the 'Elegy upon Prince Henryes Death' he expended what appears to be an extraordinary degree of care; two final corrections are found only in the printed edition of 1657, and must have been made at least thirty years after the original occasion. Something of the nature of his aims and his difficulties emerges from this long process of correction. His temptation seems to have been to load his poetry with figures of inexact application. His final choice rejected all but those capable of fusion with the subject, able to bear without contortion the weight of his meaning. For example,

---

[1] See pp. 49, 51–52, and 56 below. Some of the later poems were still being altered in the years between the copying of the earliest authoritative manuscript and the printing of the edition of 1657.

from the original opening of the 'Elegy' a personification of 'death and horror' was pruned away, and their offspring 'teeming mischief' went with them, leaving a plain statement of greater significance and greater dignity. He was concerned also to avoid repetition. Originally 'Compendious Eloquence' in line 11 stressed needlessly an idea repeated in 'Two words' (the idea which the whole structure of the poem was in any case intended to illustrate); this was changed to point the meaning of 'Plague, Fire or Swords', and became first 'O murthering Eloquence', and at last (leaving out the inappropriate moral implication of 'murthering') 'Oh killing rhetorick'; one of the final alterations was to the same end in line 18, which, when the manuscripts were copied, had read 'Throngs in this narrow compasse', but in 1657 was, more literally, 'Sounds in these fatal accents'. In its first state, the Elegy ended at line 18, with the repeated 'Henry's dead'. The apology for 'unable Poetry' was an early addition which had undergone revision before the authoritative manuscripts were copied: for the earliest 'Here then break off my Muse, thy love and phrase Is hoarse', he substituted an impersonal address to 'unable Poetry', from which 'love' (inappropriate equally to the Muse and to Poetry) has disappeared; and the figurative 'hoarse' was changed to the more literal 'weak'. In all this, the purpose was to relieve the verse of whatever irrelevance of epithet or of imagery had suggested itself, and so to bring the expression sharply into focus. Since the original conclusion (lines 17–18) had been sacrificed to the need for apology, there had to be found a new ending. At first this was a loosely applied 'sentence':

> We learn by this Mortality
> The Sun rose but to set, frail man to die.

By the time the manuscripts were copied, the whole meaning had been transmuted into the two words 'Dying Sunne', a compression which made way for the eloquent and closely applied image which now stands. By a similar process, the image of the Sybil in a later poem, 'To a Lady who sent me a copy of verses at my going to bed', was compressed, with no loss of meaning, from four lines of the first version,

> Or you some Sybill are, sent to unty
> The knotty Riddles of all Poetry:
> Whilst your smooth Numbers such perfections tell,
> As prove your self a Moderne Oracle,

into this brief parenthesis:

> Nor can I make my drowsie sense indite
> Which by your verses' musick (as a spell
> Sent from the Sybillean Oracle)
> Is charm'd . . .

In the last of his 'Elegies', King spoke of poetry as 'That Art wherewith our Crosses we beguile'.[1] An attempt has been made to indicate something of the study and experiment and effort through which he attained that art. The occasion on which he came nearest to perfection in its use was his wife's death in the winter of 1623–4. In all the manuscripts, and in the edition of 1657, 'An Exequy' is placed next after the 'Epitaph on the Earl of Dorset'. Dorset died on 28 March, and Anne King had been buried on 5 January; but the 'Epitaph' may well have been written almost at once on its occasion; and the 'Exequy' not until there had been time for the days and nights to have formed themselves into a discernible pattern. It is possibly the later composition; certainly it is Henry King's best, early or late.

Though it is alone in its excellence, I find it a characteristic work. From his earlier poems the quality of the 'Exequy' could hardly have been predicted, but from the first there had at times been apparent elements of the same art which is here used with unique effect. And on rare occasions in the early group of poems he had spoken with the same moving simplicity and warmth; there was his account of the lovers who in 'The Surrender'

> did nothing study but the way
> To love each other, with which thoughts the Day
> Rose with delight . . . and with them sett;

---

[1] 'An Elegy upon my Best Friend L. K. C.', 1657, l. 43; cf. 'The Departure', ll. 3–5, 'I could then with ease Attire my Grief in words, and so appease That Passion', and Donne, 'The triple Foole', l. 11. See R. Tuve, op. cit., p. 171.

or the future foreseen for the friend to whom he gave Overbury's
Wife,

> When you so farr love any, that you dare
> Venter your whole affection on his care.

Here we recognize for a moment the voice of transparent sin-
cerity in which he spoke, for the first time at length, on Anne's
death. In the 'Exequy' he lays hold of a situation he regards as
'Heaven's will'. Happiness is seen no longer in relation to time,
but to eternity, and the lament with its epithalamic overtones
ends in his expressed acceptance.

The choice of verse in which to 'fetter' grief (it is Donne's
phrase) fell on the eight-syllabled couplet used earlier by Jonson
for his best funeral epigrams, and by King himself in 'The
Defence' and in some of the 'Sonnets'. It moves, as his other
elegiac poems do, in long phrases of unpredictable length; and
though the couplet structure is clearly marked, pauses fall as
often in the middle of the line as at the end. The varied move-
ment of the verse seems to have an independent beauty of its
own. But it was not King's way to concern himself primarily
with the sound of his verse. The form of each paragraph of the
'Exequy' is determined by the needs of the phase reached in the
argument. He never goes far without passing into an image,
sometimes briefly, even by the use of a single word;[1] sometimes
at greater length, allowing one image to touch off another,
delaying the moment of coming to rest, and drawing out the
phrases into a melodious variety:

> Deare Losse! since thy untimely fate
> My task hath beene to meditate
> On Thee, on Thee: Thou art the Book,
> The Library whereon I look
> Though almost blind. For Thee (Lov'd Clay!)
> I Languish out, not Live the Day,
> Using no other Exercise
> But what I practise with mine Eyes.

[1] For example, in the first paragraph, *crown, strew, melted*.

> By which wett glasses I find out
> How lazily Time creepes about
> To one that mournes: This, only This
> My exercise and bus'nes is:
> So I compute the weary howres
> With Sighes dissolved into Showres.

For the most part, the imagery of the 'Exequy' comes from places which had been drawn on for King's earlier poems;[1] and perhaps there was some gain in the quality of *concinnity*, admired by James Howell,[2] from this use of material on which consideration had already been spent. The seed from which grew the cosmic imagery of the third paragraph (21–38) was the trite sentence originally considered for the conclusion of Prince Henry's elegy: here he assumes that the way is prepared, and without the interruption of establishing the metaphor, speaks at once from within it, 'Thou hast benighted me'. The different aspects of the image so introduced extend through a long paragraph, closing with her 'strange ecclipse'. With the same directness of entry he calls up by a single word the familiar image of a ship, in the passage on his journey after her (ll. 84–106):

> At Night when I betake to rest
> Next Morne I rise neerer my West
> Of Life, almost by eight Howres' *sayle*
> Then when Sleep breath'd his drowsy gale.

Here he deals swiftly with the image, compressing his voyage into four more lines, in which he draws on the equation of life with day made earlier in the poem:

> Thus from the Sunne my Bottome steares
> And my Daye's Compasse downeward beares.
> Nor labour I to stemme the Tide,
> Through which to Thee I swiftly glide.

This is more complex than the ship in 'To his unconstant

---

[1] Some parallels follow: 9 *book*: 'The Surrender', l. 5; 23 *set*, 25 *day*: 'Elegy upon Prince Henryes Death', ll. 27–28; 34 *fled star*: 'Sic Vita', l. 1; 47 *longest date*: 'The Surrender', l. 25; 65 *right and interest*: 'Sic Vita', l. 8; 81 *cold bed*: 'An Essay on Death and a Prison', l. 47; 101 *my bottom steers*: 'To his unconstant Freind', l. 65.

[2] See p. 17 above.

Freind', in which he launched off 'with triumph' in search of 'safe harbour'; and there is a suggestion here of that other 'safe harbour' of 'An Essay on Death and a Prison', the coffin.

At one point there are signs that King failed to satisfy himself. This is in the passage which deals in legal and financial terms (used by him in other places without discordance) with the earth's temporary possession of her dust. It is hardly successful; and King himself seems not to have found it so. Amongst miscellaneous manuscript copies, five have signs of trouble between lines 65 and 70, suggesting that their originals were imperfect at this point; and an indication that the difficulty here was never fully resolved survives in one of his very rare admissions of assonance, *grief/keep* in lines 66–67.

A quality which sets the 'Exequy' apart from King's other long poems is its sustained poetical intensity. Though the facts lying behind it could have been told in a very small space, much more might well have been needed to convey their full meaning in the context of thought and memory and feeling; by comparison with the compression and formality of style here, his other elegies seem to have dropped into a tone almost conversational. But even this rare quality of intensity is shared by the 'Sonnets', concerned as they are each with a single concept or incident, stated and developed through imagery exactly applied, to a final climax in epigram or paradox. The 'Exequy', having passed from one to another of a sequence of concepts so treated, ends just in the same way:

> Deare! (forgive
> The Crime) I am content to live
> Divided, with but half a Heart,
> Till wee shall Meet and Never part.

He did not again come near to the perfection of the 'Exequy', but in what he wrote after it there is vitality of a kind not often present in the earliest poems. The difference seems to lie in an increase of skill in communication; there exists between matter and form a juster proportion, creating a sense of necessity, and with it a new degree of interest in matter and in manner; and from time to time a word or an image, or some moment of verbal music, will remind his reader of the powers shown in the 'Exequy' itself. A condition for such writing seems to be that he should be contemplating an aspect of death, which so pre-occupied him that even the poem on 'the young Prince his happy Birth' has for its main topic the most sombre implication of the word 'Heir'; and a poem intended to welcome the Queen at Oxford on her visit in 1643 is partly concerned with her future 'fame and memory in death'. Nor, looking as he did at temporal things from a position a little withdrawn, could he consider the newly launched ship the *Soveraigne* without thought of her possible end, and on that thought he brings together ingenious metaphor and an unusually pictorial treatment:

> O never may crosse Wind or swelling Wave
> Conspire to make the treach'rous Sandes thy Grave:
> Nor envious Rocks in their white foamy laugh
> Rejoice to weare thy Losse's Epitaph.

Occasionally (in, for example, the second verse of 'Tell me no more', or the third verse of 'The Vow-Breaker') he seems to bring in death too lightly; and because of the general seriousness of his tone the effect is of bombast. This kind of incongruity is never found when death is his immediate concern. The 'Elegy occasioned by Sicknesse' rises from a definition of life in drab commonplace and similitude to a radiant climax, echoing Donne:

> But Faith steares up to a more glorious scope
> Which sweetens our sharp passage: And firme Hope
> Anchors our torne Barkes on a Blessed Shoare,
> Beyond the Dead Sea wee here ferry o're.
> To this Death is our Pilott . . .

'The Dirge', written on the theme of the earlier 'Sic Vita', shows the same concern for imagery and for sound as the 'Sonnets': each stanza holds an image of life subsiding into death: it is a war, a tempest, a flower, a dream, the shadow on a sun-dial, a play. Each succeeding metaphor has its own growth and its own beauty, and is applied with exact precision; and the meaning

is reflected in the sound, the momentum failing from an im-
petuous opening of three light syllables ('It is a . . .') to the
solemn conclusion. But 'The Dirge' shares with most of King's
shorter poems a limitation which, by Professor F. P. Wilson's
definition,[1] must banish it from 'the school of Donne': it lacks
what he called 'sequaciousness', it does not proceed.

From the time of the first printed appearance of King's poems
in 1657 the element of likeness which does exist between some
of his writing and Donne's has often been stressed. Richard
Marriot chose to print on his first page 'The Double Rock',
which differs from most of King's 'Sonnets' in its greater energy
of expression, in the intricate conceit of its imagery, and in its
stanzaic form; next to it was 'The Vow-Breaker', which in its
vehemence is again quite unlike King's usual tone. In both, there
was probably a conscious intention to resemble some of Donne's
'Songs and Sonets', and there are other imitative passages; but
it is as easy to find deliberate reference to Donne in verbal echo
as genuine likeness to his manner, and neither is very common.
King's first elegy, on Prince Henry's death in 1612, seems to
owe less to Donne than to a speech of Juliet's at a crisis in her
tragedy:

> Tybalt is dead and Romeo banished.
> That 'banished', that one word 'banished',
> Hath slain ten thousand Tybalts . . .
> . . . 'Romeo is banished'.
> There is no end, no limit, measure, bound,
> In that word's death; no words can that woe sound[2]—

and King's correction of this 'Elegy', described earlier, shows
him concerned to eliminate faults rather neo-Shakespearian than
neo-metaphysical. Perhaps somewhere in Shakespeare it may be
possible to find almost anything that is looked for; certainly
the Shakespeare of *Richard II* and *Romeo and Juliet* expressed
thoughts which recur, not much changed in form or in imagery,

[1] F. P. Wilson, *Elizabethan and Jacobean*, 1945, p. 58.
[2] *Romeo and Juliet*, III. ii. 112.

in King's poems. His 'Surrender' seems to be indebted to Richard II's parting from his queen; his 'Farewell' is reminiscent of Richard's despairing vision of his deposed state: 'I'll give my jewels for a set of beads; My gorgeous palace for a hermitage';[1] and there are other points of likeness.

A willingness to accept suggestion from other poets is not the same as dependence on them, and King's own manner is distinctive and independent to a degree beyond that suggested by the often-repeated phrase 'Donne's literary disciple'; he was this no more than he was Jonson's or Shakespeare's. He kept and developed in later years habits of poetic composition formed at Westminster. And much of his poetry was undertaken with a seriousness which, while it admitted close concern with poetic form, could not easily have allowed expense of effort on imitating the characteristic forms of expression of another mind.

Late in his life a kind of writing new to King grew out of his increasing preoccupation with satire. There had always been a tendency for some chance reference to bring him for a few lines into a satirical vein, rather in the manner of Jonson; he had revealed himself a little in the earlier poems by the topics of disapproval: 'pretended Witt', 'enamour'd Tristrams . . . Borne to make paper deare with [their] laments', or censorious courtiers who in fact 'doe but little knowe'.[2] None of his occasional poems of the sixteen-thirties is without a brief passage of this kind: there is one in the poem on the prince's birth, in the Elegy on Donne ('poetick eyes' who 'melt themselves in easy Elegyes') and in 'To . . . Mr. Henry Blount upon his Voyage' ('our Gadders' triviall reach'). In the Elegy on Gustavus Adolphus the satiric tone becomes unexpectedly audible in the comparison of Julius Caesar's exploits with the Swedish King's:

> the Roman thought he had done much
> Did he the Bank of Rhenus only touch.

---

[1] *Richard II*, v. i. 86 and III. iii. 147.
[2] 'Woes of Esay', 61–74; 'To his unconstant Freind', 51–52; 'To his Freinds of Christchurch', 17–24.

At last, in the 'Elegy on Sir Charls Lucas, and Sir George Lisle', 1648, satire usurps the greatest part. The poem begins in the solemn elegiac manner, but at a point where he turns to harangue the New Model Army the tone is transformed: the verse becomes swift and clear, and he strides through a strongly biased narrative, knocking home his points with quick strokes of irony, with references to parallel stories, now mainly drawn from the Bible, even with rapid jokes. This achievement of an admirable pamphlet style prepared the way for the second elegy on Charles I, which again breaks away from the elegiac manner into vigorous satirical reproach. King in this mood writes with perfect clarity and with incisive emphasis. Though his thought and his imagery show an extreme conservatism, neither his point of view nor the kind of figure chosen to convey it having changed since the earliest poems, the sound of this verse is a reminder that he had lived long enough to see, and partly to sympathize with, an age very different from that in which he had grown up. The climax of the elegy is a curious blend of the new style with sentiments familiar since the poem on Sir Walter Ralegh:

> We must impute
> That Lustre which His Sufferings contribute
> To your preposterous Wisdoms, who have done
> All your good Deeds by Contradiction:
> For as to work His Peace you rais'd this Strife,
> And often Shot at Him to Save His Life;
> As you took from Him to Encrease His wealth,
> And kept Him Pris'ner to secure His Health;
> So in revenge of your dissembled Spight,
> In this last Wrong you did Him greatest Right,
> And (cross to all You meant) by Plucking down
> Lifted Him up to His Eternal Crown.

TEXT AND CANON OF THE POEMS

King's poems survive in an edition printed during his lifetime, but without his consent, on which modern editions have been based; in three manuscript collections containing his poems alone; and in a number of miscellaneous contemporary copies, printed and manuscript.

(1) *Manuscript Collections*[1]

I take first the three manuscript collections, because for each of them a connexion can be argued with King himself. Dr. Percy Simpson, in an article on 'The Bodleian Manuscripts of Henry King', *Bodleian Quarterly Record*, v, 1926–9, p. 60, showed that MS. Eng. poet. e. 30 was corrected by King, and that the other Bodleian manuscript, Malone 22, was copied by a hand that had assisted in the corrected manuscript. In the third collection, there are signs that the copyist acquired at different times extra lines, new titles, and new poems, and it is unlikely that the source of these was far removed from King himself. All three manuscripts show an extreme degree of care both in their text and in their physical appearance. They are as follows:

H, Bodl. MS. Eng. poet. e. 30, 'Hannah's manuscript', called after Archdeacon John Hannah, who borrowed it for his edition of 1843 from his publisher William Pickering. Later it disappeared, and was not available for the editions of Mason, Saintsbury, or John Sparrow. It may be the one described in the Historical Manuscript Commission's *Second Report*, 1871, p. 7, among manuscripts belonging to the Countess Cowper and Baroness Lucas, Wrest Park, Bedfordshire (no. 51). It was acquired by the Bodleian Library in 1928.

The copyist of most of *H* was Thomas Manne, Chaplain of Christ Church, Oxford, from 1605 to 1635. His signature is in the college disbursement books during that period, and the same distinctive hand is also found in a book kept by Henry King's uncle, Philip King, as auditor of Christ Church, in papers relating to Christ Church and the Kings in the Bodleian Library, and in copies of Henry King's poems now in the British Museum;[2] Manne also started the collection of poems which is described

---

[1] I included an account of these manuscripts in 'Notes on the Physical Characteristics of some manuscripts of the poems of Donne and of Henry King', printed in *The Library*, 5th ser., xvi, 1961, pp. 121–32.   [2] Cf. pp. 197, 221.

on p. 56. For Henry King he copied in *H* fifty-four poems. His writing became increasingly shaky as the work proceeded; and the variation in appearance between one part of the manuscript and another suggests that he may have had it in hand for some time. The last dated poem he copied is 'Upon the King's Happy Returne from Scotland', 1633.

Ten more poems were added by another scribe, who apparently formed his writing on a meticulous imitation of Manne's. This was an extremely conscientious person, even more anxious for accuracy than for good appearance. His exemplary character as a copyist is revealed by the insignificance of the slips which he thought it worth while to put right. The poems he added include those relating to events of 1636–8, but, although space remained, not the 'Elegy on Mrs. Kirke', July 1641.

Henry King's corrections in *H* are of more than one kind. Where the copyist was unable to read a word in the original he left a blank, which King filled. In a few places mistakes were corrected. Titles were added to four poems, and a date to the poem on 'the Young Prince his happy Birth'. In three poems readings were altered, not so skilfully as to hide the lines in their earlier state. All through the manuscript punctuation was added.

The pages left blank at the end were later filled by another hand, which copied the funeral sermon on Katherine, Countess of Leinster (she was buried at Malpas in Cheshire, 3 July 1657), an epitaph, and King's elegy on her. For this part there is no such evidence of connexion with Henry King as that which gives authority to the two earlier sections. It is conceivable that the book was originally copied for the countess, whose death deprived the art of poetry of 'further use' for him, and who had even extracted from him a 'jest' about mourning verse; in that case it may well have seemed appropriate to whoever inherited it from her that the blank leaves should be filled with memorial verse and prose; but not all of this need be taken for King's.

M, Bodl. MS. Malone 22, was copied by Manne's imitator, whose hand in this manuscript has a more settled and regular appearance than in the additions to *H*. There are included sixty-one poems, which leave no space. *M*, alone of the three authoritative manuscripts, is in its original binding, and it appears to be complete.

Malone's books reached the Bodleian in 1821, and this manuscript was used by all King's editors.

P, Phillipps MS. 9325, earlier in the possession of the Marquis of Blandford, now owned by Sir Geoffrey Keynes, was first used by John Sparrow for his edition of 1925. There were originally included seventy-four poems, of which the last is on the death of the Earl of Essex in 1646. Down to the page (159) on which this poem ends, the writing was constant, and the practice of numbering the pages, and of ruling margins with dry point in double lines, was invariable; the uniformity of appearance suggests that this part of the work was completed in a short space of time. After p. 159 more copies follow, but the page-numbers cease, the margins are single lines, and there appear in the writing different forms of certain letters, which give a new (and comparatively ungraceful) general appearance. Four poems were added after these changes: one of them, the 'Epigram on Colonel Hammond', refers to an incident which happened in March 1647/8. Earlier in the book additional titles were written in, but not all at one time, for the ink varies. An English translation of the Latin epigram on Bishop John King was written in a space after the elegy on his death. Minor corrections to other poems were made after the hand had changed.

The copyist of *P* was less exact than Thomas Manne and his imitator, and there are some mistakes, but the general impression given is still one of great care.

Though the content and order of *H*, *M*, and *P* are not precisely the same, the textual agreement is so close in poems which are included in all three as to suggest a common origin. There is a near approach to unanimity between them in spelling, in punctuation, and in an apparently capricious use of capital letters. They are even in agreement in their rare mistakes, seeming to have encountered difficulty at the same points. For example, in

'The Woes of Esay', 110, the reading 'mounted vpon high' formerly appeared in all three manuscripts; in *H* a correction was made to 'vpp, on' and in *P* to 'vp on'. Again, in 'Sic Vita', 11, 'the Dew dry'd vp', though plainly wrong, was copied in *H* and *P*, while *M* had the sensible but wrong emendation, 'the Dews dry'd vp'; in both *M* and *P* there is a correction to 'the Dew dryes vp'. Other alterations by the scribes show that what they were copying was in places difficult to read: *H* and *P* first read in 'A Penitentiall Hymne', 8, 'can not'; both were corrected to agree with *M*, 'can nor'. In 'A Blackmore Mayd', 5, the word 'doe' was missed and had to be inserted above the line in *H* and *P*. In the elegy on Gustavus Adolphus, 37, *H* and *P* both read 'Fate' for 'Hate'; in *H*, Thomas Manne corrected himself, but in *P* the mistake was allowed to stand. The copyist of *M* seems on the whole to have had less trouble, but in 'By Occasion of the young Prince his happy Birth', 24, where *H* reads 'the Parent' and *P* 'his parent', *M* has 'his' corrected to 'the'; this is one of several cases where in *M* minor changes were made from readings of *P* to those of *H*; and probably in these places an obscurity of the original baffled the copyist of *P*, misled at first the copyist of *M*, but presented no lasting difficulty to Thomas Manne in *H*. In the notes to the poems are mentioned some other points which support the view that the three manuscripts derive from the same original copy.

Their more significant differences are mostly of a kind which would have resulted from their original's growing, as *P* grew, or from revision of the original, like King's revision of *H*. They represent successive stages. Text and content show *H* to have been the earliest, including no poem that can be dated much after 1638. When *H* was copied, there were early versions of five poems which were later to be revised: 'The Retreit', 'Love's Harvest', 'The Dirge', 'To One demanding why Wine sparkles', and 'To a Lady who sent me a copy of verses at my going to bed'; and twelve poems, which were afterwards given precise titles, then appeared merely as 'Sonnet' or 'An Elegy'. Henry King's own changes in *H* were made before the copying of *M*, in which the copyist included the same revised readings and titles as King had written in *H*, besides several more minor revisions, and two additional titles. *P* was the last. It includes with earlier work poems which belong to the years 1641–8. There were by then substantially revised versions of three of the poems mentioned above, which were included, with other slighter revisions, and six new titles.

The manuscripts do not agree in order throughout, but the same poems are found together in all three, apparently grouped according to the order of their composition, with exceptions which are for the most part accountable. At the beginning, all of them had the same group of twenty poems in the same order;[1] there are included in this collection the earliest dated poems, on the deaths of Prince Henry, 1612, of Anne King, 1623/4, and of the Earl of Dorset, 1624. After this, differences between the three manuscripts suggest an original copied on loose sheets whose arrangement could be altered. In a section containing occasional poems dating from 'The Anniverse', January 1629/30, to the elegy on Gustavus Adolphus, November 1632, *M* differs considerably from *H* in order, and is fairly closely followed by *P*; after this a series of poems including 'Upon the King's happy Returne from Scotland', 1633, appears in each manuscript with very slight variation in arrangement; with this series Manne's section of *H* ends. The next series, including occasional poems of 1636–8, was added by the second hand in *H*, and again varies in order only slightly from one manuscript to another, though part of it was omitted from *M*. After this *H* drops out, and *P* continues alone.

From the three manuscript collections together, a fairly close approach can be made to Henry King's own collection of his poems from 1612 to the spring of 1647/8. Their concurrence over spelling, punctuation, and an unpredictable use of capital

---

[1] This agreement is partly obscured, because in *H* the 'Penitentiall Hymne' was added on an unnumbered leaf before the first poem, and in *M* extra poems were introduced: 'My Midd-night Meditation' was brought in to be next to 'Sic Vita', and 'The Anniverse' next to 'An Exequy', where they are appropriately placed; the third addition in *M* is the Sonnet, 'Tell me no more'. Cf. pp. 54–55 and note.

letters can only mean that each of the scribes aimed at an exact reproduction, which they were not far from achieving; their successive versions of the text of corrected poems give the same information that a clearly corrected holograph might have done; their positive evidence as to canon is unquestionable; and from their order, additions, and omissions some idea of the order in which the poems were composed can be formed.

It is therefore from these manuscripts, and not from the printed edition, that the text and arrangement of the poems here have been taken; but the occasional poems, which in the manuscripts come in little groups interspersed among poems of other kinds, are here collected together in their chronological order at the beginning, followed by the undated poems in the order suggested by their positions in the manuscripts (the probable dates of their composition are given in the notes). The most reliable scribe was Manne's imitator, who completed *H* and copied *M*; and wherever possible his text has been followed; in the latest poems, which he did not copy, and in the final versions of revised passages the text given here follows the printed edition.

(2) *Poems, Elegies, Paradoxes, and Sonnets, 1657, and second issue, 1664*

The printed edition appeared anonymously, though it was entered in the Stationers' Register on 11 March 1656/7 as 'Poems by Dr. Hen: King, Bishop of Chicester'. The 'publishers', Richard Marriot and Henry Herringman, printed an address 'to the author', in which they made it clear that his consent had been withheld, and that what they called 'this hasty and immethodical impression' was due to their own initiative. They acknowledged the inspiration and assistance of 'friends that honour[ed]' the poet, who they said had 'furnished [them] with some papers which they thought Authentick'. A friend that honoured King, who was also a friend of Richard Marriot's, was Izaak Walton, and he could have been responsible; but I have not found evidence that he was.

The edition contains seventy-two poems, of which three—the 'Elegy on Lady Stanhope', 1654, 'The Acquittance', and 'The Forfeiture'—are not in the manuscripts. In 1664 the sheets were reissued, with four extra poems added at the end: these are three royalist elegies (of which one, on the Earl of Essex, was in *P*) and the elegy on the Countess of Leinster, 1657. The two issues are here referred to as *1657* and *1664*. A third appeared in 1700 as *Ben Johnson's Poems, Elegies, Paradoxes and Sonnets*.[1]

The publishers' remarks inspire little confidence, but when a textual comparison is made between *1657* and the manuscript collections a very close relationship appears, suggesting that the 'Authentick' papers may even have been the same that lie behind *H*, *M*, and *P*. It is unlikely that a printer working in 1657 intended to reproduce the archaic peculiarity of the manuscripts; but some characteristic oddities do appear in the printed text, in spite of the care of someone who made spelling approximately conventional, removed capital letters, took away stops from within the lines, and added them at line-endings. Apart from these differences the text of *1657* agrees almost exactly with the last manuscript, *P*.[2] What differences there are in text and content may be attributed to the continued processes of revision and growth.

The order of *1657* was new. The poems were arranged by kind, beginning with the songs and other secular poems; going on to occasional poems, with royal occasions first; and ending with religious and meditative poems. The few strays from the confines of this scheme may have been in the minds of the publishers when they spoke of their edition as 'immethodical'. One trace of the arrangement of the manuscripts survives: of the twenty poems collected in each of them at the beginning, in *1657* fourteen are found, scattered according to the new plan, but in pairs and threes, suggesting that physically they were

---

[1] See Sir Geoffrey Keynes's bibliography, *Sparrow*, p. 189.
[2] The punctuation of poems printed from *1657* in the following text has in some cases been corrected by *P*.

inseparable.[1] The probability is that these earliest poems had been copied on both sides of the leaves of a book.

(3) *Miscellaneous Copies*

The numerous other contemporary copies of King's poems in manuscript and in print add to the canon no more than one elegy; and to the text, a few variants which there is reason to accept as genuine early readings, amongst a host of differences which must be ascribed to chance.

The elegy is *A Groane* [or *A Deepe Groane, Fetch'd*] *at the Funerall of . . . Charles the First*, of which two editions were printed early in 1649, *A Groane* attributed to I.B. and *A Deepe Groane* attributed to D.H.K. Hannah thought that 'I.B.' was the corrected edition, and, partly for this reason, suspected the attribution to D.H.K., and was doubtful whether to admit the elegy to the canon. He found it much inferior to the other poem on the same subject printed in *1664*, and saw in it 'very few of the characteristics of [King's] style' (*Hannah*, p. cxxvii). John Sparrow has shown that in fact 'D.H.K.' was a corrected second edition (*Sparrow*, pp. 175–6; and see Sir G. Keynes's bibliography, op. cit., p. 187); he found in *A Deepe Groane* comparisons drawn from the same places as in the other elegy (lines 75 and 121), and stylistic devices used elsewhere in King's poetry (lines 18 and 148; see op. cit., pp. 175, 177. To the places noted by Mr. Sparrow may be added 115–20, which resemble 'Woes of Esay', 87 and final paragraph; and 214, *nephews*, with which may be compared a reference in the poem to Sandys, 32). *A Deepe Groane* is not characteristic of King at his best, but the inferiority noticed by Hannah is probably an effect of hurried composition. Its absence from *1664* would have been a stronger argument against admitting it to the canon if the publishers had not then been able to include another, and better, poem on the same subject.

[1] These are: the elegies on Prince Henry and S. W. R.; the 'Exequy' and the 'Epitaph' on the Earl of Dorset; 'The Woes of Esay' and 'An Essay on Death and a Prison'; 'To his unconstant Freind', 'Madam Gabrina', and 'The Defence'; 'Dry those fair . . .' and 'When I entreat'; 'The Farewell' and the Blackmoor poems.

Sources of variant readings in 'miscellaneous copies' are of two kinds. There are texts derived from King himself by compilers or printers, which seem to include changes made, perhaps not very deliberately, whilst copying: of this kind, examples are mentioned in the notes to the 'Penitentiall Hymne' and to the poems on Donne, Jonson, Gustavus Adolphus, Lady Anne Rich, and George Sandys. Variants of more interest are found in texts of a different kind, those derived from copies made earlier than the manuscript collections. From what the collections show of King's way of revising, it was to be expected that some changes would have been made during the twenty and more years which separate the first of them, *H*, from the composition of the first poems, and in fact some older versions have survived in isolated manuscript copies or in manuscript or printed miscellanies. In one instance, 'Love's Harvest', a miscellany reading is visible under King's correction of *H*: sometimes the miscellanies agree with *H* against the later texts of *M*, *P*, and *1657*; and more often they agree among themselves in readings which had already been revised by the time *H* was copied.

Lists of a selection of manuscripts and of the printed books containing King's poems are given on pp. 59–61. Readings have been quoted from only a few of them, and in most cases the reason for accepting their authority is given in the notes on the text of the poems concerned.

Three manuscript miscellanies contain substantial collections of King's poetry, and are of some authority. They are as follows: *TM*, Thomas Manne's notebook, in the possession of Mr. Philip Robinson, containing about a hundred poems by various authors copied at different times, not all by Manne himself. The first section, of thirty-nine poems, is in the calligraphic hand Manne used in copying *H*. It begins with the 'Exequy', followed by John King's poems on the same occasion, and includes seven more of Henry King's earlier poems. There are present in these eight poems variants which belong to an earlier stage of revision than is found in *H*. In the rest of the manuscript there are fewer variants, but it appears from readings in 'By Occasion of the young Prince his happy Birth' and 'The Dirge' that for the most part a state between *H* and the other authoritative collections is represented. The second section consists of thirty-two poems copied by Manne in a less formal style; the dated poems here belong to the early sixteen-thirties; nine of Henry King's are included. Six other hands made additions, among which are included seven more poems by Henry King. At least two leaves are missing.

The poets represented are nearly all members of Christ Church, and the King family occupies a large share of the space: besides Henry's twenty-four poems there are ten, and perhaps more, by his brother John,[1] and epitaphs and elegies on their father, on Henry's wife, on his son, and on John's children Dorothy and William. Henry King's poems belong to a wide range of date, from the elegy on Prince Henry, 1612, to the paradox, 'Fair one, why', which was probably written in 1644, added after Manne had parted with the book. Manne and his successors gave few ascriptions, but to four poems Henry King's hand has added the name 'R[ichard Earl of] Dorset'.

Harl., British Museum MSS. Harl. 6917–18. The collection of Peter Calfe, in whose varied handwriting the whole of both volumes appears to me to be:[2] towards the end of 6918 the hand is, at first intermittently, then consistently, much more cursive than at the beginning. Twenty-five poems in 6917 and six in 6918, mostly relating to the King family but not including any of Henry King's own, appear to have been copied from *TM* or from the same original. Besides these, there are seventeen of Henry King's poems in good texts from a different source. 'A Contemplation upon Flowers' is probably mistakenly attributed to H. Kinge at the end of 6917 (fol. 105ᵛ):[3] it is unlike his

---

[1] See Appendix II (i).

[2] Except fols. 94, 101ᵛ–102. But cf. *The Poems of Crashaw*, ed. L. C. Martin, 2nd ed., 1957, p. lxxvi.

[3] Printed as a 'Doubtful Poem', *Mason*, p. 177, *Sparrow*, p. 155, *Saintsbury*, p. 273; cf. p. 251 below.

usual writing in thought, in expression, and in cadence; in British Museum Add. MS. 47111 it appears again, this time attributed to Mr. R. C. Poems by John King are among those shared by *Harl.* with *TM*, and the younger brothers William and Philip are also represented. Poems initialed P. C. at the end of 6918 are imitations of Henry King.

Add. British Museum Add. MS. 25707. A manuscript first intended as a Donne collection, starting with thirty-four of his poems copied by two hands.[1] After them, the collection was continued by a third hand,[2] which added a miscellaneous selection of poems, including a great many not by Donne. On fol. 134, having left about forty leaves blank, this hand made a new start,[3] and in this section are good texts of seven of Henry King's poems, including 'On the King's Happy Return, 1633'. In this section also are a number of poems by William Skipwith,[4] who may himself have been the copyist. The manuscript was afterwards owned by someone who seems to have been intimate with the King family. He wrote at the beginning anagrams on 'Dorothie King',[5]

> For ought I ever sawe, felt, hard, or understood
> I vow, I swere as she is faire, *I think her good*,

and (perhaps because his name also was Will),

> When dainty Doll is truly understood
> Then all as well as *I will think her good.*

This writer gave a precise, though incomplete, date to Philip

---

[1] The first poems to be copied were Elegies on fols. 8–13ᵛ, numbered 2–12; in the space before them, fols. 5ᵛ–6ᵛ, a different hand, also found later in the manuscript, added 'Elegia 1'. These two hands wrote out thirty-four poems.

[2] He uses two kinds of script.

[3] Here he copied nothing of Donne's. Possibly his purpose had been altered by the appearance in 1633 of the printed edition of Donne's poems.

[4] There were Williams in the Royalist family of Skipworth of Cotes. Sir John Beaumont's *Bosworth-field*, 1629, includes (p. 163) a poem on the death of one Sir William, most probably the one who died in 1610. His son Henry was created a baronet in 1622, and may have written the 'Elegy on Charles I' which is included in this manuscript.

[5] Bishop John King's third daughter was Dorothy. She married, probably in the sixteen-thirties, Sir Richard Hubert, groom-porter to King Charles the First.

King's imitative exequy 'On his mistris deceased by a feaver', '19° 7^{mbris}' (fol. 79^v). His first copy was 'On Sr Kenelme Digbyes Lady 1633'. Good texts of eight of Henry King's poems are found written by this last hand in spaces left by the earlier copyists. Fols. 39–40 are a double sheet added by him, containing 'A letter written by Sr H: G: and J: D: alternis vicibus' and 'An Elegie on the Death of my never enough Lamented master King Charles the first' by Henry Skipwith or Skipworth.

LIST OF SEVENTEENTH-CENTURY MISCELLANIES, ETC., CONTAINING HENRY KING'S POEMS

Walter Porter, *Madrigales and Ayres*, 1632: 149 (2).[1]
Poems by Francis Beaumont, 1640: 148 (2).
Wits Recreations, 1641: 149 (1).
The Academy of Complements, 1646: 151, 168 (1), 169 (1).
Certain Elegant Poems by Dr. Corbet, 1647: 67 (2).
The Academy of Complements, 1650: 145, 151, 168 (1), 169 (1).
The Harmony of the Muses, 1654: 157 (3), 174.
Wits Interpreter, 1655: 149 (2).
Abraham Wright, *Parnassus Biceps*, 1656: 65, 145, 151, 157 (3), 160 (2).
Choyce Drollery, 1656: 160 (2).
Playford's *Select Ayres and Dialogues*, 1659: 149 (1).
John Donne the younger, *Poems by Pembroke and Ruddier*, 1660: 145, 147.
Le Prince d'Amour, 1660: 65.
The Divine Services and Anthems Usually sung in the Cathedrals and Collegiate Choires in the Church of England, by J[ames] C[lifford], 1663: 161.
A Crew of Kind London Gossips, 1663: 68.
Playford's *Select Ayres and Dialogues*, 1669: 151.
The Loyal Garland, 167[?] and 1678 (Percy Soc. Publications, xxix): 158 (1).

[1] The numbers refer to the page on which the poems concerned are printed. A second number, in brackets, is the number of the poem on that page.

LIST OF MISCELLANEOUS MANUSCRIPTS
USED

Bodleian Library, Oxford:

  MSS. Ashmole 36–37: 68.

               38: 67, (2), 81, 92, 144.

               47: 147, 151, 157 (3), 174.

  Don. c. 57: 149 (1), 149 (2), 151.

      d. 58: 68.

  Eng. misc. e. 13: 151.

           e. 262: 93.

  Eng. poet. c. 50: 67 (2), 157 (3).

           e. 14: 65, 145, 151, 157 (3).

           e. 37: 68.

           e. 97: 67 (2).

           f. 16: 151.

           f. 25: 145, 151.

  Firth d. 7: 67 (2).

       e. 4: 151, 167 (2).

  Jones 56: 92.

  Locke c. 32: 77.

  Malone 16: 157 (3).

         21: 65, 147, 151, 157 (3).

  Mus. b. 1: 147, 148 (1), 149 (1), 149 (2), 151, 158 (1), 158 (2), 162, 167 (2).

  Rawl. D. 398: 68, 174.

        692: 150.

        954: 66.

  Rawl. poet. 23: 161.

         26: 68, 76.

         65: 158 (1).

         84: 151, 157 (3).

         116: 145, 151.

         117: 144.

         160: 68, 77.

         172: 146.

         199: 151, 157 (3).

         206: 151.

         209: 65, 66, 67 (2).

  Top. Oxon. e. 380: 145, 146.

Corpus Christi College, Oxford:

  MSS. 325: 151.

       328: 66, 67 (2), 68, 145, 157 (3).

British Museum:

Add. MSS. 11811: 149 (2), 151.

        15227: 151.

        17062: 150.

        19268: 149 (2).

        21433: 142, 146, 149 (2), 157 (3).

        22582: 151.

        22602: 145.

        22603: 66, 144.

        23229: 167 (2), 168 (1), 169 (1).

        25303: 68, 142, 146, 149 (2), 157 (3).

        25707: 68, 77, 81, 146, 147, 149 (1), 149 (2), 158 (1), 159, 160 (2), 162, 167 (2), 168 (1), 170, 172.

        27408: 68, 139.

        30982: 67(2), 145, 151, 157 (3).

        33998: 83.

        47111: 139, 147, 158 (1), 177.

MSS. Burney 390: 174.

      Egerton 2013: 158 (1).

          2725: 68, 146, 147, 150, 151, 170.

      Harl. 3511: 149 (2), 151, 174.

        3910: 66.

        6057: 66, 142, 146, 157 (3).

        6346: 161.

        6917–18: 67 (1), 72 (1), 72 (2), 73, 96, 152, 159, 160 (1), 161, 162, 163, 164, 167, 168 (1), 168 (2), 172, 173.

        6931: 67 (2), 81, 151, 157 (3).

      Lansdowne 777: 66.

      Sloane 542: 67 (2), 151.

        1446: 72 (1), 72 (2), 73, 146, 148 (1), 148 (2), 149 (1), 149 (2), 151, 152, 156 (1), 158 (1), 160 (2), 162.

        1792: 67 (2), 145, 151.

      Stowe 962: 149 (1).

Cambridge Manuscripts:

University Library Add. MS. 79: 68.

St. John's College MSS. 417: 76, 77.

                 423: 147, 148 (1), 148 (2), 149 (1), 149 (2), 150, 151, 157 (3), 159.

Trinity College MS. R. 3. 12: 68, 149 (1), 151.

Mr. Philip Robinson's MS.:
  Manne's notebook: 65, 66, 67 (2), 68, 73, 76, 77, 93, 96, 136, 139, 142,
                145, 146, 148 (2), 150, 157 (3), 159, 167 (1), 170,
                172, 174, 177, 182.

Nottingham University Library:
  MS. Pw. V. 37: 68.

THE POEMS

NOTE ON THE TEXT

The poems are printed, wherever possible, from copies by King's second scribe, for reasons given on p. 49 (cf. p. 53). The poems which he did not copy are printed from the best available text, usually *1657* or *1664*; other sources are described in the notes to the poem concerned. Spelling, punctuation, and capital letters follow the originals, except that *u* and *v* are used according to modern practice, contractions have been expanded, and 'apostrophe *s*' has been introduced where its absence in the original might be confusing. Italics have been omitted from texts taken from printed copies. Variant readings are printed in the notes. The spelling of variants from miscellanies has usually been modernized.

An Elegy Upon Prince Henryes Death

Keep station Nature, and rest Heaven sure
On thy Supporter's shoulders, least past cure
Thou dash't in ruine fall, by a griefe's weight
Will make thy bases shrink, and lay thy height
Lowe as the Center! Heark, and feele it read   5
Through the astonish't Kingdom, Henry's dead.
It is enough. Who seekes to aggravate
One straine beyond this, prove more sharp his fate
Then sad our doome. The World dares not survive
To parallell this Woe's superlative.   10
Oh Killing rhetorick of Death! Two words
Breath stronger terrours, then Plague, Fire, or Swords
E're conquer'd. This were Epitaph and Verse
Worthy to be præfixt on Nature's Hearse,
Or Earth's sad dissolution; whose fall   15
Will be lesse grievous, though more generall.
For all the woe ruine e're buryed,
Sounds in these fatal accents, Henry's dead.
Cease then unable Poetry; Thy Phrase
Is weak and dull to strike us with amaze   20
Worthy thy vaster Subject. Let none dare
To coppy this sad happ, but with despaire
Hanging at his quill's point. For not a Streame
Of ink can write, much lesse improve this Theame.
Invention highest wrought by Grief or Witt   25
Must sink with Him, and on his Tombstone splitt.
Who, like the Dying Sunne, tells us the Light
And glory of our Day sett in His Night.

An Elegy Upon S. W. R.

I will not weep. For 'twere as great a Sinne
To shed a Teare for Thee, as to have bin
An Actor in thy Death. Thy Life and age
Was but a various Scæne on fortune's stage,
With whome thou tugg'st and strov'st ev'n out of breath 5
In thy long toile. Ne're master'd, till thy death;
And then, despight of traines and cruell witt,
Thou didst at once subdue malice and it.
   I dare not then so blast thy memory
As say I doe lament or pitty thee. 10
Were I to choose a Subject to bestow
My pitty on, he should be one as low
In spirit as desert. That durst not dy,
But rather were content by slavery
To purchase Life. Or I would pitty those 15
Thy most industrious and freindly foes:
Who when they thought to make thee scandall's story,
Lent thee a swifter flight to heav'n and glory.
That thought by cutting off some wither'd dayes,
(Which thou couldst spare them) to ecclipse thy praise, 20
Yet gave it brighter foile, made thy ag'd fame
Appeare more white and faire, then foule their shame;
And did promote an Execution,
Which (but for them) Nature and Age had done.
   Such worthlesse things as these were only borne 25
To live on Pittye's almes (Too meane for scorne).
Thou dy'dst an envious wonder, whose high fate
The world must still admire, scarce imitate.

To his Freinds of Christchurch upon the mislike of the Marriage of the Artes, acted at Woodstock

But is it true, the Court mislik't the Play,
That Christchurch and the Arts have lost the day?
That Ignoramus should so farr excell
Their Hobby-horse from ours hath borne the bell?
    Troth you are justly serv'd, that would present   5
Ought unto them, but shallow merriment;
Or to your Marriage-table did admitt
Guests, that are stronger farr in smell, then Witt.
    Had some quaint bawdry larded ev'ry Scæne,
Some fawning Sychophant, or courted Queane;   10
Had there appear'd some sharp, crosse-garter'd man,
Whome their loud laugh might nickname Puritan,
Cas'd up in factious breeches, and small ruff,
That hates the Surplis, and defyes the Cuff,
Then sure they would have giv'n applause to crowne   15
That which their ignorance did now cry downe.
    Let mee advise, when next you doe bestowe
Your paines on men that doe but little know,
You doe no Chorus, nor a Comment lack
Which may expound and conster ev'ry Act;   20
That it be short and slight: for if't be good
Tis long, and neither lik't, nor understood.
    Know, 'tis Court fashion still to discommend
All that which they want braine to comprehend.

An Epitaph on his most honour'd Freind Richard Earle of Dorset

Let no profane ignoble foot tread neere
This hallow'd peece of Earth; Dorsett lyes here.
A small sad relique of a Noble Spirit
Free as the Aire, and ample as his meritt:

Whose least perfection was large, and great 5
Enough to make a common man compleat.
A Soule refin'd and cull'd from many men,
That reconcil'd the Sword unto the Pen,
Using both well. No proud forgetting Lord,
But mindfull of meane names, and of his word. 10
One that did love for honour, not for ends;
And had the noblest way of making freinds
By loving first. One that did know the Court,
Yet understood it better by report
Then practise. For He nothing took from thence, 15
But the King's favour for his recompence.
   One for Religion, or his Countrye's good
That valew'd not his Fortune nor his Blood.
One high in faire Opinion, rich in praise;
And full of all wee could have wish't, but Dayes. 20

     Hee that is warn'd of this, and shall forbeare
     To vent a Sigh for him, or lend a Teare;
     May he live long and scorn'd, unpitty'd fall,
     And want a Mourner at his Funerall.

An Exequy To his Matchlesse never to be forgotten Freind

Accept, thou Shrine of my Dead Saint!
Instead of Dirges this Complaint;
And, for sweet flowres to crowne thy Hearse,
Receive a strew of weeping verse
From thy griev'd Friend; whome Thou might'st see 5
Quite melted into Teares for Thee.
   Deare Losse! since thy untimely fate
My task hath beene to meditate
On Thee, on Thee: Thou art the Book,
The Library whereon I look 10

Though almost blind. For Thee (Lov'd Clay!)
I Languish out, not Live the Day,
Using no other Exercise
But what I practise with mine Eyes.
By which wett glasses I find out   15
How lazily Time creepes about
To one that mournes: This, only This
My Exercise and bus'nes is:
So I compute the weary howres
With Sighes dissolved into Showres.   20
   Nor wonder if my time goe thus
Backward and most præposterous;
Thou hast Benighted mee. Thy Sett
This Eve of blacknes did begett,
Who wast my Day, (though overcast   25
Before thou hadst thy Noon-tide past)
And I remember must in teares,
Thou scarce hadst seene so many Yeeres
As Day tells Howres. By thy cleere Sunne
My Love and Fortune first did run;   30
But Thou wilt never more appeare
Folded within my Hemispheare:
Since both thy Light and Motion
Like a fledd Starr is fall'n and gone;
And 'twixt mee and my Soule's deare wish   35
The Earth now interposed is,
Which such a straunge Ecclipse doth make
As ne're was read in Almanake.
   I could allow Thee for a time
To darken mee and my sad Clime,   40
Were it a Month, a Yeere, or Ten,
I would thy Exile live till then;
And all that space my mirth adjourne,
So Thou wouldst promise to returne,
And putting off thy ashy Shrowd   45
At length disperse this Sorrowe's Cloud.

But woe is mee! the longest date
Too narrowe is to calculate
These empty hopes. Never shall I
Be so much blest, as to descry   50
A glympse of Thee, till that Day come
Which shall the Earth to cinders doome,
And a fierce Feaver must calcine
The Body of this World, like Thine,
(My Little World!) That fitt of Fire   55
Once off, our Bodyes shall aspire
To our Soules' blisse: Then wee shall rise,
And view our selves with cleerer eyes
In that calme Region, where no Night
Can hide us from each other's sight.   60
    Meane time, thou hast Hir Earth: Much good
May my harme doe thee. Since it stood
With Heaven's will I might not call
Hir longer Mine; I give thee all
My short liv'd right and Interest   65
In Hir, whome living I lov'd best:
With a most free and bounteous grief,
I give thee what I could not keep.
Be kind to Hir: and prethee look
Thou write into thy Doomsday book   70
Each parcell of this Rarity,
Which in thy Caskett shrin'd doth ly:
See that thou make thy reck'ning streight,
And yeeld Hir back againe by weight;
For thou must Auditt on thy trust   75
Each Grane and Atome of this Dust:
As thou wilt answere Him, that leant,
Not gave thee, my deare Monument.
    So close the ground, and 'bout hir shade
Black Curtaines draw, My Bride is lay'd.   80
    Sleep on (my Love!) in thy cold bed
Never to be disquieted.

My last Good-night! Thou wilt not wake
Till I Thy Fate shall overtake:
Till age, or grief, or sicknes must   85
Marry my Body to that Dust
It so much loves; and fill the roome
My heart keepes empty in Thy Tomb.
Stay for mee there: I will not faile
To meet Thee in that hollow Vale.   90
And think not much of my delay;
I am already on the way,
And follow Thee with all the speed
Desire can make, or Sorrowes breed.
Each Minute is a short Degree   95
And e'ry Howre a stepp towards Thee.
At Night when I betake to rest,
Next Morne I rise neerer my West
Of Life, almost by eight Howres' sayle,
Then when Sleep breath'd his drowsy gale.   100
    Thus from the Sunne my Bottome steares,
And my Daye's Compasse downward beares.
Nor labour I to stemme the Tide,
Through which to Thee I swiftly glide.
    'Tis true; with shame and grief I yeild   105
Thou, like the Vann, first took'st the Field,
And gotten hast the Victory
In thus adventuring to Dy
Before Mee; whose more yeeres might crave
A just præcedence in the Grave.   110
But hark! My Pulse, like a soft Drum
Beates my Approach, Tells Thee I come;
And, slowe howe're my Marches bee,
I shall at last sitt downe by Thee.
    The thought of this bids mee goe on,   115
And wait my dissolution
With Hope and Comfort. Deare! (forgive
The Crime) I am content to live

Divided, with but half a Heart,
Till wee shall Meet and Never part.   120

On two Children dying of one Disease, and buryed in one Grave

Brought forth in Sorrow, and bred up in Care
Two tender Children here entombed are:
One Place, one Sire, one Womb their being gave,
They had one mortall Sicknesse, and one Grave.
And though they cannot number many Yeeres   5
In their Account, yet with their Parent's teares
This comfort mingles. Though their Dayes were few,
They scarcely Sinne, but never Sorrow, knew:
So that they well might boast, they carry'd hence,
What riper Ages loose, their Innocence.   10
    You Pretty Losses, that revive the fate
Which in your Mother, Death did Antedate,
O let my high-swol'n Grief distill on You
The saddest dropps of a Parentall Dew:
You ask no other Dowre then what my eyes   15
Lay out on your untimely Exequyes:
When once I have discharg'd that mournfull skoare,
Heav'n hath decreed you ne're shall cost mee more,
Since you release, and quitt my borrow'd trust,
By taking this Inheritance of Dust.   20

The Anniverse. An Elegy

So soone grow'n old? Hast thou bin six yeares dead?
Poore Earth, once by my Love inhabited!
And must I live to calculate the time
To which thy blooming Youth could never climbe,
But fell in the ascent? Yet have not I   5
Study'd enough Thy Losse's History?

72

How happy were mankind, if Death's strict Lawes
Consum'd our Lamentations like the Cause!
Or that our grief, turning to dust, might end
With the dissolved body of a freind!   10
    But sacred Heaven! O how just thou art,
In stamping Death's impression on that heart
Which through thy favours would grow insolent,
Were it not physick't by sharp discontent.
If then it stand resolv'd in thy Decree,   15
That still I must doom'd to a Desart bee
Sprung out of my lone thoughts, which know no path
But what my owne misfortune beaten hath;
If thou wilt bind mee Living to a Coarse,
And I must slowly wast; I then of force   20
Stoop to thy great appointment, and obey
That Will, which nought availes mee to gainsay.
    For whilst in Sorrowe's maze I wander on,
I doe but follow Life's Vocation.
Sure wee were made to grieve: At our first birth   25
With Cryes wee tooke possession of the Earth:
And though the lucky man reputed be
Fortune's Adopted Sonne: Yet only hee
Is Nature's True-borne Child, who summes his yeares
(Like mee) with no Arithmetick, but Teares.   30

By Occasion of the young Prince his happy Birth. May 29. 1630

At this glad Triumph, when most Poëts use
Their Quill, I did not bridle up my Muse
For sloath or lesse devotion. I am one
That can well keep my Holy-dayes at home;
That can the blessings of my King and State   5
Better in Pray'r then Poëms gratulate;

And in their fortunes beare a Loyall part,
Though I no bon-fires light, but in my heart.

   Truth is, when I receav'd the first report
Of a New Starr Risen and seene at Court,   10
Though I felt joy enough to give a tongue
Unto a Mute, yet duty strook mee dumbe:
And thus surpriz'd by rumour, at first sight
I held it some Allegeance not to write.

   For howe're children, unto those that look   15
Their Pedigree in God's, not the Church-book,
Faire Pledges are of that eternity
Which Christians possesse not till they dy;
Yet they appeare, view'd in that Perspective
Through which wee look on men long since alive,   20
Like Succours in a Camp, sent to make good
Their place, that last upon the Watches stood.
So that in Age, or Fate, each following Birth
Doth sett the Parent so much neerer Earth:
And by this Grammer, wee our Heires may call   25
The smiling Preface to our Funerall.

   This sadded my soft Sense, to think that Hee
Who now makes Lawes, should by a bold decree
Be summon'd hence, to make Another roome,
And change His Royall Palace for a Tombe.   30
For none e're truly lov'd the present Light,
But griev'd to see it rivall'd by the Night.
And if't be Sin to wish that Light extinct,
Sorrow may make it Treason but to think't.
I know, each Malecontent, or giddy man   35
In his religion, with the Persian,
Adores the Rising Sun; And his false view
Best likes, not what is Best, but what is New.
O that wee could these Gangrenes so prevent
(For our owne Blessing and their Punishment)   40
That all such might, who for wild Changes thirst,
Rack't on a hopelesse expectation, burst

To see us fetter time, and by his stay
To a Consistence fixe the flying day;
And in a Solstice by our prayers made,   45
Reskew our Sun from Death, or Envye's shade.
  But here with Fate wee dally, and in this
Sterne Destiny mocks and controules our wish;
Informing us, if Fathers should remaine
For ever here, Children were borne in vaine;   50
And wee in vaine were Christians, should wee
In this world dreame of Perpetuitye.
Decay is Nature's Kalendar; nor can
It hurt the King to think He is a Man:
Nor grieve, but Comfort Him to heare us say   55
That His owne Children must His Scepter sway.
Why slack I then to contribute a vote
Large as the Kingdome's joy, free as my thought?
Long live the Prince, and in that Title beare
The World long witnesse that the King is here: 60
May he grow up, till all that good Hee reach
Which wee can wish, or his great Father teach:
Let Him shine long a mark to Land and Mayne,
Like that bright Spark plac't neerest to Charles' Wayne:
And like Him, lead Succession's goulden Teame,   65
Which may possesse the Brittish Diademe.
  But in the meane space, let His Royall Sire,
Who warmes our hopes with true Promethean fire,
So long his Course in Time and Glory run,
Till he estate His Vertue on His Sonne.   70
So in His Father's dayes This Happy One
Shall crowned bee, yet not usurp the Throne;
And Charles reigne still, since thus Himself will be
Heire to Himself through all Posteritye.

Upon the Death of my ever Desired Freind
Dr Donne Deane of Paules

To have liv'd Eminent, in a degree
Beyond our loftyst flights, that is, like Thee;
Or t'have had too much meritt, is not safe;
For such Excesses find no Epitaph.
At common graves wee have poëtick eyes   5
Can melt themselves in easy Elegyes;
Each quill can dropp his tributary Verse,
And pin it, with the Hatchments, to the Hearse:
But at Thine, Poëme, or Inscription
(Rich Soule of Witt and Language!) wee have none.   10
Indeed a Silence does that Tombe befitt,
Where is no Herald left to blazon it.
Widdow'd Invention justly doth forbeare
To come abroad, Knowing Thou art not here,
Late hir great Patrone, whose Prærogative   15
Maintain'd and cloath'd hir so, as none alive
Must now presume to keep her at Thy rate,
Though he the Indyes for her dowre Estate.
Or else that awfull fire, which once did burne
In thy cleare braine, now fall'n into thy Urne   20
Lives there to fright rude Empericks from thence,
Which might profane thee by their Ignorance.
Who ever writes of Thee, and in a Stile
Unworthy such a Theame, does but revile
Thy pretious Dust, and wake a Learned Spiritt   25
Which may revenge his rapes upon thy meritt.
For all a lowe-pitch't Phant'sie can devise
Will prove, at best, but hallow'd injuryes.
   Thou, like the dying Swann, didst lately sing
Thy mournfull Dirge in audience of the King;   30
When pale Lookes, and faint accents of thy breath
Presented so to Life, that Peece of Death,

That it was fear'd and prophesy'd by all,
Thou thither camst to preach Thy Funerall.
O! hadst thou in an Elegiack Knell   35
Rung out unto the world thine owne Farwell,
And in thy high victorious Numbers beat
The solemne measure of thy griev'd Retreat;
Thou mightst the Poet's service now have mist
As well, as then Thou didst prevent the Priest,   40
And never to the World beholden bee
So much as for an Epitaph for Thee.
   I doe not like the Office. Nor is't fitt
Thou, who didst lend our Age such summes of witt,
Shouldst now re-borrow from her bankrupt Mine   45
That Ore to bury Thee, which once was Thine.
Rather still leave us in thy debt; And Know
(Exalted Soule!) more glory tis to owe
Unto thy Hearse, what wee can never pay,
Then with embased Coine those Rites defray.   50
   Committ wee then Thee to Thyself: Nor blame
Our drooping Loves, which thus to Thy owne fame
Leave Thee Executor. Since, but Thy owne,
No Pen could doe Thee Justice, nor Bayes crowne
Thy vast desert; save That, wee nothing can   55
Depute to be thy Ashes' Guardian.
   So Jewellers no Art, or Mettall trust
   To forme the Diamond, but the Diamond's Dust.

An Elegy
Upon the most victorious King of Sweden
Gustavus Adolphus

Like a cold Fatall Sweat which ushers Death
My Thoughts hang on mee; and my lab'ring Breath
Stop't up with Sighes; My Phant'sy bigg with woes
Feeles Two Twinn'd Mountaines struggle in her Throwes;

Of boundlesse Sorrow one, T'other of Sinne: 5
For lesse let no one rate it, To Beginne
Where Honour Ends. In Great Gustavus' flame
That Stile burnt out, and wasted to a Name
Does barely live with us. As, when the Stuff
That fed it failes, the Taper turnes to Snuff.   10
With this poore Snuff, this Aiery Shadow, wee
Of Fame and Honour must contented bee;
Since from the vaine grasp of our Wishes fled
Their glorious Substance is, now Hee is Dead.

   Speak it againe; and lowder; Lowder yet;   15
Else, whilst wee heare the Sound, wee shall forgett
What it delivers. Let hoarse Rumour cry,
Till shee so many Ecchoes multiply,
Those may like numerous Witnesses confute
Our unbeleeving Soules, that would Dispute   20
And Doubt this Truth for ever. This one way
Is left our Incredulity to sway,
To waken our deaf Sense, and make our Eares
As open and dilated as our Feares;
That wee may feele the Blow, and feeling grieve   25
At what wee would not faine, but must beleeve.
And in that horrid Faith behold the world,
From her proud height of Expectation hurl'd,
Stooping with Him: As if shee strove to have
No Lower Center now, then Sweden's Grave.   30
   O! could not all thy purchas'd Victoryes,
Like to thy Fame, thy Flesh immortalize?
Were not thy vertue, nor thy valour charmes
To guard thy Body, from those outward harmes
Which could not reach thy Soule? could not thy Spirit   35
Lend somewhat, which thy Frailty might inheritt
From thy Diviner part, that Death, nor Hate
Nor Envye's bulletts e're could penetrate?
Could not thy early Trophyes in sterne fight
Torne from the Dane, the Pole, the Moscovite?   40

78

(Which were thy Triumphe's Seedes; as pledges sow'n,
That when thy Honour's harvest was ripe grown,
With full-summ'd wing Thou Falcon-like wouldst fly,
And cuff the Eagle in the German Sky:
Forcing his Iron Beak and Feathers feele   45
They were not proof 'gainst thy Victorious steele.)
Could not all these protect Thee? or prevaile
To fright that Coward Death, who oft grew pale
To look Thee, and Thy Battailes in the face?
   Alas they could not! Destiny gives place   50
To None. Nor is it seene that Princes' Lives
Can saved be by their Prærogatives.
No more was Thine: who clos'd in thy cold Lead
Dost from Thyself a mournfull Lecture read
Of Man's short dated Glory. Learne you Kings!   55
You are, like Him, but penetrable Things,
Though You from Demi-Gods derive your Birth,
You are at best but Honourable Earth:
And, howe're sifted from that courser bran
Which does Compound and Knead the Common man,   60
Nothing's immortall, or from Earth refin'd
About You, but your Office, and your Mind.
Here then break your False Glasses, which present
You Greater, then your Maker ever meant.
Make Truth your Mirrour now; since You find all   65
That flatter You, confuted by His Fall.
   Yet since it was decreed, Thy Life's bright Sun
Must be Ecclips'd e're Thy full Course was run,
Be proud, Thou didst in Thy Black Obsequyes
With greater Glory Sett, then Others Rise.   70
For in thy Death, as Life, Thou heldest One
Most just and regular proportion.
Look how the Circles draw'n by Compasse meet
Indivisibly joyned head to feet,
And by continued pointes which them unite   75
Grow at once Circular and Infinite:

So did Thy Fate and Honour now contend
To match Thy Brave Beginning with Thy End.
Therfore Thou hadst, insteed of Passing Bells,
The Drumms' and Cannons' Thunder for thy Knells;   80
And in the Field Thou didst Triumphing Dy,
Closing thy Ey-lids with a Victory.
That so by Thousands, who there lost their Breath,
King-like Thou mightst be waited on in Death.

    Liv'd Plutarch now, and would of Cæsar tell,   85
He could make none, but Thee, his Parallell,
Whose Tide of Glory swelling to the brim
Needes borrow no addition from Him.
When did great Julius in any clime
Atchieve so much, and in so small a time?   90
Or if He did, yet shalt Thou in That Land
Single for Him, and unexampled stand.
When ore the Germans first his Eagle towr'd,
What saw the Legions which on them he powr'd?
But massy Bodyes, made their Swords to try,   95
Subjects not for his *Fight, but Slavery.
In that so vast expanded peece of ground
(Now Sweden's Theater and Tomb) he found
Nothing worth Cæsar's Valour or his Feare,
No conqu'ring Army, nor a Tilley there;   100
Whose strength, nor wiles, nor practise in the warre
Might the fierce Torrent of Thy Triumphs barre,
But that Thy winged Sword Twise made him yeeld,
Both from his Trenches beat, and from the Feild.

    Besides the Roman thought he had done much,   105
Did he the bank of Rhenus only touch:
But though his March was bounded by the Rhine,
Not Oder, nor the Danube Thee confine;
And, but thy Frailty did thy Fame prevent,
Thou hadst Thy Conquests stretch't to such extent,   110
Thou mightst Vienna reach, and after Span
From Mulda to the Baltick Ocean.

*Magis
triumphati
quam victi.
Tacit. De
Mor. Germ.

But Death hath Spann'd Thee. Nor must wee divine
What Heire thou leavst to finish Thy Designe;
Or who shall Thee succeed, as Champion   115
For Liberty and for Religion.
   Thy Task is done. As in a Watch the Spring
Wound to the height relaxes with the String:
So thy Steele nerves of Conquest, from their steep
Ascent declin'd, ly slack't in thy Last Sleep.   120
   Rest then Triumphant Soule! for ever rest!
And, like the Phœnix in hir Spicy nest,
Embalm'd with thine owne Meritt, upward fly,
Borne in a Cloud of Perfume to the Sky.
Whilst, as in Deathlesse Urnes, each noble mind   125
Treasures Thy Ashes which are left behind.
   And if perhapps no Cassiopëian Spark
(Which in the North did Thy first Rising mark)
Shine o're Thy Hearse: The Breath of our just Praise
Shall to the Firmament Thy Vertues Raise: 130
Then Fixe, and Kindle Them into a Starre,
Whose Influence may crowne Thy Glorious Warre.

>   *— O Famâ ingens ingentior armis*
>   *Rex Gustave, quibus Cælo te laudibus æquem?*
>   Virgil. Æneid. *lib.* 11.

Upon the King's happy Returne from Scotland

So breakes the Day, when the Returning Sun
Hath newly through his Winter Tropick run:
As You (Great Sir!) in this Regresse come forth
From the remoter Climate of the North.
   To tell You now what Cares, what feares wee past,   5
What clouds of Sorrow did the Land o'recast,
Were lost, but unto such as have beene there
Where the absented Sun benightes the Yeere:
Or have those Countryes travail'd, which ne're feele
The warmth and vertue of his flaming Wheele.   10

How happy yet were wee! that when You went,
You left within Your Kingdome's Firmament
A Partner Light, whose Luster may despise
The nightly glim'ring Tapers of the Skyes,
Your Peerlesse Queene; and at each hand a Starre,   15
Whose Hopefull Beames from You enkindled are.
Though (to say truth) the Light which they could bring,
Serv'd but to lengthen out our Evening.
Heav'n's Greater Lamps illumine it; Each Spark
Adds only this, to make the Sky lesse dark.   20
Nay Shee, who is the Glory of Hir Sexe
Did sadly droop for lack of your Reflexe:
Oft did Shee hir faire Brow in lonenesse shrowd,
And dimly shone, like Venus in a Cloud.

Now are those gloomy Mists dry'd up by You,   25
As the World's Ey scatters the Ev'ning Dew:
And You bring home that Blessing to the Land
Which Absence made us rightly understand.

Here may You henceforth stay! There need no Charmes
To hold You, but the Circle of Hir armes,   30
Whose fruitfull Love yeilds You a rich encrease,
Seales of your Joy, and of the Kingdome's Peace.
O may those Pretious Pledges fix You here,
And You grow old within that Christall Sphære!

Pardon this bold detention. Else our Love   35
Will meerly an officious trouble prove.
Each busy Minute tells us, as it flyes,
That there are better Objects for your Eyes.
To them let us leave You. Whilst wee goe Pray,
Raising this Triumph to a Holyday.   40

And may that Soule the Churche's blessing want,
May his Content be short, his Comforts scant;
Whose Bosome Altar does no Incense burne,
In thankfull Sacrifice for Your Returne.

To my Noble and Judicious Friend Mr Henry Blount upon his Voyage

Sir I must ever owne my self to be
Possest with humane curiositee
Of seeing all that might the Sense invite
By those two baites of profit and delight.
And since I had the witt to understand   5
The Termes of Native or of Forraine land;
I have had strong and oft desires to tread
Some of those Voyages which I have read.
Yet still so fruitlesse have my wishes prov'd
That from my Countrye's smoak I never mov'd: 10
Nor ever had the fortune (though design'd)
To satisfy the wandrings of my mind.
    Therfore at last I did with some content,
Beguile my self in Time which Others spent,
Whose Art to Provinces small Lines allots,   15
And represents large Kingdomes but in Spots.
Thus by Ortelius' and Mercator's aid
Through most of the discover'd World I stray'd.
I could with ease double the Southerne Cape,
And in my passage Africk's wonders take: 20
Then, with a speed proportion'd to the Scale,
Northward againe as high as Zemla saile.
Oft hath the travaile of my Ey out-run
(Though I sate still) the journey of the Sun:
Yet made an end, ere his declining beames   25
Did nightly quench themselves in Thetis' streames.
Oft have I gone through Ægypt in a day,
Not hinder'd by the droughtes of Lybia;
In which, for lack of Water, Tides of Sand
By a dry diluge overflow the Land.   30
There I the Pyramids and Cairo see,
Still famous for the Warrs of Tomombee,

And its owne Greatnes; Whose Immured Fence
Takes Fourty miles in the Circumference.
Then without Guide or stronger Caravan   35
Which might secure the wild Arabian,
Back through the scorched Desarts passe, to seek,
Once the Worlde's Lord, now the beslaved Greek:
Made by a Turkish Yoake and Fortune's hate
In Language, as in Mind, degenerate.   40
    And here all rap't in pitty and Amaze
I stand, whilst I upon the Sultan gaze.
To think how Hee, with Pride and Rapine fir'd
So vast a Territory hath accquir'd:
And by what daring stepps he did become   45
The Asian feare, and scourge of Christendome:
How he atchiev'd, and kept; and by what artes
He did concenter those divided Partes,
And how He holdes that monstrous Bulk in awe,
By settled Rules of Tyranny, not Law.   50
So Rivers large, and rapid Streames began,
Swelling from Dropps into an Ocean.
    Sure who e're shall the just Extraction bring
Of this Gygantick Power from the Spring
Must there confesse a Higher Ordinance   55
Did it for terrour to the Earth advance.
For mark, how 'mongst a Lawlesse Straggling Crew
Made up of Arab, Saracen and Jew,
The worlde's disturber, faithlesse Mahomet
Did by Impostures an Opinion get: 60
O're whome He first usurpes as Prince, and than
As Prophet does obtrude his Alcoran.
Next, how fierce Ottoman his claime made good
From that unblest Religion, by Bloud;
Whilst he the Easterne Kingdomes did deface,   65
To make their ruin his proud Empire's base.
Then like a Comet blazing in the skyes
How Death-portending Amurath did rise;

When he his Horned Crescents did display
Upon the fatall Plaines of Servia: 70
And farther still his Sanguin Tresses spread,
Till Croya Life and Conquests limited.
Lastly how Mahomet, thence stil'd the Great,
Made Constantine's his owne Imperiall Seat
After that he in one Victorious bond   75
Two Empires grasp't, of Greece and Trabezond.
   This, and much more then this, I gladly read,
Where my relatours it had Storyed;
Besides That People's Manners and their Rites,
Their Warlike discipline, and order'd fightes;   80
Their des'prate valour, hardned by the Sense
Of unavoyded Fate and Providence:
Their Habit, and their Houses; who confer
Lesse cost on them, then on their Sepulcher:
Their frequent washings, and the severall Bath   85
Each Meschit to it self annexed hath:
What honour they unto the Mufty give,
What to the Soveraigne under whome they live:
What quarter Christians have; how just and free
To in-offensive Travailours they bee.   90
Though I confesse, Like stomackes fed with Newes,
I took them in for wonder, not for use,
Till your Experienc'd and authentick pen
Taught mee to know the Places and the Men;
And made all those suspected Truthes become   95
Undoubted now, and cleare as Axiome.
   Sir, for this work more then my thankes is due:
I am at once inform'd and cur'd by You.
So that, were I assur'd I should live o're
My periods of Time run out before;   100
Ne're needed my Erratick wish transport
Mee from my Native lists, to that Resort
Where many at Outlandish Martes unlade
Ingenuous manners, and doe only trade

For Vices and the Language. By your Eyes   105
I here have made my full Discoveryes;
And all your Countreyes soe exactly seene,
As in the Voyage I had sharer beene.
By This You make mee soe: And the whole Land
Your debtour. Which can only understand   110
How much Shee owes You, when hir Sons shall try
The solid depthes of your rare History.
Which lookes above our Gadders' triviall reach,
The common place of Travailours, who teach
But Table-talk; and seldomly aspire   115
Beyond the Countrye's Dyett or Attire.
Wheras your piercing judgment does relate
The Policy, and Manage of Each State.
And since Shee must here without envy grant
That You have farther journey'd the Levant   120
Then any noble Spiritt by hir bred
Hath in your way as yet adventured;
I cannot lesse in justice from hir look
Then that shee henceforth Canonize your Book
A Rule to all hir Travailours; And You   125
The brave Example. From whose equall view
Each knowing Reader may himself direct,
How he may Goe Abroad to some effect,
And not for Forme: what Distance and what Trust
In those remoter Partes observe he must: 130
How he with Jealous People may converse,
Yet take no hurt himself by that Commerce.
So when he shall embark'd in daungers be,
Which witt and wary caution not foresee;
If he partake your valour and your Braine,   135
He may perhapps come safely off againe
As You have done: Though not soe richly fraught
As this Returne hath to our Staple brought.
   I know your modesty shuns vulgar praise:
And I have none to bring: But only raise   140

This Moniment of Honour and of Love.
Which your long know'n deserts so farr emprove,
They leave mee doubtfull in what stile to end;
Whither more your Admirer or your Friend.

To my Dead Friend Ben: Johnson

I see that Wreath, which doth the Wearer arme
'Gainst the quick Strokes of Thunder, is no Charme
To keep off Death's pale Dart. For, Jonson, then
Thou hadst beene number'd still with Living men.
Time's Sithe had fear'd Thy Laurell to invade,   5
Nor Thee this Subject of our Sorrow made.
   Amongst those many Votaryes who come
To offer up their Girlonds at thy Tombe,
Whilst some more lofty Pens in their bright Verse
(Like Glorious Tapers flaming on thy Hearse)   10
Shall light the dull and thanklesse World to see
How great a maime it suffers wanting Thee:
Let not thy Learned Shadow scorne, that I
Pay meaner Rites unto thy memory;
And since I nought can add but in desire,   15
Restore some Sparkes, which leapt from Thine owne Fire.
   What endes soever others' Quills invite,
I can protest, it was no itche to write,
Nor any vaine ambition to be read,
But meerly Love and Justice to the Dead,   20
Which rais'd my famelesse Muse, and caus'd hir bring
These Dropps, as Tribute throw'n into that Spring,
To whose most rich and fruitfull Head wee owe
The purest streames of Language, which can flow.
   For 'tis but truth. Thou taught'st the ruder age   25
To speak by Grammar, and Reformd'st the Stage:
Thy Comick Sock induc'd such purged Sense,
A Lucrece might have heard without offence.

Amongst those Soaring Wits that did dilate
Our English, and advance it to the rate 30
And value it now holdes: Thy self was one
Helpt lift it up to such proportion,
That thus Refin'd and Rob'd, It shall not spare
With the full Greek or Latine to compare.
For what Tongue ever durst, but Ours, Translate 35
Great Tullye's Eloquence, or Homer's State?
Both which in their unblemish't Lustre shine,
From Chapman's pen, and from thy Catiline.
　　All I would ask for Thee, in recompence
Of thy successfull toile and Time's expence, 40
Is only this poore Boone: That those who can
Perhaps read French, or talk Italian,
Or doe the lofty Spaniard affect,
To shew their skill in Forraine Dialect,
Prove not themselves so'unnaturally wise 45
They therfore should Their Mother Tongue despise
(As if Hir Poëts both for Stile and Witt
Not æquall'd, or not pass'd Their Best that writt)
Untill by studying Jonson they have know'n
The Height, and Strength, and Plenty of their Owne. 50
　　Thus in what low Earth or neglected roome
Soe're Thou Sleep'st, Thy Book shall be Thy Tombe.
Thou wilt goe downe a happy Coarse, bestrew'd
With Thine owne Flowr's; and feele Thy self renew'd,
Whilst Thy Immortall never with'ring Bayes 55
Shall yeerly flourish in thy Readers' praise.
And when more spreading Titles are forgot,
Or, spight of all their Lead and Searcloth, rot,
Thou, wrap't and shrin'd in Thine owne Sheetes, wilt ly
A Relick fam'd by all Posterity. 60

To my honourd friend Mr. George Sandys

It is, Sir, a confess'd intrusion here
That I before Your Labours doe appeare,
Which no lowd Herald need, that may proclaime
Or seek acceptance, but the Authour's fame.
Much lesse that should this happy Work commend,   5
Whose Subject is Its License; and doth send
It to the World to be Receav'd and Read,
Farre as the glorious beames of Truth are spread.
   Nor let it be imagin'd that I look
Only with custome's ey upon your Book;   10
Or in this service that 'twas my intent
T'exclude your Person from your Argument.
I shall profess, much of the love I owe
Doth from the Root of our Extraction grow.
To which though I can little contribute,   15
Yet with a Naturall joy I must impute
To Our Tribe's honour, what by You is done
Worthy the Title of a Prælate's Sonne.
   And scarsly have Two Brothers farther borne
A Father's Name, or with more Value worne   20
Their Owne, then Two of You; whose Pens and Feet
Have made the Distant Points of Heav'n to meet;
He by exact Discoveryes of the *West
Yourself by painfull Travailes in the East.

> *Sr. Edwin Sandys survay of Religion in the West

   Some more like You might pow'rfully confute   25
Th'Opposers of Priestes' Marriage by the Fruit.
And (since 'tis know'n, for all their strait vow'd Life,
They like the Sexe in any Stile but Wife)
Cause them to chaunge their Cloister for That State
Which keepes men chast by Vowes Legitimate: 30
Nor shame to Father their Relations,
Or under Nephewes' names disguise their Sonnes.
This Child of Yours borne without spurious blot,
And fairly Midwiv'd as it was begot

Doth so much of the Parent's goodnesse weare,   35
You may be proud to owne It for Your Heire.
Whose choice acquites You from the common sin
Of such, who Finish worse then they Begin.
You mend upon Yourself, and Your last straine
Does of Your first the start in judgment gaine.   40
Since what in Curious Travaile was begun,
You here conclude in a Devotion.

    Where in delightfull raptures wee descry,
As in a Mapp, Sion's Chorography
Lay'd out in soe direct and smooth a Line   45
Men need not goe about through Palestine.
Who seek Christ here will the streight Rode prefer,
As neerer much then by the Sepulcher.
For not a Limme growes here, but is a Path
Which in God's Citty the blest Center hath: 50
And doth soe sweetly on each passion strike,
The most phantastick tast will somwhat like.

Job. To the unquiet Soule Job still from hence
Pleades in th'Example of his Patience.
Ecclesiastes. The Mortify'd may heare the Wise King Preach,   55
When his Repentance made him fit to teach.

The Act of Parliament for publique Thanksgiving on the 5th of November set to a Tune by H. Dod a Tradesman of London at the end of his Psalmes which stole from the Presse Anno Dom: 1620. Nor shall the singing Sisters be content
To chaunt at home the Act of Parliament
Turn'd out of Reason into Rhime by one
Free of his Trade, though not of Helicon;   60
Who did in his poëtick zeale contend
Sternolde's edition, by a worse, to mend.

Hymnes. Here are choice Hymnes and Carrowles for the Glad,
Lamentations. With melancholy Dirges for the Sad:
Psalmes. And David (as he could his skill transfer)   65
Speakes like Himself by an Interpreter.
Your Muse rekindled hath the Prophet's fire,
And Tun'd the Strings of his neglected Lyre;
Making the Note and Ditty so agree,
They now become a perfect Harmony.   70

I must confesse, I have long wish'd to see
The Psalmes reduc'd to this conformitie:
Grieving the Songs of Sion should be sung
In Phrase not diff'ring from a Barbarous Tongue.
As if, by Custome warranted, wee may   75
Sing that to God wee would be loath to say.
Farre be it from my purpose to upbraid
Their honest meaning, who first offer made
That Book in Meter to compile, which You
Have mended in the Forme, and built anew.   80
And it was well, considering the time,
Which hardly could distinguish Verse and Rhime.
But now the Language, like the Church, hath won
More Luster since the Reformation,
None can condemne the Wish or Labour spent   85
Good Matter in Good Wordes to represent.
    Yet in this jealous Age some such There be,
So without cause afraid of Novelty,
They would not (were it in their pow'r to choose)
An Old Ill Practise for a Better loose.   90
Men who a Rustick Plainesse so affect
They think God served best by their Neglect.
Holding the Cause would be Prophan'd by it,
Were they at charge of Learning or of Wit.
And therfore bluntly (what comes next) they bring   95
Course and unstudy'd Stuffes for Offering;
Which, like th'old Tabernacle's Cov'ring, are
Made upp of Badgers' skinns, and of Goates' haire.
But these are Paradoxes they must use,
Their Sloth and bolder Ignorance t'excuse.   100
Who would not laugh at One, will Naked goe,
'Cause in old Hangings Truth is pictur'd soe?
Though Plainess be reputed Honour's note,
They Mantles use to beautify the Coat;
So that a curious (un-affected) dress   105
Adds much unto the Bodye's comelinesse:

And where so e're the Subject's Best, the Sense
Is Better'd by the Speaker's Eloquence.
   But, Sir, to You I shall no Trophee raise
From other men's Detraction or Dispraise.   110
That Jewell never had inhærent worth
Which ask'd such Foiles as these to sett it forth.
If any quarrell Your Attempt or Stile,
Forgive them: Their owne folly they revile.
Since, 'gainst themselves, their Factious Envy shall   115
Allow this Work of Yours Canonicall.
Nor may you feare the Poët's common lot,
Read, and Commended, and then quite Forgot:
The Brazen Mines and Marble Rocks shall wast,
When Your Foundation will unshaken last.   120
'Tis Fame's best Pay, that You Your Labours see
By their Immortall Subject crowned bee.
For ne're was Writer in Oblivion hid
Who Firm'd his Name on such a Pyramid.

A Salutation of His Majestye's Shipp
The Soveraigne

Move on thou Floating Trophee built to Fame!
And bid Hir Trump spread Thy Majestick Name;
That the blew Tritons, and those petty Gods
Which sport themselves upon the dancing Floods,
May bow as to their Neptune, when they feele   5
The awfull pressure of thy potent Keele.
   Great Wonder of the Time! whose Forme unites
In one aspect Two warring Opposites,
Delight and Horrour; and in them portends
Diff'ring events both to thy Foes and Friends.   10
To These thy Radiant brow, Peace's bright Shrine,
Doth like that Golden Constellation shine

Which guides the Seaman with auspitious Beames
Safe and unshipp-wrack't through the troubled Streames.
But, as a Blazing Meteor, to Those   15
It doth ostents of bloud and death disclose.
For thy Rich Decks Lighten, like Heaven's fires
To usher forth the Thunder of thy Tires.
   O never may crosse Wind or swelling Wave
Conspire to make the treach'rous Sandes thy Grave: 20
Nor envious Rocks in their white foamy laugh
Rejoice to weare thy Losse's Epitaph.
But may the smoothest, most successfull Gales
Distend thy Sheat, and wing thy flying Sailes:
That all Designes which must on Thee embarke   25
May be securely plac't, as in the Arke.
Mayst Thou, where're thy Streamers shall display,
Enforce the bold Disputers to obay:
That They, whose Pens are sharper then their Swordes,
May yeeld in Fact, what they Deny'd in Wordes.   30
Thus when th'amazed World Our Seas shall see
Shut from Usurpers, to Their Owne Lord Free,
Thou may'st, returning from the conquer'd Maine,
With thine owne Triumphes be crown'd Soveraigne.

An Elegy Upon the immature losse of the
most vertuous Lady Anne Riche

I envy not thy mortall triumphes, Death!
(Thou Enemy to Vertue as to Breath!)
Nor doe I wonder much, nor yet complaine
The weekly numbers by thy Arrow slaine.
The whole world is thy Factory, and wee   5
Like Traffick driven, and retail'd by Thee.
And where the Springs of Liͤe fill up so fast,
Some of the Waters needes must run to wast.
   It is confest. Yet must our Griefes dispute
That which Thine owne Conclusion doth refute   10

E're wee begin. Hearken. For if thy Eare
Be to Thy Throat proportion'd, Thou canst heare.
Is there no Order in the work of Fate?
Nor Rule, but blindly to anticipate
Our growing seasons? or think'st Thou 'tis just   15
To sprinkle our fresh Blossomes with thy Dust?
Till by abortive Funeralls thou bring
That to an Autumne, Nature mean't a Spring?
Is't not enough for thee, that wither'd Age
Lyes the unpitty'd Subject of thy rage,   20
But, like an ugly Amorist, Thy Crest
Must be with spoiles of Youth and Beauty drest?
In other Campes, Those which sate downe to day
March first to morrow: and they longest stay
Who last came to the Service. But in Thine   25
Only Confusion stands for Discipline.
Wee fall in such promiscuous heapes, none can
Put any diff'rence 'twixt thy Rere or Van:
Since oft the youngest lead thy Files. For this
The grieved World here thy Accuser is,   30
And I a Plaintive, 'mongst those many Ones
Who wett this Ladye's Urne with zealous Moanes
As if Hir Ashes quick'ning into Yeares
Might be againe embodyed by Our Teares.
  But all in vaine. The moisture wee bestow   35
Shall make as soone Hir curled Marble grow,
As render Heat or Motion to that Bloud,
Which through Hir Veines branch't like an azure Flood;
Whose now still current in the Grave is lost,
Lock't up and fetter'd by eternall frost.   40
  Desist from hence, doting Astrologye!
To search for hidden Wonders in the Sky;
Or from the Concourse of malignant starres
Foretell Diseases generall as our Warrs:
What barren Droughtes, forerunners of leane Dearth,   45
Threaten to starve the Plenty of the Earth:

What horrid formes of Darknes must affright
The sickly World, hast'ning to that Long Night
Where it must end. If there no Portents are,
No black Eclipses for the Kalendar,   50
Our Time's sad Annalls will remembred be
I'th'Losse of bright Northumberland and Thee.
Two Starrs of Court, who in one fatall Yeare
By most untimely Set drop't from their Spheare.
Shee in the Winter took Hir flight: and soone   55
As Hir perfections reach't the point of Noone,
Wrap't in a cloud, contracted Hir wish't Stay
Unto the measure of a short-liv'd Day.
But Thou in Summer, like an early Rose
By Death's cold hand nipp'd as Thou didst disclose,   60
Took'st a long day to run that narrow Stage,
Which in Two gasping Minutes summ'd thy Age.
And, as the fading Rose when the Leaves shed
Lyes in its native sweetnes buryed,
Thou in thy vertues bedded and inhearst   65
Sleep'st with those Odours thy pure Fame dispers't.
Where till that Rising Morne thou must remaine,
In which Thy wither'd Flow'rs shall Spring againe.
And greater Beautyes thy Wak't Body vest
Then were at thy Departure here possest.   70
    So with full Eyes wee close thy Vault. Content
(With what Thy Losse bequeaths us) to Lament,
And make that use of thy griev'd Funerall
As of a Christall broken in the fall;
Whose pitty'd fractures gather'd up, and set,   75
May smaller Mirrours for thy Sexe begett;
There let them view themselves, untill they see
The end of all their Gloryes shew'n in Thee.
    Whilst in the truth of this sad tribute, I
    Thus strive to canonize Thy Memory.   80

An Elegy Upon Mrs. Kirk unfortunately drowned in Thames

For all the Ship-wracks, and the liquid graves
Lost men have gain'd within the furrow'd waves
The Sea hath fin'd, and for our wrongs paid use
When its wrought foam a Venus did produce.
  But what repair wilt thou unhappy Thames   5
Afford our losse? Thy dull unactive streames
Can no new beauty raise, nor yet restore
Her, who by thee was ravisht from our shore:
Whose death hath stain'd the glory of thy flood
And mixt the guilty Channel with her blood.   10
  O Neptune! was thy favour onely writ
In that loose Element where thou dost sit?
That after all this time thou should'st repent
Thy fairest blessing to the Continent?
Say, what could urge this Fate? Is Thetis dead,   15
Or Amphitrite from thy wet armes fled?
Was't thou so poor in Nymphs, that thy moist love
Must be maintain'd with pensions from above?
If none of these, but that whilst thou did'st sleep
Upon thy sandy pillow in the deep,   20
This mischief stole upon us: May our grief
Waken thy just revenge on that slie thief,
Who in thy fluid Empire without leave,
And unsuspected, durst Her Life bereave.
Henceforth invert thy order, and provide   25
In gentlest floods a Pilot for our guide.
Let rugged Seas be lov'd, but the Brook's smile
Shunn'd like the courtship of a Crocodile;
And where the Current doth most smoothly pass
Think for Her sake that stream Death's Looking-Glass. 30
To shew us our destruction is most neer
When pleasure hath begot least sense of fear.

Else break thy forked Scepter 'gainst some Rock
If thou endure a flatt'ring calm to mock
Thy far-fam'd pow'r, and violate that Law   35
Which keeps the angry Ocean in aw.
Thy Trident will grow useless, which doth still
Wild Tempests, if thou let Tame Rivers kill.
   Mean time we ow thee nothing. Our first debt
Lies cancell'd in thy wat'ry Cabinet.   40
We have, for Her thou sent'st us from the Main,
Return'd a Venus back to thee again.

To the Queen at Oxford

Great Lady! That thus quite against our use,
We speak your welcome by an English Muse,
And in a vulgar Tongue our zeales contrive
Is to confess your large Prerogative:
Who have the pow'rful freedom to dispense   5
With our strict Rules, or Custome's difference.
   'Tis fit, when such a Star deigns to appeare
And shine within the Academick Spheare,
That ev'ry Colledge grac't by Your Resort
Should onely speak the Language of Your Court;   10
As if Apollo's learned Quire, but You
No other Queen of the Ascendent knew.
   Let those that list invoke the Delphian Name,
To light their verse, and quench their doting flame
In Helicon. It were High Treason now   15
Did any to a feign'd Minerva bow:
When You are present, whose chast vertues stain
The vaunted glories of her Maiden Brain.
   I would not flatter. May that dyet feed
Deform'd and vicious soules: They onely need   20
Such physick, who grown sick of their decayes
Are onely cur'd with surfets of false praise;

Like those, who fall'n from Youth or Beautie's grace
Lay colours on which more bely the face.
    Be You still, what You are, a glorious Theme   25
For Truth to crown. So when that Diademe
Which circles Your fair brow drops off, and Time
Shall lift You to that pitch our prayers climbe,
Posterity will plat a nobler wreath
To crown Your fame and memory in death.   30
This is sad truth and plain: which I might fear
Would scarce prove welcome to a Princesse' Ear.
And hardly may you think that Writer wise
Who preaches there, where he should poetize,
Yet where so rich a bank of goodness is   35
Triumphs and Feasts admit such thoughts as this:
Nor will Your vertue from her Client turn
Although he bring his tribute in an urn.
    Enough of this: who knowes not when to end
Needs must by tedious diligence offend.   40
'Tis not a Poet's office to advance
The precious value of allegiance.
And least of all the rest do I affect
To word my duty in this dialect.
    My service lies a better way: whose tone   45
Is spirited by full devotion.
Thus whilst I mention You, Your Royal Mate,
And Those which Your Blest Line perpetuate,
I shall such votes of happiness reherse
Whose softest accents will out-tongue my Verse.   50

An Elegy
Upon the death of Mr. Edward Holt

Whether thy Father's, or Disease's rage,
More mortal prov'd to thy unhappy age,
Our sorrow needs not question; since the First
Is known for Length and Sharpness much the Worst.

Thy Feaver yet was kind; which the ninth day   5
For thy misfortunes made an easie way.
When th'other barbarous and Hectick fit
In nineteen winters did not intermit.
    I therefore vainly now not ask thee why
Thou didst so soon in thy Youth's mid-way dy: 10
But in my sence the greater wonder make
Thy long oppressed heart no sooner brake.
Of force must the neglected blossom fall
When the tough root becomes unnaturall,
And to his branches doth that sap deny   15
Which them with life and verdure should supply.
For Parent's shame, Let it forgotten be:
And may the sad example die with Thee.
    It is not now thy grieved friend's intent
To render thee dull Pitie's argument.   20
Thou hast a bolder title unto fame
And at Edge-Hill thou didst make good the claime:
When in thy Royal Master's Cause and Warre
Thy ventur'd Life brought off a noble skarre.
Nor did thy faithful services desist   25
Till Death untimely strook thee from the List.
    Though in that prouder vault then, which doth tomb
Thy ancestors, thy body find not room,
Thine own deserts have purchas'd thee a place,
Which more renowned is then all thy race;   30
For in this earth thou dost ennobled ly
With marks of Valour and of Loyalty.

On the Earl of Essex

Essex twice made unhappy by a Wife,
Yet Marry'd worse, unto the People's strife:
He who by two Divorces did untie
His Bond of Wedlock, and of Loyalty:

Who was by Easiness of Nature bred   5
To lead that Tumult, which first Him misled;
Yet had some glimm'ring Sparks of Virtue lent
To See (though late) his Errour, and Repent:
Essex lies here, like an inverted Flame
Hid in the Ruins of his House and Name;   10
And as He, Frailtie's sad Example, lies,
Warns the Survivours in His Exequies.

    He shews what wretched bubbles Great Men are
Through their Ambition grown too Popular:
For They, built up from weak Opinion, stand   15
On Bases false as Water, loose as Sand.
Essex in differing Successes try'd
The fury and the falshood of each Tide,
Now with applauses Deify'd, and then
Thrown down with Spightfull infamy agen.   20

    Tells them, what Arts soever them support
Their Life is meerly Time and Fortune's sport,
And that no Bladders blown by Common breath
Shall bear them up amidst the Waves of Death.

    Tells them no Monstrous Birth, with Pow'r endu'd   25
By that more Monstrous Beast the Multitude,
No State-Coloss' (though Tall as that bestrid
The Rhodian Harbour where their Navy rid)
Can hold that ill-proportion'd Greatness still,
Beyond His Greater, most Resistless Will,   30
Whose dreadfull Sentence written on the Wall
*Belshazar, Did sign the Temple Robbing *Tyrant's fall.
Dan. 5.   But Spight of their vast Priviledge, which strives
T'exceed the Size of ten Prerogatives,
Spight of Their Endless Parliament, or Grants,   35
(In Order to those Votes and Covenants
When, without Sense of their black Perjury
They Sware with Essex they would Live and Dye)
With Their Dead General ere long They must
Contracted be into a Span of Dust.   40

Epigram

Hammond his Master's Cabbanet broke ope,
Yet nothing found included but a Rope:
A fatall Embleme, which in Justice might
A treach'rous Heart, and guilty conscience fright;
And shewes what mortall dangers 'gainst him lye   5
Who into Prince's secrets dares to pry.
   That Casket thinke thy Lottery, false man!
Where thou thy End may'st calculated skan:
To which Two Tytles thy corrupted fayth
Both as a Picklock and a Traytor hath.   10
And were thy wages measur'd by that Line
Haman's tall Gallowes scarce should Equall Thine.

An Elegy on Sir Charls Lucas, and Sir George Lisle

In measures solemn as the groans that fall
From the hoarse Trumpet at some Funerall;
With trayling Elegy and mournfull Verse
I wait upon two Pearless Souldiers' Hearse:
Though, I acknowledge must, my sorrowe's dress   5
Ill matched to the cause it should Express;
Nor can I, at my best Invention's cost,
Sum up the Treasure which in them we lost:
   Had they with other Worthies of the Age,
Who late upon the Kingdome's bloody Stage,   10
For God, the King, and Laws, their Valour try'd,
Through Warr's stern chance in heat of Battel Dy'd,
We then might save much of our grief's expence
Reputing it not duty, but offence.
They need no tears nor howling Exequy,   15
Who in a glorious undertaking Dye;
Since all that in the bed of honour fell
Live their own Monument and Chronicle.

But these, whom horrid danger did not reach,
The wide-mouth'd Cannon, nor the wider Breach,   20
These, whom till cruel want and coward fate
Penn'd up like famish'd Lions in a Grate,
Were for their daring Sallies so much fear'd
Th'Assailants fled them like a frighted Heard;
Resolving now no more to fight, but lurk   25
Trench'd in their Line or earth'd within a Work.
Where not like Souldiers they, but Watchmen, creep,
Arm'd for no other office but to sleep:
They, whose bold charge whole Armies did amaze,
Rendring them faint and heartless at the Gaze,   30

*Sir George Lisle *at* Newbury *charged in his Shirt and Routed them.*

To see Resolve and *Naked Valour charmes
Of higher Proof than all their massy Armes:
They whose bright swords ruffled the proudest Troop
(As fowl unto the towring Falcon stoop)
Yet no advantage made of their Success   35
Which to the conquer'd spake them merciless;
(For they, when e'r 'twas begg'd did safety give,
And oft unasked bid the vanquish'd live;)
Ev'n these, not more undaunted in the Field
Than mild and Gentle unto such as yield,   40
Were, after all the shocks of battails stood,
(Let me not name it) murther'd in cold blood.

    Such poor revenge did the enraged Greek
Against (till then) victorious Hector seek,
Triumphing o'r that Body bownd and dead   45
From whom in Life the Pow'rs of Argos fled.
Yet might Achillis borrow some excuse
To colour, though not warrant the abuse:

*Patroclus

His dearest *Friend in the fierce combate foyl'd
Was by the Trojan's hand of Life despoyl'd;   50
From whence unruly grief grown wild with rage
Beyond the bownds of Honour did engage.
But these, confirm'd in their unmanly hate,
By Counsels cruel yet deliberate,

Did from the Stock of bleeding honour hew   55
Two of the noblest Branches ever grew;
And (which our grief and Pitty must improve)
When brought within their reach with shews of Love:
For by a Treaty they entangled are,
And Rendring up to Mercy is the Snare;   60
Whence we have learn'd when e'r their Saint-Ships Treat,
The ends are mortall, and the means a Cheat;
In which the World may read their black intent,
Drawn out at large in this sad President.
Who (though fair promis'd) might no Mercy have,   65
But such as once the faithless *Bashaw gave,
When to his trust deluded Bragadine
Himself and Famagosta did resign.
Whose envy'd Valour thus to bonds betray'd
Was soon the mark of barb'rous slaughter made: 70
So gallant Shipps which rocks and storms had past,
Though with torn Sails and spending of their Mast,
When newly brought within the sight of Land,
Have been suckt up by some devouring Sand.

   You wretched Agents for a Kingdom's fall,   75
Who yet your selves the Modell'd Army call;
Who carry on and fashion your Design
By Syllae's, Syllae's red proscription's Line,
(Rome's Comet once, as You are Ours) for shame
Henceforth no more usurp the Souldier's Name: 80
Let not that Title in fair Battails gain'd
Be by such abject things as You profan'd;
For what have you atchiev'd, the world may guess
You are those Men of Might which you profess.
Where ever durst You strike, if you met foes   85
Whose Valour did your odds in men oppose?
Turn o're the Annalls of your vaunted Fights
Which made you late the People's Favourites;
Begin your course at Naseby, and from thence
Draw out Your Marche's full circumference,   90

Famagosta defended most Valiantly by Signior Bragadino in the time of Selymus 2.d was upon Honourable terms surrendred to Mustapha the Bashaw, who observing no Conditions, at his Tent Murthered the Principal Commanders, invited thither under shew of Love, and flayed Bragadine Alive.

Bridgwater, Bristol, Dartmouth, with the rest
Of Your well-plotted renders in the West;
Then to the angry North Your compass bend
Untill Your spent careere in Scotland end,
(This is the perfect Scale of our mishap   95
Which measures out your conquest by the Mapp)
And tell me he that can, What have you won,
Which long before Your progress was not done?
What Castle was besieg'd, what Port, what Town,
You were not sure to carry 'ere sat down?   100
There needed no Granadoes, no Petard,
To force the passage, or disperse the Guard.
No, Your good Masters sent a Golden Ramm
To batter down the gates against You came.

*The Swedes
hired Anno
164[3] to in-
vade the King
of Denmark,
provided to as-
sist his Nephew
the King of
England.

Those blest Reformers who procur'd the *Swead   105
His armed Forces into Denmark lead,
'Mongst them to kindle a sharp warr for hire,
Who in mear pitty meant to quench our fire,
Could where they pleased with the King's own coyn
Divert His Aids and Strengths at home purloyn.   110
     Upon Sea Voyages I sometimes find
Men trade with Lapland Witches for a Wind,
And by those purchas'd Gales, quick as their thought,
To the desired Port are safely brought.
We need not here on skillfull Hopkins call   115
The States allow'd Witch-finder General.
For (though Rebellion wants no Cad nor Elfe,
But is a perfect Witchcraft of it self)
We could with little help of art reveal
Those learn'd Magitians with whom You deal: 120
We all Your Juggles both for Time and Place
From Darby-house to Westminster can Trace,
The Circle where the factious Jangle meet
To Trample Law and Gospel under feet;
In which, like Bells Rung backward, they proclaim   125
The Kingdom by their Wild-fire set on flame,

And, quite Perverting their First Rules, invent
What mischief may be done by Parliament:
We know Your holy Flamens, and can tell
What Spirits Vote within the Oracle;   130
Have found the spells and Incantations too,
By whose assistance You such Wonders do.
For divers Years the credit of Your warrs
Hath been kept up by these Familiars,
Who that they may their providence express   135
Both find you Pay and purchase Your Success:
No wonder then You must the Garland wear,
Who never fought but with a Silver Spear.

   We grant the Warrs unhappy consequence
With all the num'rous Plagues which grow from thence, 140
Murthers and Rapes, threats of Disease and Dearth,
From You as from the proper Spring take birth:
You may for Laws enact the Publick Wrongs,
With all fowl Violence to them belongs;
May bawl aloud the People's Right and Pow'r   145
Till by Your Sword You both of them Devour,
(For this brave Liberty by You up-cry'd
Is to all others but Your-selves deny'd,)
May with seditious fires the Land embroyl,
And in pretence to quench them take the Spoyl: 150
You may Religion to Your lust subdue,
For these are actions only Worthy You:
Yet when your Projects, crownd with wish'd event,
Have made You Masters of the ill You meant,
You never must the Souldier's glory share,   155
Since all your Trophies Executions are:
Not thinking your Successes understood,
Unless Recorded and Scor'd up in Blood.

   In which, to Gull the People, you pretend,
That *Military Justice was Your end;   160
As if we still were Blind, not knowing this
To all your other Virtues suited is;

*See the Letter
sent to Edward
Earl of
Manchester,
Speaker of the
House of Peers
pro tempore,
from T. Fair-
fax, Dated
August 29.
1648. at
Hieth.

Who only Act by your great Grandsires' Law,
The Butcher Cade, Wat Tyler, and Jack Straw,
Whose Principle was Murther, and their Sport   165
To cut off those they fear'd might do them hurt:
Nay, in your Actions we compleated find
What by those Levellers was but design'd,
For now Committees, and your Arm'd supplies,

Canton the Land in *petty Tyrannies,   170
And for one King of Commons in each Shire,
Four hundred Commons rule as Tyrants here.
Had you not meant the Copies of each Deed
Should their Originals in ill exceed,
You would not practice sure the Turkish Art,   175
To Ship your taken Pris'ners for a Mart,
Least if with Freedome they at Home remain,
They should (which is your Terrour) Fight again.
A thing long since by Zealous Rigby mov'd,
And by the Faction like himself approv'd;   180
Though you uncounsell'd can such Outrage try,
Scarce sampled from the basest Enemy.
Naseby of Old, and late St. *Fagans Fare,
Of these inhumane Truckings witness are;

At which the Captiv'd Welch in Couples led   185
Were Marketted, like Cattel, by the Head.
Let it no more in History be told,
That Turks their Christian Slaves for Aspers sold;
When we the Saints selling their Brethren see,
Who had a Call (they say) to set them free;   190
And are at last by Right of Conquest grown
To claim our Land of Canaan for their own.
Though luckless Colchester in this out-vies
Argiers' or Tunis' shamefull Merchandise;
Where the Starv'd Souldiers (as th'agreement was)   195
Might not be suffer'd to their Dwelling pass,
Till, led about by some insulting Band,
They first were shew'd in Triumph through the Land:

*Wat-Tyler and his Complices design was to take away the King and chief Men, and to erect petty Tyrannies to themselves in every Shire. And already one Littistar a Dyar had taken upon him in Norfolk the Name of King of Commons, and Robert Westborn in Suffolk, Rich. 2. Anno 1381. Speed.

*At St. Fagans in Glamorganshire near Cardiff, The Welsh unarmed were taken in very great Numbers, and Sold for twelve pence a piece to certain Merchants, who bought them for Slaves to their Plantation.

In which for lack of Dyet, or of Strength
If any Fainted through the Marche's length,   200
Void of the Breasts of Men, *this Murth'rous Crew
All those they could drive on no further, Slew;
What Bloody Riddle's this? They mercy give,
Yet those who should enjoy it, must not Live.
Indeed we cannot less from such expect,   205
Who for this Work of Ruine are Elect:
This Scum drawn from the worst, who never knew
The Fruits which from Ingenuous Breeding grew;
But take such low Commanders on their Lists,
As did revolted Jeroboam Priests: 210
Thus 'tis our Fate, I fear, to be undone
Like Ægypt once with Vermin over-run.
If in the Rabble some be more refin'd
By fair Extractions of their birth or mind,
Ev'n these corrupted are by such allays,   215
That no Impression of their Vertue stays.
As Gold embased by some mingled Dross
Both in its Worth and Nature suffers Loss.
   Else had that Sense of Honour still Surviv'd
Which Fairfax from his Ancestors deriv'd,   220
He ne'r had shew'd Himself, for hate or fear,
So much degen'rous from renowned Vere
(The Title and Alliance of whose Son
His Acts of Valour had in Holland won),
As to give up by his rash dooming Breath   225
This precious Pair of Lives to timeless death;
Whom no brave Enemy but would esteem,
And, though with hazard of his own, redeem.
For 'tis not vainly by the world surmis'd
This Blood to private Spleens was sacrifis'd.   230
Half of the guilt stands chardgd on Whaley's score,
By Lisle affronted on his guards before;
For which his spight by other hands was shew'n,
Who never durst dispute it with his own.

*Grimes *now a Captain, former-ly a Tinker at St.* Albans, *with his own hand Killed four of the Prisoners, being not able for Faintness to go on with the rest, of which number Lieutenant Woodward was one: Like-wise at* Thame, *and at Whateley, some others were Kill'd.*

Twice guilty coward! first by Vote, then Eye,   235
Spectator of the shamefull Tragedy.
But Lucas elder cause of quarrell Knew,
From whence his Critical Misfortune grew;
Since he from Berkley Castle with such scorn
Bold Ransborough's first Summons did return,   240
Telling him Loudly at the Parley's Beat,
With Rogues and Rebells He disdain'd to Treat;
   Some from this hot contest the world perswade
His sleeping vengeance on that ground was laid:
If so, for ever blurr'd with Envie's brand,   245
His Honour gain'd by Sea, was lost at Land:
Nor could he an impending Judgment shun
Who did to this with so much fervour run,
When late himself, to quit that Bloody stain,
Was, midst his Armed Guards, at Pomfret slain.   250
But all in vain we here expostulate
What took them hence, private or publick hate:
Knowledge of acted Woes small comforts add,
When no repair proportion'd can be had:
And such are ours, which to the Kingdome's eyes   255
Sadly present ensuing miseries,
Fore-telling in These Two some greater ill
From Those who now a Pattent have to Kill.
Two, whose dear loss leaves us no recompence,
Nor them attonement, which in weight or Sense   260
With These shall never into Ballance come
Though all the Army fell their Hecatomb.
Here leave them then; and be't our last relief
To give their merit Value in our grief.
Whose blood however yet neglected must   265
Without revenge or Rites mingle with Dust;
Nor any falling drop shall ever dry
Till to a Weeping Spring it multiply,
Bath'd in whose tears their blasted Laurell shall
Grow green, and with fresh Garlands Crown their fall. 270

From this black region then of Death and Night
Great Spirits take your everlasting flight:
And as your Valours' mounting fires combine,
May they a brighter Constellation shine
Than Gemini, or than the Brother-Starrs   275
Castor and Pollux fortunate to warrs.
That all fair Souldiers by Your sparkling light
May find the way to Conquer when they Fight,
And by those Paterns which from you they take
Direct their course through Honou's Zodiak: 280
But upon Traitors frown with dire Aspect,
Which may their perjuries and guilt reflect;
Unto the Curse of whose Nativity,
Prodigious as the Caput Algol be,
Whose pale and ghastly Tresses still portend   285
Their own despair or Hangman for their end.
And that succeeding ages may keep safe
Your Lov'd remembrance in some Epitaph,
Upon the ruins of your glorious Youth
Inscribed be this Monumentall Truth: 290

> Here ly the Valiant Lucas and brave Lysle,
> With Amasa betray'd in Joab's smile:
> In whom revenge of Honour taking place
> His great Corrivall's stabb'd in the Embrace.

And as it was the Hebrew Captain's stain   295   1 *Kings* 2
That he two Greater than himself had Slain,   32. vers.
Shedding the Blood of Warr in time of Peace,
When Love pretended was, and Arms did cease,
May the fowl Murtherers expect a fate
Like Joab's, Blood with Blood to expiate: 300
Which quick as Lightning, and as Thunder sure,
Prevention's wisest arts nor shun, nor cure.
O may it fall on their perfidious head!
That when, with Joab to the Altar fled,
Themselves the Sword and reach of vengeance flee   305
No Temple may their Sanctuary be.

Last, that nor frailty nor devouring time
May ever lose impressions of the Crime,
Let loyal Colchester (who too late try'd
To Check, when highest wrought, the Rebels' Pride,   310
Holding them long, and doubtfull at the bay,
Whilest we by looking on gave all away)
Be only Nam'd: which like a Columne built
Shall both enhearse this blood un-nobly spilt,
And live, till all her Towres in rubbish lye   315
The Monuments of their base Cruelty.

A Deepe Groane, fetch'd at the Funerall of that incomparable and Glorious Monarch, Charles the First, King of Great Britaine, France, and Ireland, &c.

On whose Sacred Person was acted that execrable, horrid, & prodigious Murther, by a trayterous Crew and bloudy Combination at Westminster, January the 30. 1648.

— Heu fausta Britannia quondam
Tota peris ea morte sua, Mors non fuit ejus
Sed tua, non una hæc, sed publica mortis imago.

To speake our Griefes at full over Thy Tombe
(Great Soul) we should be Thunder-struck, and dumbe:
The triviall Off'rings of our bubling eyes
Are but faire Libels at such Obsequies.
When Griefe bleeds inward, not to sense, 'tis deep;   5
W'have lost so much, that 'twere a sin to weep.
The wretched Bankrupt counts not up his summes
When his inevitable ruine comes.
Our losse is finite when we can compute;
But that strikes speechlesse, which is past recruit.   10
     W'are sunke to sense; and on the Ruine gaze,
As on a curled Comet's fiery blaze:

As Earth-quakes fright us, when the teeming earth
Rends ope her bowels for a fatall birth:
As Inundations seize our trembling eyes   15
Whose rowling billowes over Kingdomes rise.
Alas! our Ruines are cast up, and sped
In that black Totall—Charles is Murthered.
Rebellious Gyant hands have broake that Pole,
On which our Orbe did long in Glory roule.   20
That Roman Monster's wish in Act we see,   *Caligula.*
Three Kingdoms' necks have felt the Axe in Thee.
The Butchery is such, as when by Caine,
The fourth Division of the world was slaine.
The mangled Church is on the shambles lay'd,   25
Her Massacre is on thy Blocke display'd.
Thine is Thy people's epidemicke Tombe:
Thy Sacrifice a num'rous Hecatombe.
The Powder-mine's now fir'd; we were not freed,
But respited by Traytours thus to bleed.   30
November's plots are brew'd and broach't in worse,
And January now compleats the Curse.
Our Lives, Estates, Lawes, and Religion, All
Lye crush'd, and gasping at this dismall fall.

    Accursed Day that blotted'st out our Light!   35
May'st Thou be ever muffled up in Night.
At Thy returne may sables hang the skie;
And teares, not beames, distill from Heaven's Eye.
Curs'd be that smile that guilds a Face on Thee,
The Mother of prodigious Villanie.   40
Let not a breath be wafted, but in moanes;
And all our words be but articulate groanes.
May all Thy Rubrick be this dismall Brand:
Now comes the miscreant Doomes-day of the Land.
Good-Friday wretchedly transcrib'd; and such   45
As Horrour brings alike, though not so much.
May Dread still fill Thy minutes, and we sit
Frighted to thinke, what others durst commit.

A Fact that copies Angels when they fell,
And justly might create another Hell.   50
Above the scale of Crimes; Treason sublim'd,
That cannot by a parallell be rim'd.
Raviliack's was but under-graduate sin,
And Goury here a Pupill Assassin.
Infidell wickednesse, without the Pale!   55
Yet such as justifies the Canniball.
Ryot Apochryphall, of Legend breed;
Above the Canon of a Jesuite's Creed.
Spirits-of-witch-craft! quintessentiall guilt!
Hel's Pyramid! another Babell built!   60
Monstrous in bulke! above our Fancies' span!
A Behemoth! a Crime Leviathan!
So desperately damnable, that here
Ev'n Wild smels Treason, and will not appeare.
That Murdering-peece of the new Tyrant-State,   65
By whom't hath Shot black Destinies of late;
He that belch'd forth the Loyall Burleigh's doome,
Recoyles at this so dreadfull Martyrdome.
What depth of Terrour lies in that Offence,
That thus can grind a seared Conscience?   70
    Hellish Complotment! which a League renewes,
Lesse with the men, then th'Actions of the Jewes.
Such was their Bedlam Rabble, and the Cry
Of Justice now, 'mongst them was Crucifie:
Pilate's Consent is Bradshaw's Sentence here;   75
The Judgement-hall's remov'd to Westminster.
Hayle to the Reeden Scepter; th' Head, and knee
Act o're againe that Cursed Pageantrie.
The Caitiffe crew in solemne pompe guard on
Mock'd Majesty as not to th'Block, but Throne: 80
The Belch agrees of those envenom'd Lyes;
There a Blasphemer, here a Murd'rer dyes.
If that goe first in horrour, this comes next,
A pregnant Comment on that gastly Text.

The Heav'ns ne're saw, but in that Tragicke howre, 85
Slaughter'd so great an Innocence, and Power.
  Bloud-thirsty Tygars! could no streame suffice
T'allay that Hell within your Breasts but This?
Must you needs swill in Cleopatra's Cup,
And drinke the price of Kingdomes in a sup? 90
Cisterns of Loyalty have deeply bled,
And now y'have damm'd the Royall Fountain Head.
Cruell Phlebotomie! at once to draine
The Median, and the rich Basilick veine!
The tincture's great that popular murther brings, 95
'Tis scarlet-deep, that's dy'd in bloud of Kings.
  But what! could Israel find no other way
To their wish'd Canaan than through This Red Sea?
Must God have here his leading Fire and Cloud,
And He be th'Guide to this outragious Crowd? 100
Shall the black Conclave counterfeit His hand,
And superscribe Their Guilt, Divine Command?
Doth th'ugly Fiend usurpe a Saint-like grace?
And Holy-water wash the Devil's face!
Shall Dagon's Temple the mock'd Arke inclose? 105
Can Esau's hands agree with Jacob's voyce?
Must Molech's Fire now on the Altar burne?
And Abel's bloud to Expiation turne?
Is Righteousnesse so lewd a Bawd? and can
The Bible's Cover serve the Alcoran? 110
Thus when Hel's meant, Religion's bid to shine;
So Faux his Lanterne lights him to his Mine.
Here, here is sin's *non ultra*, when one Lie
Kils This, and stabs at Higher Majestie.
  And though His sleepy Arme suspend the scourge, 115
Nor doth loud Bloud in winged Vengeance urge:
Though the soft houres a while in pleasures flie,
And conquering Treason sing her Lullabie:
The guilt at length in fury he'l inroule
With barbed Arrows on the trayt'rous Soule. 120

Time may be when that John-à-Leyden King
His Quarters to this Tombe an Offring bring,
And that Be-Munster'd Rabble may have eyes
To read the Price of their deare Buttcheries.
Yet if just Providence reprieve the Fate,   125
The Judgement will be deeper, though 't be late.
And After-times shall feele the curse enhanc'd
By how much They've the sin bequeath'd, advanc'd.
    Meane time (most blessed shade) the Loyall eye
Shall pay her Tribute to Thy Memory.   130
Thy Aromatic Name shall feast our sense,
'Bove Balmie Spiknard's fragrant Redolence;
Whilst on Thy loathsome Murderers shall dwell
A plague-sore-blast, and rotten ulcer's smell.
    Wonder of Men and Goodnesse! stamp'd to be   135
The Pride, and Flourish of all History.
Thou hast undone the Annals, and engross'd
All th'Heroes' Glory which the Earth e're lost.
Thy Priviledge 'tis onely to commence
Laureate in Sufferings, and in Patience.   140
Thy wrongs were 'bove all Sweetnesse to digest;
And yet thy Sweetnesse conquer'd the sharp test:
Both so immense, and infinitely vast,
The first could not be reach'd, but by the last.
Meane Massacres are but in death begun;   145
But Thou hast Liv'd an Execution,
Close coffin'd up in a deceased Life;
Hadst Orphan Children, and a Widow-Wife,
Friends, not t'approach, or comfort, but to mourne
And weep their unheard plaints, as at Thy Urne?   150
Such black Attendants Colonied Thy Cell,
But for thy Presence, Car'sbrooke had been Hell.
Thus basely to be Dungeon'd, would enrage
Great Bajazet beyond an Iron Cage.
That deep indignity might yet have layne   155
Something the lighter from a Tamerlaine.

But here Sidonian Slaves usurp the Reines,
And lock the Scepter-bearing Armes in chaines,
The spew'd-up surfeit of this glut'nous Land,
Honour'd by Scorne, and cleane beneath all brand.   160
For such a Varlot-brood to teare all downe,
And make a common Foot-ball of the Crowne;
T'insult on wounded Majesty, and broach
The bloud of Honour by their vile reproach;
What Royall Eye but Thine could sober see,   165
Bowing so Low, yet bearing up so high?
What an unbroken sweetnesse grac'd Thy Soule,
Beyond the World's proud conquest, or controule?
Maugre grim cruelty, thou kept'st Thy Hold;
Thy Thorny Crowne was still a Crowne of Gold.   170
Chast Honour, Might enrag'd could ne're defloure,
Though others th'Use, Thou claim'dst the Right of Power.
The brave Athenian thus (with lopp'd-off Hands)   *Cynegirus.*
A stop to swelling sailes by 's mouth commands.
New Vigour rouz'd Thee still in Thy Embroyles,   175
Antæus-like, recruiting from Thy Foyles.
Victorious fury could not terrour bring,
Enough to quell a captivated King.
So did that Roman Miracle withstand   *Horatius*
Hetrurian shoales, but with a single hand.   180   *Cocles.*
The Church in Thee had still her Armies; thus
The World once fought with Athanasius.
The Gantlet thus upheld; It is decreed,
(No safety else for Treason) Charles must bleed.
Traytor and Soveraigne now inverted meet;   185
The wealthy Olive's dragg'd to th'Bramble's feet.
The Throne is metamorphiz'd to the Barre,
And despicable Batts the Eagle dare.
Astonishment! yet still we must admire
Thy courage growing with Thy conflicts high'r.   190
No palsied hands or trembling knees betray
That Cause, on which Thy Soule sure bottom'd lay.

So free and undisturbed flew thy Breath,
Not as condemn'd, but purchasing a death.
Those early Martyrs in their funerall pile   195
Embrac'd their Flames with such a quiet smile.
Brave Cœur-de-Lyon Soule, that would'st not vaile
In one base syllable to beg Thy Bayle!
How didst Thou blush to live at such a price,
As ask'd thy People for a sacrifice!   200

Codrus. Th'Athenian Prince in such a pitch of zeale
Redeem'd his destin'd Hoast, and Common-weale;
Who brib'd his cheated Enemies to kill,
And both their Conquest, and their Conquerour fell.

Thus Thou our Martyr died'st: but Oh! we stand   205
A Ransome for another Charles his Hand;
One that will write Thy Chronicle in Red,
And dip His Pen in what Thy Foes have bled;
Shall Treas'nous Heads in purple Caldrons drench,
And with such veines the Flames of Kingdomes quench.   210
Then Thou at last at Westminster shal't be
Fil'd in the Pompous List of Majestie.
Thy Mausolœum shall in Glory rise,
And Teares and wonder force from Nephews' Eyes.
Till when (though black-mouth'd Miscreants engrave   215
No Epitaph, but Tyrant, on Thy Grave)
A Vault of Loyalty shall keep Thy Name,
An orient, and bright Olibian flame.
On which, when times succeeding foot shall tread,
Such Characters as these shall there be read.   220

Here Charles the best of Monarchs butcher'd lies;
The Glory of all Martyrologies.
Bulwarke of Law; the Churche's Cittadell;
In whom they triumph'd once, with whom they fell:
An English Salomon, a Constantine;   225
Pandect of Knowledge, Humane and Divine.
Meeke ev'n to wonder, yet of stoutest Grace,
To sweeten Majesty, but not debase.

So whole made up of Clemencie, the Throne
And Mercy-seat, to Him were alwaies one. 230
Inviting Treason with a pardoning looke,
Instead of Gratitude, a Stab He tooke.
With passion lov'd, that when He murd'red lay,
Heav'n conquered seem'd, and Hell to bear the sway.
   A Prince so richly good, so blest a Reigne, 235
   The World ne're saw but once, nor can againe.

Scilicet, Humano generi Natura benigna
Nil dedit, aut tribuet moderato hoc Principe majus
In quo vera Dei, vivensque eluxit Imago:
Hunc quoniam scelerata cohors violavit, acerbas 240
Sacrilego Deus ipse petet de Sanguine pœnas
Contemptumque sui Simulachri haud linquet inultum.

     Parodia ex Buchanani Genethliacon Jacobi sexti Regis
                  Scotorum.

An Elegy upon the most Incomparable King Charls the First

Call for amazed thoughts, a wounded sense
And bleeding Hearts at our Intelligence.
Call for that Trump of Death the Mandrake's Groan
Which kills the Hearers: This befits alone
Our Story which through time's vast Kalendar 5
Must stand without Example or Repair.
What spouts of melting Clouds, what endless Springs,
Powr'd in the Ocean's lap for Offerings,
Shall feed the hungry Torrent of our grief
Too mighty for expression or belief? 10
Though all those moistures which the brain attracts
Ran from our eyes like gushing Cataracts,
Or our sad accents could out-tongue the Cryes
Which did from mournful Hadadrimmon rise,

Since that remembrance of Josiah slain   15
In our King's murther is reviv'd again.
   O pardon me that but from Holy Writ
Our loss allowes no Parallel to it:
Nor call it bold presumption that I dare
Charls with the best of Judah's Kings compare: 20
The vertues of whose life did I prefer
The Text acquits me for no Flatterer.
For he like David perfect in his Trust,
Was never stayn'd like Him, with Blood or Lust.
   One who with Solomon in Judgment try'd,   25
Was quick to comprehend, Wise to decide,
(That even his Judges stood amaz'd to hear
A more transcendent Mover in their Sphear)
Though more Religious: for when doting Love
A while made Solomon Apostate prove,   30
Charls nev'r endur'd the Truth which he profest
To be unfixt by bosome interest.
Bold as Jehosaphat, yet forc'd to Fight,
And for his own, no unconcerned Right.
Should I recount His constant time of Pray'r,   35
Each rising Morn and Ev'ning Regular,
You'ld say his practice preach'd, They ought not Eat
Who by devotion first not earn'd their Meat:
Thus Hezekiah He exceeds in Zeal,
Though not (like him) So facile to reveal   40
The Treasures of God's House, or His own Heart,
To be supplanted by some forein art.
And that he might in fame with Joash share
When he the ruin'd Temple did repair,
His cost on Paul's late ragged Fabrick spent   45
Must (if no other) be His Monument.
   From this Survey the Kingdom may conclude
His Merits, and her Losse's Magnitude:
Nor think he flatters or blasphemes, who tells
That Charls exceeds Judea's Parallels,   50

In whom all Vertues we concentred see
Which 'mongst the best of them divided be.

   O weak built Glories! which those Tempests feel
To force you from your firmest bases reel,
What from the stroaks of Chance shall you secure,   55
When Rocks of Innocence are so unsure?
When the World's only mirrour slaughter'd lies,
Envie's and Treason's bleeding sacrifize;
As if His stock of Goodness could become
No Kalendar, but that of Martyrdom.   60

   See now ye cursed Mountebanks of State,
Who have Eight years for Reformation sate;
You who dire Alva's Counsels did transfer,
To Act his Scenes on England's Theater;
You who did pawn your Selves in Publick Faith   65
To slave the Kingdom by your Pride and Wrath;
Call the whole World to witness now, how just,
How well you are responsive to your trust,
How to your King the promise you perform,
With Fasts, and Sermons, and long Prayers sworn,   70
That you intended Peace and Truth to bring
To make your Charls Europe's most Glorious King.
Did you for this Lift up your Hands on high,
To Kill the King, and pluck down Monarchy?
These are the Fruits by your wild Faction sown,   75
Which not Imputed are, but Born your own:
For though you wisely seem to wash your Hands,
The Guilt on every Vote and Order stands;
So that convinc'd, from all you did before,
Justice must lay the Murther at your Door.   80
Mark if the Body does not Bleed anew,
In any Circumstance approach'd by You,
From whose each motion we might plain descry
The black Ostents of this late Tragedy.

   For when the King through Storms in Scotland bred 85
To his Great Councel for his shelter fled,

Sparguntur in omnes, In te mista fluunt ...
Claudian.

Call'd the Councel of Troubles.

The form of taking the Covenant, June 1643.

When in that meeting every Error gain'd
Redresses sooner granted, than Complain'd:
Not all those frank Concessions or Amends
Did suit the then too Powerfull Faction's ends: 90
No Acts of Grace at present would Content,
Nor Promise of Triennial Parl'ament,
Till by a formal Law the King had past
This Session should at Your pleasure last.

    So having got the Bitt, and that 'twas known   95
No power could dissolve You but Your own,
Your graceless Junto make such use of this,

Diodorus
Siculus lib. 2.
As once was practis'd by Semiramis;
Who striving by a subtile Sute to prove
The largeness of her Husband's Trust and Love,   100
Did from the much abused King obtain
That for Three dayes She might sole Empress reign;
Before which time expir'd, the bloody Wife
Depriv'd her Lord both of his Crown and Life.
There needs no Comment when your deeds apply   105
The Demonstration of her Treachery.

    Which to effect, by Absolon's foul wile
You of the People's Heart your Prince beguile;
Urging what Eases they might reap by it
Did you their Legislative Judges sit.   110
How did you fawn upon, and Court the Rout,
Whose Clamour carry'd your whole Plot about?
How did you thank Seditious men that came
To bring Petitions which your selves did frame?
And lest they wanted Hands to set them on,   115
You lead the way by throwing the first stone.
For in that Libel after Midnight born,
Wherewith your Faction labour'd till the Morn,

Remonstrance
of the State
of the Kingdom,
Dec. 15. 1641.
That Famous Lye, you a Remonstrance name;
Were not Reproaches your malicious aim?   120
Was not the King's dishonour your intent,
By Slanders to traduce his Government?

All which your spightfull Cunning did contrive;
Men must receive through your false Perspective,
In which the smallest Spots improved were,   125
And every Mote a Mountain did appear.
Thus Cæsar by th'ungratefull Senate found
His Life assaulted through his Honour's Wound.
   And now to make Him hopeless to resist,
You guide His Sword by Vote, which as you list   130 *Ord.* Feb. 29.
Must, Strike or Spare (for so you did enforce   *Voted* March
His Hand against His Reason to divorce   15.
Brave Strafford's Life,) then wring it quite away   *The Navy*
By your usurping each Militia: *seiz'd* Mar.
                                           28. 1642.
Then seize His Magazines, of which possest   135 *The* London
You turn the Weapons 'gainst their Master's Breast.   *Tumults*. Jan.
                                          10.1641[/2].
   This done, th'unkennell'd crew of Lawless men
Led down by Watkins, Pennington, and Ven,
Did with confused noise the Court invade;
Then all Dissenters in Both Houses Bay'd.   140
At which the King amaz'd is forc'd to flye,
The whilst your Mouths laid on mantain the Cry.
   The Royal Game dislodg'd and under Chase,
Your hot Pursute dogs Him from place to place:
Not Saul with greater fury or disdain   145
Did flying David from Jeshimon's plain
Unto the barren Wilderness pursue,
Than Cours'd and Hunted is the King by you.
The Mountain Partridge or the Chased Roe
Might now for Emblemes of His Fortune go,   150
And since all other May-games of the Town
(Save those you selves should make) were Voted down,
The Clam'rous Pulpit Hollaes in resort,
Inviting men to your King-catching Sport.
Where as the Foyl grows cold you mend the Scent   155
By crying *Privilege of Parliament*,
Whose fair Pretensions the first sparkles are,
Which by your breath blown up enflame the War,

And Ireland (bleeding by design) the Stale
Wherewith for Men and Money you prevail.   160
    Yet doubting that Imposture could not last,
When all the Kingdom's Mines of Treasure waste,
You now tear down Religion's sacred Hedge
To carry on the Work by Sacriledge;
Reputing it Rebellion's fittest Pay   165
To take both God's and Cæsar's dues away.
    The tenor of which execrable Vote
Your over-active Zelots so promote,
That neither Tomb nor Temple could escape,
Nor Dead nor Living, your Licentious Rape.   170
Statues and Grave-stones o'r men buried
Rob'd of their Brass, the *Coffins of their Led;
Not the Seventh Henry's gilt and curious Skreen,
Nor those which 'mongst our Rarities were seen,
The *Chests wherein the Saxon Monarchs lay,   175
But must be basely sould or thrown away.
May in succeeding times forgotten be
Those bold Examples of Impiety,
Which were the Age's wonder and discourse,
You have Their greatest ills improv'd by worse.   180
    No more be mention'd Dionysius' Theft,
Who of their Gold the Heathen Shrines bereft;
For who with Yours His Robberies confer,
Must him repute a petty Pilferer.
    Nor Julian's Scoff, who when he view'd the State   185
Of Antioch's Church, the Ornaments and Plate,
Cry'd, Meaner Vessels would serve turn, or None
Might well become the birth of Mary's Son:
    Nor how that spightfull Atheist did in scorn
Pisse on God's Table, which so oft had born   190
The Hallow'd Elements, his death present:
    Nor he that fould it with his Excrement,
Then turn'd the Cloth unto that act of shame,
Which without trembling Christians should not name.

*At Basing—
Chapel Sold
Dec. 29. 1643.

*At Win-
chester.

Lactant.
l. 2. c. 4.

Julian.
Praefectus
Ægypti.
Theodoret.
l. 3. c. 11.

ibid.

Gaguin. l. 6.

Nor John of Leyden, who the pillag'd Quires   195
Employ'd in Munster for his own attires;
His pranks by Hazlerig exceeded be,
A wretch more wicked and as mad as he,
Who once in triumph led his Sumpter Moil
Proudly bedecked with the Altar's spoyl.   200 *The Carpet*
    Nor at Bizantium's sack how Mahomet   *belonging to*
In St. Sophia's Church his Horses set.   *the Com-*
                                                            munion Table
                                                            of Winchester
    Nor how Belshazzar at his drunken Feasts   *Cathedral*
Carows'd in holy Vessels to his Guests: Dec. 18. 1642.
    Nor he that did the Books and Anthems tear,   205 Adrian *Emp.*
Which in the daily Stations used were.
    These were poor Essayes of imperfect Crimes,
Fit for beginners in unlearned times,
Siz'd onely for that dull Meridian
Which knew no Jesuit nor Puritan,   210
(Before whose fatal Birth were no such things
As Doctrines to Depose and Murther Kings.)
But since Your prudent care Enacted well
That there should be no King in Israel,
England must write such Annals of Your Reign   215
Which all Records of elder mischiefs stain.
    Churches unbuilt by order, others burn'd;
Whilst Paul's and Lincoln are to Stables turn'd;
And at God's Table you might Horses see
By (those more Beasts) their Riders manger'd be,   220
Some Kitchins and some Slaughter-houses made,   *At* Winch-
Communion-boards and Cloths for Dressers laid: comb *in*
                                                           Glocester-
Some turn'd to loathsome Gaols, so by you brought   shire.
Unto the Curse of Baal's House, a Draught.
The Common Prayers with the Bibles torn,   225
The Coaps in Antick Moorish Dances worn,
And sometimes, for the wearers' greater mock,
The Surplice is converted to a Frock.
Some bringing Dogs the Sacrament revile,
Some with Copronimus the Font defile.   230

O God! canst Thou these prophanations like?
If not, why is thy Thunder slow to strike
The cursed Authors? who dare think that Thou
Dost, when not punish them, their acts allow.
All which outragious Crimes, though your pretence   235
Would fasten on the Souldiers' insolence,
We must believe, that what by them was done
Came licens'd forth by your probation.
For, as your selves with Athaliah's Brood
In strong contention for precedence stood,   240

Whitehall,
Windsor.
Feb. 5. 1643.

You robb'd Two Royal Chapels of their Plate,
Which Kings and Queens to God did dedicate;
Then by a Vote more sordid than the Stealth,
Melt down and Coyn it for the Common-wealth;
That is, give't up to the devouring jaws   245
Of your great Idol Bell, new styl'd The Cause,
And though this Monster you did well devise
To feed by Plunder, Taxes, Loans, Excise;
(All which Provisions You the People tell
Scarce serve to diet Your Pantagruel)   250
We no Strew'd Ashes need to trace the Cheat,
Who plainly see what Mouthes the Messes eat.
    Brave Reformation! and a through one too,
Which to enrich Your selves must All undo.
Pray tell us (those that can) What fruits have grown   255
From all Your Seeds in Blood and Treasure sown?
What would you mend? when Your Projected State
Doth from the Best in Form degenerate?
Or why should You (of All) attempt the Cure,
Whose Facts nor Gospel's Test nor Law's endure?   260
But like unwholsome Exhalations met
From Your Conjunction onely Plagues beget,
And in Your Circle, as Imposthumes fill
Which by their venome the whole Body kill;
For never had You Pow'r but to Destroy,   265
Nor Will, but where You Conquer'd to Enjoy.

This was your Master-prize, who did intend
To make both Church and Kingdom's prey Your End.
'Gainst which the King (plac'd in the Gap) did strive
By His (till then unquestion'd) Negative,   270
Which finding You lack'd Reason to perswade,
Your Arguments are into Weapons made;
So to compell him by main force to yield,
You had a Formed Army in the Field
Before his Reared Standard could invite   275
Ten men upon his Righteous Cause to fight:
Yet ere those raised Forces did advance,
Your malice struck him dead by Ordinance,
When your Commissions the whole Kingdom swept
With Blood and Slaughter, Not the King Except.   280
   Now hardned in Revolt, You next proceed
By Pacts to strengthen each Rebellious Deed,
New Oaths, and Vows, and Covenants advance,
All contradicting your Allegiance,
Whose Sacred knot you plainly did unty,   285
When you with Essex swore to Live and Dye.
These were your Calves in Bethel and in Dan,
Which Jeroboam's Treason stablish can,
Who by strange Pacts and Altars did seduce
The People to their Laws' and King's abuse;   290
All which but serve like Shibboleth to try
Those who pronounc'd not your conspiracy;
That when your other Trains defective are,
Forc'd Oaths might bring Refusers to the Snare.
And lest those men your Counsels did pervert   295
Might when your Fraud was seen the Cause desert,
A fierce Decree is through the Kingdom sent,
Which made it Death for any to Repent.
What strange Dilemmaes doth Rebellion make?
'Tis mortal to Deny, or to Partake: 300
Some Hang who would not aid your Traiterous Act,
Others engag'd are Hang'd if they Retract.

*E. of Essex'
Army*, Aug. 1.
1642. *The
Standard at*
Notingham,
Aug. 25. 1642.

June 27.
1643.

*Declaration and
Resolution of
Parl.* Aug. 15.
1642.

*History of
English and*

Scotish
Presbytery,
p. 320.

So Witches who their Contracts have unsworn,
By their own Devils are in pieces torn.

    Thus still the rageing Tempest higher grows,   305
Which in Extreams the King's Resolvings throws.
The face of Ruin every where appears,
And Acts of Outrage multiply our fears;
Whilst blind Ambition by Successes fed
Hath You beyond the bound of Subjects led,   310
Who tasting once the sweet of Regal Sway,
Resolved now no longer to obey.
For Presbiterian pride contests as high
As doth the Popedom for Supremacy.
Needs must you with unskilfull Phaeton   315
Aspire to guide the Chariot of the Sun,
Though your ill-govern'd height with lightning be
Thrown headlong from his burning Axle-tree.

The 19
Propos.

You will no more Petition or Debate,
But your desire in Propositions state,   320
Which by such Rules and Ties the King confine,
They in effect are Summons to Resign.
Therefore your War is manag'd with such sleight,
'Twas seen you more prevail'd by Purse than Might;
And those you could not purchase to your will,   325
You Brib'd with Sums of Money to sit still.

    The King by this time hopeless here of Peace,
Or to procure His wasted People's ease,
Which He in frequent Messages had try'd,
By you as oft as Shamelesly deny'd;   330
Wearied by faithless Friends and restless Foes,
To certain hazard doth His Life Expose:

April 27.
1646.

When through your Quarters in a mean disguise
He to His Country-men for succour flies,

May 5. 1646.

Who met a brave occasion then to save   335
Their Native King from His untimely Grave,
Had he from them such fair Reception gain'd
Wherewith ev'n Achish David entertain'd.

But Faith to Him or Hospitable Laws
In your Confederate Union were no Clause,   340
Which back to you their Rendred Master sends
To tell how He was us'd among his Friends.
Far be it from my thoughts by this black Line
To measure all within that Warlike Clime;
The still admir'd Montross some Numbers lead   345
In his brave steps of Loyalty to tread.
I only Tax a furious Party there,
Who with our Native Pests Enleagued were.
Then 'twas you follow'd Him with Hue and Cry,
Made Midnight Searches in Each Liberty,   350   *This Order*
Voting it Death to all without Reprieve,   *publish'd by*
Who should their Master Harbour or Relieve.   *beat of Drum,*
Ev'n in pure pity of both Nations' Fame,   *May 4. 1646*
I wish that Act in Story had no Name.
When all your mutual Stipulations are   355
Converted at Newcastle to a Fair,
Where (like His Lord) the King the Mart is made,
Bought with Your Money, and by Them Betraid;
For both are Guilty, They that did Contract,
And You that did the fatal Bargain Act.   360
Which who by equal Reason shall peruse,
Must yet conclude, They had the best Excuse:
For doubtless They (Good men) had never Sold,
But that you tempted Them with English Gold;
And 'tis no wonder if with such a Sum   365
Our Brethren's frailty might be overcome.
What though hereafter it may prove their Lot
To be compared with Iscariot?
Yet will the World perceive which was most wise,
And who the Nobler Traitor by the Price;   370
For though 'tis true Both did Themselves undo,
They made the better Bargain of the Two,
Which all may reckon who can difference
Two hundred thousand Pounds from Thirty Pence.

However something is in Justice due,   375
Which may be spoken in defence of You;
For in your Master's Purchase you gave more,
Than all your Jewish Kindred paid before.
And had you wisely us'd what then you bought,
Your Act might be a Loyal Ransome thought,   380
To free from Bonds your Captive Soveraign,
Restoring Him to his lost Crown again.

But You had other Plots, your busie hate
Ply'd all advantage on His fallen State,
And shew'd You did not come to bring Him Bayl,   385
But to remove Him to a stricter Gaol,
To Holmby first, whence taken from His Bed,
He by an Army was in Triumph led;
Till on pretence of safety Cromwel's wile
Had juggl'd Him into the Fatal Isle,   390
Where Hammond for his Jaylor is decreed,
And Murderous Rolf as Lieger-Hangman fee'd,
Who in one fatal Knot Two Counsels tye,
He must by Poison or by Pistol Dye.
Here now deny'd all Comforts due to Life,   395
His Friends, His Children, and His Peerless Wife;
From Carisbrook He oft but vainly sends,
And though first Wrong'd, seeks to make you Amends;
For this He sues, and by his restless Pen
Importunes Your deaf Ears to Treat agen.   400
Whilst the proud Faction scorning to go less,

Jan. 3.
1647[/8].
Jan. 9.
1647[/8].

Return those Trait'rous Votes of Non Address,
Which follow'd were by th'Armies thundering
To Act without and quite against the King.
Yet when that Cloud remov'd, and the clear Light   405
Drawn from His weighty Reasons, gave You sight
Of Your own Dangers, had not Their Intents

Colchester
Siege.

Retarded been by some cross Accidents;
Which for a while with fortunate Suspence
Check'd or diverted Their swoln Insolence: 410

When the whole Kingdom for a Treaty cry'd,
Which gave such credit to Your falling side,
That you Recall'd those Votes, and God once more
Your Power to save the Kingdome did restore,
Remember how Your peevish Treators sate,   415
Not to make Peace, but to prolong Debate;
How You that precious time at first delay'd,
And what ill use of Your advantage made,
As if from Your foul Hands God had decreed
Nothing but War and Mischief should succeed.   420
For when by easie Grants the King's Assent
Did your Desires in greater things prevent,
When He did yield faster than You intreat,
And more than Modesty dares well repeat;
Yet not content with this, without all sense   425
Or of His Honour or His Conscience,
Still you prest on, till you too late descry'd
'Twas now less safe to stay than be deny'd:
For like a Flood broke loose the Armed Rout,
Then Shut Him closer up, And Shut You out,   430
Who by just Vengeance are since Worried
By those Hand-wolves You for His Ruine bred.
  Thus like Two smoaking Firebrands, You and They
Have in this Smother choak'd the Kingdom's Day:
And as you rais'd Them first, must share the Guilt,   435
With all the Blood in these Distractions spilt.
For though with Sampson's Foxes backward turn'd,
(When he Philistia's fruitfull Harvest burn'd)
The face of your Opinions stands averse,
All your Conclusions but one Fire disperse;   440
And every Line which carries your Designs
In the same Centre of Confusion joyns.
Though then the Independants end the Work,
'Tis known they took their Platform from the Kirk;
Though Pilate Bradshaw with his pack of Jews   445
God's High Vice-gerent at the Bar accuse,

June 30.
1648.

Treaty Voted,
July 28.
1648.

They but reviv'd the Evidence and Charge,
Your poys'nous Declarations laid at large;
Though they Condemn'd or made his Life their Spoil,
You were the Setters forc'd him to the Toil: 450
For you, whose fatal hand the Warrant writ,
The Prisoner did for Execution fit;
And if their Ax invade the Regal Throat,
Remember you first Murther'd Him by Vote.
Thus They receive Your Tennis at the bound,   455
Take off that Head which you had first Un-crown'd;
Which shews the Texture of our Mischief's Clew,
If Ravell'd to the Top, begins in You,
Who have for ever stain'd the brave Intents
And Credit of our English Parliaments: 460
And in this One caus'd greater Ills, and more,
Than all of theirs did Good that went before.

　　Yet have You kept your word against Your will,
Your King is Great indeed and Glorious still,
And You have made Him so. We must impute   465
That Lustre which His Sufferings contribute
To your preposterous Wisdoms, who have done
All your good Deeds by Contradiction:
For as to work His Peace you rais'd this Strife,
And often Shot at Him to Save His Life;   470
As you took from Him to Encrease His wealth,
And kept Him Pris'ner to secure His Health;
So in revenge of your dissembled Spight,
In this last Wrong you did Him greatest Right,
And (cross to all You meant) by Plucking down   475
Lifted Him up to His Eternal Crown.

　　With This Encircled in that radiant Sphear,
Where Thy black Murtherers must ne'r appear;
Thou from th'enthroned Martyrs' Blood-stain'd Line
Dost in thy Virtue's bright Example shine.   480
And when Thy Darted Beam from the moist Sky

Nightly salutes Thy grieving People's Eye,
Thou, like some Warning Light rais'd by our fears,
Shalt both provoke and still supply our Tears,
Till the Great Prophet wak'd from his long Sleep   485
Again bids Sion for Josiah weep:
That all Successions by a firm Decree
May teach their Children to Lament for Thee.
   Beyond these Mournfull Rites there is no Art
Or Cost can Thee preserve. Thy better Part   490
Lives in despight of Death, and will endure
Kept safe in Thy Unpattern'd Portraicture:
Which though in Paper drawn by thine own Hand,
Shall longer than Corinthian-Marble stand,
Or Iron Sculptures: There thy matchless Pen   495
Speaks Thee the Best of Kings as Best of Men:
Be this Thy Epitaph; for This alone
Deserves to carry Thy Inscription.
And 'tis but modest Truth: (so may I thrive
As not to please the Best of Thine Alive,   500
Or flatter my Dead Master, here would I
Pay my last Duty in a Glorious Lye)
In that Admired Piece the World may read
Thy Virtues and Misfortunes Storied;
Which bear such curious Mixture, Men must doubt   505
Whether Thou Wiser wert or more Devout.
   There live Blest Relick of a Saint-like mind,
With Honours endless, as Thy Peace, Enshrin'd;
Whilst we, divided by that Bloody Cloud,
Whose purple Mists Thy Murther'd Body shroud,   510
Here stay behind at gaze: Apt for Thy sake
Unruly murmurs now 'gainst Heav'n to make,
Which binds us to Live well, yet gives no Fence
To Guard her dearest Sons from Violence.
But He whose Trump proclaims, Revenge is Mine,   515
Bids us our Sorrow by our Hope confine,
And reconcile our Reason to our Faith,

Which in thy Ruine such Conclusions hath;
It dares Conclude, God does not keep His Word
If Zimri dye in Peace that slew his Lord.   520

From my sad Retirement
March 11. 1648[/9].

CaroLVs stVart reX angLIæ seCVre CœsVs
VIta CessIt trICesIMo IanVarII.

An Elegy
Occasioned by the losse of the most incomparable Lady Stanhope, daughter to the Earl of Northumberland

Lightned by that dimme Torch our sorrow bears
We sadly trace thy Coffin with our tears;
And though the Ceremonious Rites are past
Since thy fair body into earth was cast;
Though all thy Hatchments into ragges are torne,   5
Thy Funerall Robes and Ornaments outworn;
We still thy mourners without Shew or Art,
With solemn Blacks hung round about our heart,
Thus constantly the Obsequies renew
Which to thy precious memory are due.   10

Yet think not that we rudely would invade
The dark recess of thine untroubled shade,
Or give disturbance to that happy peace
Which thou enjoy'st at full since thy release;
Much less in sullen murmurs do complain   15
Of His decree who took thee back again,
And did e're Fame had spread thy vertues' light,
Eclipse and fold thee up in endless night.
This like an act of envy not of grief
Might doubt thy bliss, and shake our own belief,   20

132

Whose studi'd wishes no proportion bear
With joyes which crown thee now in glorie's sphere.

   Know then blest Soul! we for our selves not thee
Seal our woe's dictate by this Elegie:
Wherein our tears united in one streame   25
Shall to succeeding times convey this theme,
Worth all men's pity who discern how rare
Such early growths of fame and goodness are.
Of these part must thy sexe's loss bewail
Maim'd in her noblest Patterns through thy fail;   30
For 'twould require a double term of life
To match thee as a daughter or a wife:
Both which Northumberland's dear loss improve
And make his sorrow equal to his love.
The rest fall for ourselves, who cast behind   35
Cannot yet reach the Peace which thou dost find;
But slowly follow thee in that dull stage
Which most untimely poasted hence thy age.

   Thus like religious Pilgrims who designe
A short salute to their beloved Shrine,   40
Most sad and humble Votaries we come
To offer up our sighs upon thy Tomb,
And wet thy Marble with our dropping eyes
Which till the spring which feeds their current dries
Resolve each falling night and rising day   45
This mournfull homage at thy Grave to pay.

An Elegy
Upon my Best Friend
L. K. C.

Should we our Sorrows in this Method range,
Oft as Misfortune doth their Subjects change,
And to the sev'rall Losses, which befall,
Pay diff'rent Rites at ev'ry Funeral;

Like narrow Springs drain'd by dispersed Streams, ·   5
We must want Tears to wail such various Themes,
And prove defective in Death's mournfull Laws,
Not having Words proportion'd to each Cause.
   In your Dear loss my much afflicted Sense
Discerns this Truth by sad experience,   10
Who never Look'd my Verses should survive,
As wet Records, That you are not Alive;
And less desir'd to make that Promise due,
Which pass'd from Me in jest, when urg'd by You.
   How close and slily doth our Frailty work!   15
How undiscover'd in the Body lurk!
That Those who this Day did salute you well,
Before the Next were frighted by your Knell.
O wherefore since we must in Order rise,
Should wee not Fall in equal Obsequies?   20
But bear th'Assaults of an uneven Fate,
Like Feavers which their Hour anticipate;
Had this Rule constant been, my long wish'd End
Might render you a Mourner for your Friend:
As He for you, whose most deplor'd surprise   25
Imprints your Death on all my Faculties;
That hardly my dark Phant'sie or Discourse
This final Duty from the Pen inforce:
   Such Influence hath your Eclipsed Light,
It doth my Reason like my Self benight.   30
   Let me, with Luckless Gamesters, then think best
(After I have Set up and Lost my Rest)
Grow'n desp'rate through mischance, to Venture last
My whole remaining Stock upon a Cast,
And flinging from me my now Loathed Pen,   35
Resolve for your Sake nev'r to Write agen:
For whilst Successive days their Light renew,
I must no Subject hope to Equal you,
In whose Heroick Brest as in their Sphear,
All Graces of your Sex concentred were.   40

Thus take I my long Farewell of that Art,
Fit only glorious Actions to impart;
That Art wherewith our Crosses we beguile,
And make them in Harmonious numbers smile:
Since you are gone, This holds no further use,   45
Whose Virtue and Desert inspir'd my Muse.
O may She in your Ashes Buried be,
Whilst I my Self become the Elegie.

　　And as it is observ'd when Princes Dye,
(In honour of that sad Solemnity)   50
The now unoffic'd Servants crack their Staves,
And throw them down into their Masters' Graves:
So this last Office of my broken Verse,
I solemnly resign upon your Hearse;
And my Brain's moisture, all that is unspent,   55
Shall melt to nothing at the Monument.
Thus in moist Weather when the Marble weeps,
You'l think it only his Tears reck'ning keeps,
Who doth for ever to his Thoughts bequeath
The Legacy of your lamented Death.   60

The Woes of Esay

Woe to the worldly men, whose covetous
Ambition labours to joyne house to house,
Lay field to field; till their Enclosures edge
The Playne, girdling a Country with one hedge:
That leave no place unbought, no peece of Earth   5
Which they will not engrosse, making a dearth
Of all Inhabitants, untill they stand
Unneighbour'd, as unblest, within their Land.
  This Sinne cryes in God's eare, who hath decree'd
The ground they sowe shall not returne the Seed.   10
They that unpeopled Countryes to create
Themselves sole Lords; made many desolate
To build up their owne house, shall find at last
Ruine and fearefull desolation cast
Upon themselves. Their Mansion shall become   15
A Desart, and their Palace prove a Tombe.
Their vines shall barren be, Their Land yeild Tares;
Their house shall have no dwellers; They no heires.

Woe unto those that with the morning Sunne
Rise to drink wine, and sitt till he have runne   20
His weary course; not ceasing untill night
Have quench't their understanding with the Light:
Whose raging thirst, like fire, will not be tam'd,
The more they poure, the more they are enflam'd.
Woe unto them that only mighty are   25
To wage with wine; in which unhappy warre
They who the glory of the day have won,
Must yeild them foil'd and vanquisht by the Tun.
Men that live thus, as if they liv'd in jest,
Fooling their time with Musick, and a Feast;   30

That did exile all sounds from their soft eare
But of the Harp, must this sad discord heare
Compos'd in threats: The feet which measures tread
Shall in Captivity be fettered:
Famine shall scourge them for their vast excesse,   35
And Hell revenge their monstrous Drunkennesse;
Which hath enlarg'd itself, to swallowe such,
Whose throats ne're knew enough, though still too much.

   Woe unto those that countenance a Sinne,
Siding with Vice, that it may credit winne   40
By their unhallow'd Vote. That doe benight
The Truth with Errour, putting Dark for Light,
And Light for Dark. That call an Evill, Good,
And would by Vice have Vertue understood.
That with their frowne can sowre an honnest cause,   45
Or sweeten any bad by their applause.
That justify the wicked for reward,
And voyd of morall goodnes or regard,
Plott with Detraction, to traduce the fame
Of him, whose meritt hath enroll'd his name   50
Among the Just. Therfore God's vengefull ire
Glowes on his People, and becomes a fire,
Whose greedy and exalted flame shall burne
Till they, like straw or chaffe, to nothing turne.
Because they have rebell'd against the right,   55
To God and Law perversly opposite;
As Plants, which Sun nor Shewres did ever blesse,
So shall their Root convert to Rottennes:
And their Succession's Budd, in which they trust,
Shall (like Gomorrah's fruit) moulder to dust.   60

   Woe unto those that drunk with self conceit
Value their owne designes at such a rate
Which humane wisdome cannot reach; That sitt
Enthron'd, as sole Monopolists of Witt:

That out-look reason, and suppose the Ey 65
Of Nature blind to their discovery,
Whilst they a title make to understand
What ever Secret's bosom'd in the Land.
But God shall imp their pride, and let them see
They are but fooles in a sublime degree: 70
He shall bring downe, and humble those proud Eyes
In which false glasses only they lookt wise:
That all the world may laugh, and learne by it,
There is no folly to pretended Witt.

Woe unto those that draw Iniquity 75
With cordes: and by a vaine security
Lengthen the sinfull trace; Till their owne Chayne
Of many linkes, form'd by laborious paine,
Doe pull them into Hell: That, as with Lines
And Cartroapes, dragg on their unwilling Crimes: 80
Who, rather then they will committ no Sinne,
Tempt all occasions to let it in.
As if there were no God, who must exact
The strict account for e'ry vitious fact,
Nor Judgment after Death. If any bee, 85
Let Him make speed (say they) that wee may see.
Why is his Work retarded by delay?
Why doth himself thus linger on the way?
If there be any Judge, or future Doome,
Let It and Him with speed together come. 90

Unhappy men that challenge and defy
The comming of that dreadfull Majesty!
Better by much for You, he did reverse
His purpos'd Sentence on the Universe;
Or that the creeping Minutes might adjourne 95
Those flames, in which You, with the Earth, must burne:
That Time's revolting hand could lagg the Yeere,
And so put back His Day, which is too neere.

Behold his Signes advanc't, like Colours fly,
To tell the World that His approach is nigh;   100
And in a furious March Hee's comming on,
Swift as the raging Inundation,
To scowre the sinfull World. 'Gainst which is bent
Artillery that never can be spent:
Bowes strung with vengeance and Flame-feather'd Darts 105
Headed with Death, to wound transgressing Hearts.
His Charriot Wheeles rapt in the Whirlewinde's gyre,
His Horses hoov'd with flint, and shod with fire.
In which amaze where e're they fixe their Eye,
Or on the melting Earth, or upp, on high,   110
To seek Heav'ns shrunk Lights, nothing shall appeare
But Night and Horrour in their Hemisphære:
Nor shall th' affrighted Sense more objects know,
Then dark'ned Skyes above, and Hell below.

An Essay on Death and a Prison

A Prison is in all things like a Grave,
Where wee no better priviledges have
Then Dead men, nor so good. The Soule once fled
Lives freer now, then when she'e was cloystered
In walles of flesh; and though shee Organs want   5
To act her swift designes, yet all will grant
Her Facultyes more cleare, now separate,
Then if the same Conjunction, which of late
Did marry her to earth, had stood in force,
Uncapable of Death, or of Divorce: 10
But an imprison'd Mind, though Living, dyes,
And at one time feeles two Captivityes;
A narrow Dungeon which her body holds,
But narrower Body which her self enfolds.
Whilst I in Prison ly, nothing is free,   15
Nothing enlarg'd, but Thought and Misery;

Though e'ry chink be stop't, the doores close barr'd,
Despight of walles and Lockes, through e'ry ward
These have their Issues forth; may take the aire,
Though not for health, but only to compare   20
How wretched those men are who freedome want,
By such as never suff'red a restraint.
In which unquiet travaile could I find
Ought that might settle my distemper'd mind,
Or of some comfort make discovery,   25
It were a Voyage well employ'd: But I,
Like our raw Travailers, that crosse the Seas
To fetch home Fashions, or some worse Disease,
Instead of quiet a new torture bring
Home t'afflict mee, malice and murmuring.   30
What is't I envy not? no Dog, nor Fly
But my desires preferr, and wish were I;
For they are free, or if they were like mee,
They had no Sense to know Calamity.
But in the Grave no sparkes of envy live,   35
No hott comparisons that causes give
Of quarrell, or that our affections move
Any condition, save their owne, to love.
There are no Objects there but Shades and Night,
And yet that Darknes better then the Light.   40
There lives a silent harmony, no jarr
Or discord can that sweet soft consort marr.
The Grave's deaf eare is clos'd against all noise
Save that which Rockes must heare, the Angell's voice:
Whose Trump shall wake the World, and raise up men   45
Who in Earth's bosome slept, bedd-rid till then.
What man then would, who on Death's pillow slumbers,
Be re-inspir'd with Life, though golden numbers
Of blisse were powr'd into his breast: though hee
Were sure in change to gaine a Monarchy?   50
A Monarch's glorious state compar'd with his
Lesse safe, lesse free, lesse firme, lesse quiet is.

For ne're was any Prince advanc't so high
That he was out of reach of misery:
Never did Story yet a Law report 55
To banish Fate or Sorrow from his Court.
Where e're he moves, by Land, or through the maine,
These goe along, sworne Members of his traine.
But he, whome the kind Earth hath entertain'd,
Hath in her Womb a sanctuary gain'd, 60
Whose Charter and Protection arme him so,
That he is priviledg'd from future Woe.
The Coffin's a safe harbour, where he rides
Land-bound, belowe crosse Windes, or churlish Tides.
For Grief, sprung up with Life, was man's half brother, 65
Fedd by the Tast, brought forth by Sinne, the Mother.
And since the first seduction of the Wife,
God did decree to Grief a Lease for life.
Which Patent in full force continue must,
Till Man, that disobey'd, revert to Dust. 70
So that Life's sorrowes, ratify'd by God,
Cannot expire, or find their period,
Untill the Soule and Body disunite,
And by two diff'rent wayes from each take flight.
But they dissolved once, our woes disband, 75
Th'Assurance cancell'd by one fatall hand:
Soone as the passing-bell proclaimes mee dead,
My Sorrowes sink with mee, ly buryed
In the same heap of dust, the self same Urne
Doth them and mee alike to nothing turne. 80
   If then of these I might election make,
Whether I would refuse, and whether take,
Rather then like a sullen Anchorite
I would live cas'd in Stone, and learne to write
A Prisoner's Story, which might steale some teares 85
From the sad eyes of him that reades or heares,
Give mee a peacefull death, and let mee meet
My freedome seal'd up in my winding sheet.

Death is the pledge of rest, and with one Bayle
Two Prisons quitts, the Body and the Jayle.   90

To his unconstant Freind

But say, thou very Woman, why to mee
This fitt of weaknes and inconstancy?
What forfeit have I made of word or vow
That I am rack't on thy displeasure now?
If I have done a fault, I doe not shame   5
To cite it from thy Lipps, give it a name:
I ask the Bannes, stand forth and tell mee why
Wee should not in our wonted Loves comply.
Did thy cloy'd appetite urge thee to try
If any other man could love as I?   10
I see freinds are like Cloathes, lay'd up whilst new,
But after wearing cast, though ne're so true.
Or did thy feirce ambition long to make
Some Lover turne a Martyr for thy sake?
Thinking thy beauty had deserv'd no name   15
Unlesse some one do perish in that flame:
Upon whose loving dust this Sentence lyes
Herc's one was murther'd by his Mistris' Eyes.
Or was't because my love to thee was such
I could not choose but blab it? sweare how much   20
I was thy Slave, and doting let thee know,
I better could my self, then Thee forgoe?
Hearken yee men that e're shall love like mee,
I'le give you counsaile gratis: If you bee
Possest of what you like, let your faire freind   25
Lodge in your bosome, but no secrets send
To seek their lodging in a female breast,
For so much is abated of your rest.
The Steed that comes to understand his strength
Growes wild, and casts his Manager at length: 30

And that tame Lover who unlocks his heart
Unto his Mistris, teaches her an art
To plague himself, shewes hir the secret way
How shee may tyrannize another day.
   And now my Faire Unkindnes! thus to thee;   35
Mark how wise Passion and I agree;
Heare and be sorry for't. I will not dy
To expiate thy crime of Levity:
I walk (not crosse-arm'd neither) eat and live,
Yea live to pitty thy neglect, not grieve   40
That thou art from thy faith and promise gone,
Nor envy him who by my losse hath won.
Thou shalt perceave thy changing Moon-like fitts
Have not infected mee, or turn'd my Witts
To Lunacy. I doe not meane to weep   45
When I should eat, or sigh when I should sleep;
I will not fall upon my pointed quill,
Bleed ink and poëms, or invention spill
To contrive Ballads, or weave Elegyes
For Nurses wearing when the Infant cryes.   50
Nor like th'enamour'd Tristrams of the time,
Despaire in Prose, and hang my self in Rhime.
Nor thither run upon my Verses' feet,
Where I shall none but fooles or madmen meet,
Who midst the silent shades, and Myrtle walkes   55
Pule and doe Penance for their Mistris' faultes.
I'me none of those poëtick Malecontents
Borne to make paper deare with my laments;
Or wild Orlando that will raile and vexe,
And for thy sake fall out with all the Sexe.   60
No, I will love againe, and seek a prize
That shall redeeme mee from thy poore despise.
I'le court my fortune now in such a shape
That will no faint dy, nor starv'd colour take.
   Thus launch I off with triumph from thy shoare,   65
To which my last farwell; for never more

Will I touch there. I putt to sea againe
Blowne with the churlish wind of thy disdaine.
Nor will I stopp this Course, till I have found
A Coast that yeilds safe harbour and firme ground.　　70
　　Smile yee Love-starres; wing'd with desire I fly,
To make my wishes' full discovery:
Nor doubt I, but, for One that proves like You,
I shall finde Tenn as faire, and yet more true.

Madam Gabrina, Or the Ill-favourd Choice

Con mala Muger el remedio
Mucha Tierra por el medio.

　　I have oft wondred, why Thou didst elect
Thy Mistris of a stuff none could affect
That wore his Eyes in the right place. A Thing
Made up, when Nature's powers lay slumbering.
One, where all pregnant imperfections mett　　5
To make hir Sexe's scandall: Teeth of Jett,
Haire dy'd in Orpment, from whose fretfull hue
Canidia her highest witchcrafts drew:
A Lipp most Thin and Pale, But such a Mouth
Which, like the Poles, is stretched North and South:　　10
A Face so colour'd, and of such a forme,
As might defyance bidd unto a Storme:
And the complexion of her sallow hide
Like a wrack't Body wash't up by the Tide:
Eyes small: A Nose so to hir Vizard glew'd　　15
As if 'twould take a Plannet's Altitude:
Last, for her Breath; 'tis somwhat like the smell
That does in Ember-weekes on Fishstreet dwell:
Or as a man should fasting sent the Rose
Which in the savoury Bear-garden growes.　　20
If a Fox cures the Paralyticall,
Hadst thou ten Palseys, shee'd out-stink them all.

But I have found thy plott: sure thou didst try
To put Thyself past Hope of Jealousy:
And whilst unlearned Fooles their Senses please,   25
Thou cur'st thy Appetite by a Disease;
As many use, to kill an Itch withall,
Quicksilver, or some biting Minerall.

Dote upon handsome things each common man
With little study and lesse labour can: 30
But to make Love to a Deformity,
Only commends thy great ability,
Who from hard-favour'd Objects drawst content,
As Estriches from Iron nutriment.

Well take hir, and like mounted George, in bed   35
Boldly atchieve thy Dragon's mayden-head:
Where (though scarce sleep) thou may'st Rest, confident
None dares beguile thee of thy Punishment.
The sinne were not more foule he should committ,
Then is that Shee, with whome he acted it.   40

Yet take this comfort. When old age shall raze
Or Sicknes ruine many a good Face,
Thy choice cannot impaire. No cunning curse
Can mend that Night-peece: That is, Make her worse.

The Defence

Piensan los Enamorados
Que tienen los otros los oios quebrantados.

Why slightest thou what I approve?
Thou art no Peere to try my Love.
Nor canst discerne where her forme lyes,
Unlesse thou sawst her with my Eyes.

Say shee were foule, and blacker than   5
The Night, or Sun-burnt African,
If lik't by mee, tis I alone
Can make a beauty where was none.

For rated in my Phant'sy, shee
Is so, as shee appeares to mee.   10
   But 'tis not feature or a face
That does my free Election grace,
Nor is my liking only lead
By a well-tempred White and Red:
Could I enamour'd grow on those,   15
The Lilly and the blushing Rose
United in one stalk, might bee
As deare unto my thoughts, as shee.
   But I look farther, and doe find
A richer Beauty in her mind: 20
Where somthing is so Lasting Faire,
As Time, or Age cannot empaire.
Hadst thou a Perspective so cleare,
Thou couldst behold my Object there;
When thou hir Vertues shouldst espy,   25
They'ld force thee to confesse, that I
Had cause to like Hir; And Learne thence
To love by Judgment, not by Sense.

The Surrender

My once Deare Love; Happlesse that I no more
Must call thee so: The rich affection's store
That fed our hopes, lyes now exhawst and spent,
Like Summes of Treasure unto Bankerupts lent.
   Wee that did nothing study but the way   5
To love each other, with which thoughts the Day
Rose with delight to us, and with them sett,
Must learne the hatefull Art, how to forgett.
   Wee that did nothing wish that Heav'n could give
Beyond our selves, nor did desire to live   10
Beyond that Wish, all these now cancell must,
As if not writt in faith, but Words, and Dust.

Yet witnes those cleere Vowes which Lovers make!
Witnes the chast Desires, that never brake
Into unruly heates; Witnes that breast   15
Which in thy bosome anchor'd his whole rest,
Tis no default in us. I dare acquite
Thy Mayden-faith, thy purpose faire and white
As thy pure self. Crosse Plannets did envy
Us to each other, and Heav'n did unty   20
Faster then Vowes could bind. O that the Starrs
When Lovers meet, should stand oppos'd in Warrs!
   Since then some higher Destinyes command
Let us not strive, nor labour to withstand
What is past help. The longest date of grief   25
Can never yeild a hope of our releife.
And though wee wast our selves in moist laments,
Teares may drowne us, but not our discontents.
   Fold back our armes, take home our fruitlesse Loves,
That must new fortunes try, like Turtle Doves   30
Dislodged from their hauntes. Wee must in teares
Unwind a Love knitt up in many Yeares.
In this last kisse I here surrender thee
Back to Thyself. Lo thou againe art free.
Thou in another, sad as that, resend   35
The truest heart that Lover e're did lend.
   Now turne from each. So fare our sever'd Hearts
As the Divorc't Soule from her Body parts.

Sonnet

Dry those faire, those Christall Eyes
Which like growing fountaines rise
To drowne their bankes. Greife's sullen Brooks
Would better flow in furrow'd lookes.
     Thy lovely face was never meant   5
     To be the Shoare of discontent.

Then cleare those wat'rish Starrs againe
Which else portend a lasting raine;
Least the cloudes which settle there
Prolong my Winter all the Yeare: 10
   And the Example others make
   In love with Sorrow for thy sake.

Sonnet

When I entreat, either thou wilt not heare,
Or else my suit arriving at thy eare
Cooles and Dyes there. A straunge extremity
To freeze i'th' Sun, and in the Shade to Fry.
Whilst all my blasted Hopes decline so soone,   5
'Tis Evening with mee, though at high Noone.
  For pitty to thy self, if not to mee,
Think Time will ravish, what I loose, from Thee.
If my scorch't Heart wither through thy delay,
Thy Beauty withers too; and swift decay   10
Arrests thy Youth. So Thou, whilst I am slighted,
Wilt be too soone with Age or Sorrow Nighted.

Sic Vita

  Like to the Falling of a Starr;
  Or as the Flightes of Eagles are;
  Or like the fresh Spring's gawdy hew;
  Or Silver Dropps of Morning Dew;
  Or like a Wind that chafes the flood;   5
  Or Bubbles which on Water stood;
  Even such is Man, whose borrow'd Light
  Is streight Call'd in, and Pay'd to Night.

   The Wind blowes out, The Bubble Dyes;
   The Spring entomb'd in Autumne lyes: 10

The Dew dryes up: The Starr is shott:
The Flight is past: And Man Forgott.

Sonnet

  I prethee turne that face away
Whose splendour but benightes my day.
Sad eyes like mine, and wounded hearts
Shun the bright rayes which Beauty darts.
    Unwelcome is the Sun that pryes   5
    Into those shades where Sorrow lyes.

  Goe shine on happy things. To mee
That blessing is a misery:
Whome thy feirce Sun not warmes, but burnes,
Like that the Sooty Indian turnes.   10
    I'le serve the Night, and there confin'd
    Wish Thee lesse faire, or else more kind.

Sonnet

Tell mee you Starrs that our affections move
Why made yee mee that Cruell one to Love?
Why burnes my Heart hir scorned Sacrifice
Whose breast is hard as Christall, cold as Ice?
  God of Desire! if all thy Votaryes   5
Thou thus repay, Succession will grow wise;
No Sighes, for Incense, at thy shrine shall smoak,
Thy Rites will be despis'd, thy Altars broak.

  O! or give hir my flame, to melt that snow
Which, yet unthaw'd, does on hir Bosome grow: 10
Or make mee Ice; and with Hir Christall chaines
Bind up all Love within my frozen Veines.

The Farwell

Splendidis longum valedico nugis

Farwell fond Love, under whose childish whipp
I have serv'd out a weary prentishipp;
Thou that hast made mee thy scorn'd property,
To dote on Rocks, but yielding Loves to fly:
Go bane of my dear quiet and content,   5
Now practise on some other Patient.

Farwell false Hope, that fann'd my warme desire
Till it had rais'd a wild unruly fire,
Which nor Sighes coole, nor teares extinguish can,
Allthough my Eyes out-flow'd the Ocean: 10
Forth of my thoughts for ever, Thing of Aire,
Begun in Errour, finish't in Despaire.

Farwell vaine World, upon whose restlesse Stage
Twixt Love and Hope I have fool'd out my Age;
Henceforth, ere sue to thee for my redresse,   15
I'le wooe the Wind, or court the Wildernesse,
And buryed from the Daye's discovery,
Study a slow, yet certaine way to Dy.

My wofull Monument shall be a Cell,
The murmur of the purling brook my Knell.   20
My lasting Epitaph the Rock shall groane:
Thus when sad Lovers ask the weeping Stone,
What wretched thing does in that Center ly?
The hollow Eccho will reply, 'Twas I.

A Blackmore Mayd wooing a faire Boy: sent to the Author by Mr. Hen. Rainolds

Stay lovely Boy, why fly'st thou mee
That languish in these flames for Thee?
I'me black, 'tis true: why so is Night,
And Love does in dark Shades delight.
The whole World, doe but close thine Ey, 5
Will seeme to thee as black as I,
Or op't, and see what a black shade
Is by thine owne faire Body made,
That followes thee where e're thou goe;
(O who allow'd would not doe so?) 10
Let mee for ever dwell so nigh,
And thou shalt need no other shade then I.

The Boy's answere to the Blackmore

Black Mayd, complayne not that I fly,
When Fate commaundes Antipathy:
Prodigious might that Union prove, 15
Where Night and Day togither move,
And the Conjunction of our lipps
Not Kisses make, but an Ecclypse,
In which the mixed Black and White
Portends more Terrour then Delight. 20
Yet if my Shadow Thou wilt bee,
Enjoy thy dearest wish. But see
Thou take my Shadowe's property,
That hasts away when I come nigh:
Else stay till Death hath blinded mee, 25
And then I will bequeath my self to Thee.

A Letter

I ne're was drest in Formes; nor can I bend
My Pen to flatter any, nor commend,
Unlesse desert or honour doe present
Unto my verse a worthy argument.
    You are my Freind, and in that word to mee   5
Stand blazon'd in your noblest Heraldry;
That Stile presents you full, and does relate
The Bounty of your Love, and my owne Fate,
Both which conspir'd to make mee Yours. A Choice
Which needes must in the giddy people's voice,   10
That only judge the outside, and like Apes
Play with our names, and comment on our Shapes,
Appeare too light: But it lyes you upon
To justify the disproportion.
    Truth be my record, I durst not presume   15
To seek to you; Twas you that did assume
Mee to your Bosome. Wherein you subdu'd
One that can serve you, though ne're could intrude
Upon Great Titles; nor knowes how t'invade
Acquaintance: Like such as are only pay'd   20
With great men's smiles, If that the Passant Lord
Let fall a forc't salute, or but afford
The Nod Regardant. It was Test enough
For mee, You ne're did find such servile stuff
Couch't in my temper. I can freely say,   25
I doe not love you in that common way
For which Great ones are lov'd in this false Time:
I have no wish to gaine, nor will to climbe;
I cannot pawne my freedome, nor outlive
My Liberty, for all that you can give.   30
And sure, you may retaine good cheap such freinds,
Who not your Fortune make, but You, their Ends.

I speak not this to vaunt in my owne Story;
All these additions are unto your glory.
Who, counter to the World, use to elect, 35
Not to take up on trust, what you affect.
Indeed 'tis seldome seene, that such as you
Adopt a Friend, or for acquaintance sue;
Yet you did this vouchsafe, you did descend
Belowe your self, to raise an humble freind, 40
And fix him in your Love: where I will stand
The constant Subject of your free command.
Had I no aiery thoughts, sure, you would teach
Mee higher then my owne dull Spheare to reach:
And by Reflexe instruct mee to appeare 45
Somthing (though course and plaine) fitt for your weare.

    Know, Best of Freinds, however wild report
May justly say I am unapt to sort
With your opinion or society,
(Which truth would shame mee did I it deny) 50
There's something in mee sayes, I dare make good,
When honour calls mee, all I want in Blood.

    Putt off your Gyant Titles, then I can
Stand in your judgment's blank an equall man.
Though Hills advanced are above the Plaine, 55
They are but higher Earth; nor must disdaine
Allyance with the Vale: wee see a Spade
Can levell them, and make a Mount a Glade.
Howe're wee differ in the Herald's Book,
He that Mankind's Extraction shall look 60
In Nature's Rolles, must graunt, wee all agree
In our Best part's Immortal Pedigree.
You must by that Perspective only view
My Service, else 'twill ne're shew worthy You.

    You see I court you bluntly, like a Freind, 65
Not like a Mistris; My Muse is not penn'd
For smooth and oyly flights: And I indent
To use more Honesty then Complement.

But I have done; In liew of all you give
Receave his thankfull Tribute, who must live   70
Your vow'd Observer, and devotes a Heart
Which will in Death seale the bold Counterpart.

Upon a Table-book presented to a Lady

When your faire hand receaves this Little Book,
You must not there for Prose or Verses look.
Those empty regions which within you see,
May by your self planted and peopled bee.
And though wee scarce allow your Sex to prove   5
Writers (unlesse the argument be Love)
Yet without crime or envy You have roome
Here both the Scribe and Authour to become.

To the same Lady
Upon Overburye's Wife

Madam, who understands you well, would sweare
That You the Life, and this Your Coppy were.

To the same Lady
Upon Mr. Burton's Melancholy

If in this Glasse of Humours you doe find
The Passions or Diseases of your Mind;
Here without paine you safely may endure
Though not to suffer, yet to Read your Cure:
But if you nothing meet you can apply,   5
Then e're you need, you have a Remedy.
    And I doe wish You never may have cause
To be adjoudg'd by these Phantastick Lawes.
But that this Booke's Example may be know'n
By others' Melancholy, not your Owne.   10

To a Freind upon Overburie's Wife given to Hir

I know no fitter Subject for your view
Then this, a meditation ripe for You,
As You for it. Which when you read you'le see
What kind of Wife your self will one Day bee.
Which happy day be neere you, and may this   5
Remaine with you as earnest of my wish;
When you so farr love any, that you dare
Venter your whole affection on his care,
May he, for whome you change your Virgin life,
Prove good to you, and Perfect as this Wife.   10

To A. R. upon the same

Not that I would instruct or tutor you
What is a Wife's behest, or Husband's due,
Give I this Widdow-Wife. Your early date
Of knowledge makes such præcepts slowe and late;
This Book is but your glasse. Where you shall see   5
What your self are, what other Wives should be.

Upon a Braid of Haire in a Heart sent by Mris. E. H.

In this small Character is sent
My Love's eternall Monument:
Whilst wee shall live, know, this Chain'd Heart
Is our affection's Counterpart:
And if wee never meet, Think, I   5
Bequeath'd it as my Legacy.

An Epitaph On Niobe turn'd to Stone

This Pile thou see'st, built out of Flesh not Stone,
Containes no Shrowd within, nor mouldring Bone:

This Blood-lesse Trunk is destitute of Tombe,
Which may the Soule-fledd Mansion enwombe.

This seeming Sepulchre (to tell the troth)   5
Is neither Tomb, nor Body; and yet Both.

Epigram

Quid faciant Leges ubi sola pecunia regnat? &c:
Petron: Arbit.:

To what serve Lawes where only mony reignes?
Or where a poore man's cause no right obtaines?
Even those that most austerity prætend,
Hire out their Tongues, and words for profitt lend.
    What's Judgment then? but publique merchandise;   5
And the Court sitts but to allow the Price.

Epigram

Casta suô gladium cum traderet Arria Pæto. &c:
Martial:

When Arria to her Pætus had bequeath'd
The Sword, in her chast bosome newly sheath'd:
Trust mee (quoth shee) My owne wound feeles no smart,
Tis thine (my Pætus) grieves and kills my heart.

Epigram

Pro captu lectoris habent sua fata libelli.

The fate of Bookes is diverse as man's Sense:
Two Criticks nere shar'd one intelligence.

Epigram

Qui Pelago credit, magno se fænore tollit &c:
                                    Petron: Arbit:

He whose advent'rous keele ploughes the rough Seas,
Takes Interest of Fate for wealth's increase.
He that in Battaile trafficks, and pitch't fields,
Reaps with his Sword rich Harvests, which warre yeelds.
Base parasites repose their drunken heads,   5
Laden with Sleep and Wine, on Tyrian beds.
And he that melts in Lust's adult'rous fire
Getts both reward and pleasure for his hire.
But Learning only, midst this wanton heat,
Hath (save it self) nothing to weare or eat;   10
Faintly exclaiming on the looser Times,
That value Witt and Artes belowe their Crimes.

Epigram

Nolo quod cupio statim tenere:
Nec victoria mi placet parata.
                                    Petron: Arb:

I would not in my Love too soone prevaile:
An easy Conquest makes the Purchase stale.

My Midd-night Meditation

Ill busy'd Man! why should'st thou take such care
To lengthen out thy Life's short Kalendar?
When e'ry Spectacle Thou look'st upon
Presents and Actes thy Execution.
    Each drooping Season, and each Flower doth cry   5
    Foole! As I fade and wither, Thou must Dy.

157

The beating of thy Pulse (when Thou art well)
Is just the Tolling of thy Passing Bell.
Night is thy Hearse, whose sable Canopy
Covers alike Deceased Day and Thee.   10
 And all those weeping Dewes which nightly fall,
 Are but the Teares shed for thy Funerall.

Sonnet

 Tell mee no more how faire shee is;
  I have no mind to heare
 The Story of that distant Blisse
  I never shall come neere.
  By sad experience I have found   5
  That Hir perfection is my wound.

 And tell mee not how fond I am
  To tempt a daring Fate,
 From whence no triumph ever came
  But to repent too late.   10
  There is some hope ere long I may
  In silence dote my self away.

 I aske no Pitty (Love!) from thee,
  Nor will thy Justice blame;
 So that thou wilt not envy mee   15
  The glory of my Flame:
  Which crownes my Heart, when e're it dyes,
  In that it falles Hir Sacrifice.

Sonnet

 Were thy heart soft, as Thou art faire,
 Thou wert a wonder, past compare.
 But frozen Love and feirce Disdaine
 By their Extreames thy Graces staine.

Cold coynesse quenches the still fires 5
Which glowe in Lovers' warme desires;
And scorne, like the quick Light'ning's blaze,
Darts Death against affection's gaze.
  O Heavens, what prodigy is this
  When Love in Beauty buryed is! 10
  Or that Dead Pitty thus should bee
  Tomb'd in a Living Cruelty.

Silence. A Sonnet

Peace my Hearte's blabb, be ever dumbe;
Sorrowes speak loud without a Tongue:
And my perplexed Thoughts forbeare
To breath your selves in any eare:
  Tis scarse a true or manly grief 5
  Which gadds abroad to find releef.

Was ever stomack that lack't meat
Nourish't by what another eat?
Can I bestow it, or will woe
Forsake mee when I bid it goe? 10
  Then I'le beleeve a wounded breast
  May heale by shrift, and purchase rest.

But if, imparting it, I doe
Not ease my self, but trouble Two;
Tis better I alone possesse 15
My treasure of unhappinesse:
  Engrossing that, which is my owne
  No longer then it is unknowne.

If Silence be a kind of Death,
He kindles grief who gives it breath. 20
But let it rak't in Embers ly
On thine owne hearth, 'twill quickly dy;
  And, spight of fate, that very womb
  Which carryes it shall prove its Tombe.

Sonnet. To Patience

Downe stormy Passions, downe: no more
Let your rude Waves invade the Shoare
Where blushing Reason sitts, and hides
Hir from the fury of your Tides.
Fitt only 'tis where you beare sway   5
That Fooles or Franticks doe obay.
Since Judgment, if it not resists,
Will loose it self in your blind Mists.

Fall easy Patience, fall like Rest
Whose soft Spells charme a troubled breast: 10
And where those Rebells you espy,
O in your silken Cordage ty
Their malice up! So shall I raise
Altars to thank your Pow'r, and praise
The soveraigne Vertue of your Balme,   15
Which cures a Tempest by a Calme.

The Vow-Breaker

When first the Magick of thine Ey
Usurp't upon my Liberty,
Triumphing in my Heart's spoyle, Thou
Didst lock up Thine in such a Vow:
When I prove false, may the bright Day   5
Be govern'd by the Moone's pale Ray.
(As I too well remember) This
Thou saydst, and sealdst it with a Kisse.

O Heavens! and could so soone that Ty
Relent in slack Apostacy?   10
Could all thy Oathes and morgag'd trust
Vanish? like Letters form'd in Dust
Which the next Wind scatters. Take heed,
Take heed Revolter; Know this deed
Hath wrong'd the world, which will fare worse   15
By thy Example, then thy Curse.

Hide that false Brow in Mists. Thy shame
Ne're see Light more, but the dimme flame
Of funerall Lamps. Thus sitt and moane,
And learne to keep thy guilt at home.   20
Give it no vent; For if agen
Thy Love or Vowes betray more men,
At length (I feare) thy perjur'd breath
Will blow out Day, and waken Death.

A Penitentiall Hymne

Hearken, O God! unto a wretche's cryes
Who low dejected at thy footstoole lyes.
Let not the clamour of my heynous Sin
Drowne my requests: which strive to enter in
At those bright Gates, which alwayes open stand   5
To such as begg remission at thy hand.

Too well I know, if Thou in justice deale
I can nor pardon ask, nor yet appeale:
To my hoarse voyce Heav'n will no audience grant,
But deaf as brasse, and hard as Adamant   10
Beat back my words; Therfore I bring to Thee
A gratious Advocate to plead for mee.

What though my leaprous Soule no Jordan can
Recure? nor floods of the lav'd Ocean
Make cleane? yet from my Saviour's bleeding Side 15

Two large and med'cinable Rivers glide:
Lord wash mee where those Streames of Life abound,
And new Bethesdaes flow from ev'ry wound.

If I this pretious lather may obtaine,
I shall not then dispaire for any staine: 20
I need no Gilead's balme, nor oyle, nor shall
I for the Purifying Hysop call:
My spotts will vanish in His purple flood,
And Crimson there grow white, though wash't in blood.

See Lord! with broken heart, and bended knee   25
How I addresse my humble suit to Thee.
O give that Suit admittance to thine eares
Which floates to thee, not in my words, but Teares.
And let my sinfull Soule this mercy crave
Before I fall into the silent grave.   30

Sonnet

Goe Thou, that vainly dost mine eyes invite
To tast the softer comforts of the Night,
And bidst mee coole the Feaver of my braine
In those sweet balmy Dewes which slumber paine:
   Enjoy thine owne peace in untroubled Sleep,   5
   Whilst my sad thoughts æternall vigills keep.

O! couldst Thou for a Time change brests with mee,
Thou in that broken Glasse should'st plainly see,
A Heart, which wasts in the slowe smoth'ring fire
Blowne by Despaire, and fed by false Desire,   10
   Can only reap such sleepes as Seamen have,
   When fierce winds rock them on the foaming wave.

The Departure. An Elegy

Were I to leave no more than a Good Freind,
Or but to heare the Summons to my End,
(Which I have long'd for) I could then with ease
Attire my Grief in Words, and so appease
That Passion in my Bosome, which out-growes   5
The Language of strict Verse, or largest Prose.
But here I am quite lost; writing to You
All that I pen or think is forct and new.
My Facultyes run crosse, and prove as weak
T'indite this melancholy task, as speak.   10
Indeed all words are vaine. Well might I spare
This rendring of my tortur'd thoughts in aire,
Or sighing paper. My infectious grief
Strikes inward, and affords mee no releef,
But still a deeper wound, To loose a sight   15
More lov'd then Health, and dearer then the Light.
But all of us were not at the same time
Brought forth; nor are wee billeted in one clime.
Nature hath pitch't mankind at severall rates,
Making our Places diverse as our Fates.   20
Unto that universall Law I bow,
Though with unwilling knee, and doe allowe
Hir cruell justice, which dispos'd us so
That wee must counter to our wishes goe.
'Twas part of Man's first curse, which order'd well   25
Wee should not alway with our Likings dwell.
Tis only the Triumphant Church where wee
Shall in unsever'd Neighbourhood agree.

　　Goe then Best Soule, and where You must appeare
Restore the Day to that dull Hemisphære.   30
Ne're may the happlesse Night You leave behind
Darken the Comforts of your purer mind.
May all the Blessings wishes can invent
Enrich your Dayes, and crowne them with content.

And though You travaile downe into the West   35
May your Life's Sun stand fixed in the East
Farre from the weeping Sett; nor may my Eare
Take in that killing whisper, You once were.
    Thus kisse I your faire hands, taking my leave
As Prisoners at the Barr their Doome receive.   40
All joyes goe with You. Let sweet Peace attend
You on the way, and waite your journeye's end.
But let your Discontents and sowrer fate
Remaine with mee, borne off in my Retrait.
Might all your Crosses, in that Sheet of Lead   45
Which folds my heavy Heart, ly Buryed;
Tis the last service I would doe You, and the best
My Wishes ever meant, or Tongue profest.
Once more I take my leave. And once for all:
Our parting shewes so like a Funerall,   50
It strikes my Soule, which hath most right to bee
Chief Mourner at this sad Solemnity.
    And think not Dearest! cause this parting knell
Is rung in Verses, that at your Farwell
I only mourne in Poëtry and Ink: 55
No, my pen's melancholy Plommets sink
So lowe, they dive where th'hid Affections sitt,
Blotting that Paper where my mirth was writt.
    Beleev't, that Sorrow truest is, which lyes
Deep in the Breast, not floating in the Eyes: 60
And he with saddest Circumstance doth part,
Who seales his Farwell with a Bleeding Heart.

An Acknowledgment

My best of Friends! what needes a Chaine to ty
One by your meritt bound a Votary?
Think You I have some plott upon my Peace,
I would this Bondage chaunge for a Release?

Since 'twas my fate your Prisoner to be,   5
Heav'n knowes I nothing feare but Liberty.
    Yet you doe well, that study to prevent
After so rich a stock of favour spent
On one so worthlesse, least my memory
Should let so deare an Obligation dy   10
Without Record. This made my pretious Freind
Hir Token, as an Antidote to send
Against forgetfull poysons. That as they
Who Vespers late, and early Mattins say
Upon their Beades; so on this linked skoare   15
In Golden Numbers I might reckon o're
Your Vertues and my debt, which does surmount
The triviall Lawes of popular Account.
For that within this Emblematick Knott
Your Beauteous Mind, and my owne Fate is wrott.   20
    The Sparkling Constellation which combines
The Lock, is your Deare self, whose worth outshines
Most of your Sexe: so solid and so cleare
You like a perfect Diamond appeare,
Casting from your Example fuller Light   25
Then those dimme Sparkes which glaze the brow of Night;
And gladding all your friends, as doth the ray
Of that East starr which wakes the cheerfull Day.
    But the black Mapp of Death and Discontent
Behind that Adamantine Firmament,   30
That lucklesse figure which like Calvary
Stands strew'd and Coppy'd out in Skulls, is I:
Whose Life your Absence clowdes, and makes my time
Move blindfold in the dark Ecliptick Line.
Then wonder not, if my removed Sun   35
So lowe within the Westerne Tropick run,
My Eyes no day in this Horizon see,
Since, where You are not, all is Night to mee.
    Lastly the Anchor which enfast'ned lyes
Upon a paire of Deaths, sadly applyes   40

That Monument of Rest, which harbour must
Our Shipwrack't Fortunes in a Road of Dust.
   So then, how late so 'ere my joylesse Life
Be tired out in this Affection's strife;
Though my Tempestuous Phant'sy, like the Sky,   45
Travaile with Stormes, and through my watry Ey
Sorrowe's high going waves spring many a Leak;
Though Sighes blow loud, till my Heart's Cordage break;
Though Faith, and all my Wishes prove untrue,
Yet Death shall fixe and anchor mee with You.   50
   Tis some poore Comfort, that this Mortall scope
Will Period, though never Crowne, my Hope.

To my Sister Anne King who chid mee in verse for being angry

Deare Nan! I would not have thy Counsaile lost,
Though I last night had twise so much beene crost:
Well is a Passion to the Markett brought,
When such a Treasure of Advise is bought
With so much Drosse. And could'st thou mee assure   5
Each Vice of mine should meet with such a Cure,
I would Sin oft, and on my guilty brow
Weare ev'ry imperfection that I owe,
Open and visible. I should not hide
But bring my faultes abroad, to heare thee chide   10
In such a Note, and with a Quill so sage
It Passion tunes, and calmes a Tempest's rage.
   Well I am charm'd; and promise to redresse
What, without Shrift, my follyes doe confesse
Against my self. Wherefore let mee entreat   15
When I fly out in that distemper'd heat
Which fretts mee into Fasts, Thou wilt reprove
That froward Spleene in Poëtry and Love.
So though I loose my Reason in such fitts,
Thou'lt Rhime mee back againe into my Witts.   20

The Pink

Faire one, you did on mee bestow
Comparisons too sweet to owe.
And, but I found them sent from You,
I durst not think they could be true.
    But 'tis your uncontrolled Power   5
Goddess-like to produce a flower,
And by your breath, without more seed,
Make that a Pink which was a Weed.
    Because I would be loath to misse
So sweet a Metamorphosis,   10
Upon what stalk soe're I grow
Disdaine not You somtimes to blow,
And cherish by your Virgin Ey
What in your frowne would droop and dy.
    So shall my thankfull Leaf repay   15
Perfumed wishes ev'ry day:
And o're your fortune breath a spell,
Which may his Obligation tell,
Who, though he nought but Aire can give,
Must ever your (Sweet) Creature live.   20

Sonnet. The Double Rock

Since Thou hast view'd some Gorgon, and art grow'n
        A solid Stone:
To bring againe to softnesse thy hard Heart
        Is past my art.
Ice may relent to water in a thaw;   5
But Stone made Flesh Love's Chimistry nere saw.

Therfore by thinking on thy Hardnes, I
        Will petrify:
And so within our double Quarrye's womb
        Digg our Love's Tomb.   10

Thus strangly will our difference agree,
And, with our selves, amaze the world, to see
How both Revenge and Sympathy consent
To make Two Rocks each others Monument.

The Retreit

Pursue no more (My Thoughts!) that False Unkind.
You may assoone emprison the North Wind;
Or catch the Lightning as it leapes; or reach
The leading Billow, first ran downe the Breach;
Or undertake the flying Cloudes to track   5
In the same path they yesterday did rack.
   Then, like a Torch turn'd downward, let the same
   Desire which nourish't it, put out your flame.

Loe! thus I doe divorce Thee from my breast,
False to Thy Vowe, and Traitour to my Rest!   10
Henceforth Thy Teares shall be (though thou repent)
Like Pardons after Execution sent.
Nor shalt thou ever my Love's story read,
But as some Epitaph of what is dead.
   So may my Hope on future blessings dwell,   15
   As tis my firme Resolve, and last Farwell.

The Forlorne Hope

How long (vaine Hope!) dost thou my joyes suspend?
Say! must my Expectation know no end?
Thou wast more kind unto the wandring Greek,
Who did ten Yeeres his Wife and Country seek.
   Ten lazy Winters in my glasse are run,   5
   Yet my Thoughts travaile seemes but new begun.

Smooth Quicksand, which the easy World beguiles!
Thou shalt not Bury mee in thy false smiles.
They that in hunting Shadowes pleasure take,
May benefitt of thy illusion make.　　　　　　　10
　　Since thou hast banish't mee from my content
　　I here pronounce thy finall Banishment.

Farwell thou Dreame of Nothing! Thou meere Voice!
Gett thee to Fooles, that can feed fatt with noise.
Bid wretches mark't for Death look for Reprieve,　　15
Or men broke on the Wheele perswade to live.
　　Henceforth my Comfort, and best Hope shall bee,
　　By scorning Hope, ne're to rely on Thee.

Love's Harvest

Fond Lunatick forbeare. Why dost thou sue
For thy Affection's Pay ere it is due?
Love's Fruites are Legall use; and therfore may
Be only taken on the Marriage day.
　　Who for this Interest too early call,　　　　　5
　　By that Exaction loose the Principall.

Then gather not those immature delights,
Untill their riper Autumne thee invites.
He that Abortive Corne cutts off his Ground,
No Husband, but a Ravisher is found.　　　　　　10
　　So those that reap their Love, before they Wed,
　　Do in effect but Cuckold their own Bed.

Being waked out of my Sleep
by a Snuff of Candle which offended
mee, I thus thought

Perhapps 'twas but Conceit. Erroneous Sense!
Thou art thine owne Distemper and Offence.
Imagine then, that sick unwholsome steame
Was thy Corruption breath'd into a Dreame.

Nor is it straunge, when wee in Charnells dwell,   5
That all our Thoughts of Earth and Frailty smell.
   Man is a Candle, whose unhappy Light
Burnes in the Day, and smothers in the Night.
And as you see the Dying Taper wast,
By such degrees does he to Darknes hast.   10
   Here is the Diff'rence. When our Bodye's Lamps
Blinded by Age, or choak't with mortall Damps,
Now faint and dimme and sickly 'gin to wink,
And in their hollow Socketts lowly sink;
When all our vitall Fires ceasing to burne   15
Leave nought but Snuff and Ashes in our Urne:
   God will restore those Fallen Lights againe,
   And kindle Them to an Eternall Flame.

The Legacy

My Dearest Love! When Thou and I must part,
And th'Icy hand of Death shall seize that Heart
Which is all Thine: within some spatious Will
I'le leave no Blanks for Legacyes to fill.
   Tis my ambition to Dy one of those   5
   Who but Himself hath nothing to dispose.

And since that is already Thine, what need
I to regive it by some newer deed?
Yet take it once againe. Free Circumstance
Does oft the value of meane things advance.   10
   Who thus repeates what he bequeath'd before,
   Proclaimes his Bounty richer then his Store.

But let mee not upon my Love bestowe
What is not worth the giving. I doe owe
Somwhat to Dust: My Bodye's pamper'd care   15
Hungry Corruption and the Worme will share.
   That mouldring Relick which in Earth must ly
   Would prove a guift of horrour to thine Ey.

With this cast Ragg of my Mortalitye
Let all my faultes and Errours buryed bee.   20
And as my Sear-cloth rotts, so may kind fate
Those worst acts of my Life incinerate.
   Hee shall in Story fill a glorious roome,
   Whose Ashes and whose Sins sleep in one Tombe.

If now to my cold Hearse Thou deigne to bring   25
Some melting Sighes as thy last Offering,
My peacefull Exequyes are crown'd. Nor shall
I ask more honour at my Funerall.
   Thou wilt more richly balme mee with thy Teares
   Then all the Narde fragrant Arabia beares.   30

And as the Paphian Queene by her greife's show'r
Brought up her Dead Love's Spirit in a Flow'r:
So by those pretious dropps rain'd from thine Eyes
Out of my Dust, o may some Vertue rise!
   And like thy Better Genius thee attend   35
   Till Thou in my dark Period shalt end.

Lastly my constant Truth let mee commend
To Him Thou choosest next to be thy Freind.
For (witnesse all things good!) I would not have
Thy Youth and Beauty marry'd to my Grave.   40
   'Twould shew Thou didst repent the Stile of Wife,
   Shouldst Thou relapse into a Single Life.

They with præposterous grief the World delude
Who mourne for their lost Mates in Solitude.
Since Widdowhood more strongly doth enforce   45
The much lamented Lott of their Divorce.
   Themselves then of their Losses guilty are
   Who may, yet will not suffer a Repaire.

Those were Barbarian Wives that did invent
Weeping to Death at th'Husband's Moniment.　　　　50
But in more Civill Rites Shee doth approve
Her First, who ventures on a Second Love.
　　For else it may be thought, if shee refraine,
　　Shee sped so ill shee durst not try againe.

Up then my Love! and choose some worthyer One　　55
Who may supply my roome when I am gone.
So will the Stock of our Affection thrive
No lesse in Death, then were I still Alive.
　　And in my Urne I shall rejoice, that I
　　Am both Testatour thus, and Legacy.　　　　60

An Elegy Upon the Bishopp of London
John King

Sad Relick of a Blessed Soule! whose trust
Wee sealed up in this religious Dust.
O doe not thy low Exequyes suspect
As the cheap Arguments of our neglect.
'Twas a commaunded duty, that Thy Grave　　　　5
As little Pride, as Thou Thy self, should have.
　　Therfore thy Covering is an humble Stone,
Resurgam. 　　And but a Word for thy Inscription.
When those that in the same Earth neighbour thee
Have each his Chronicle and Pedigree.　　　　10
They have their waving Pennons and their Flagges,
(Of Matches and Allyance formall braggs:)
When Thou (although from Ancestours Thou came
Old as the Heptarchy; Great as Thy Name)
Sleepst there enshrin'd in thy admired Parts,　　　　15
And hast no Heraldry but thy Desarts.
Yet let not them their prowder Marbles boast,
For they rest with lesse honour, though more cost.

Goe, search the world, and with your Mattocks wound
The groaning Bosome of the patient ground: 20
Digg from the hidden veines of her dark womb
All that is rare and pretious for a Tomb:
Yet when much Treasure, and more Time is spent,
You must grant His the Nobler Monument,
   Whose Faith stands o're Him for a Hearse, and hath   25
The Resurrection for his Epitaph.

The Labyrinth

Life is a crooked Labyrinth, and wee
Are dayly lost in that Obliquity.
'Tis a perplexed Circle, in whose round
Nothing but Sorrowes and new Sins abound.
How is the faint Impression of each good   5
Drown'd in the vitious Channell of our blood?
Whose Ebbes and Tides by their vicissitude
Both our Great Maker and our selves dilude.
   O wherfore is the most discerning Ey
Unapt to make its owne discovery?   10
Why is the clearest and best judging Mind
In her owne Ill's prevention dark and blind?
Dull to advise, to act præcipitate,
Wee scarce think what wee doe, but when too late.
Or if wee think, that fluid Thought like Seed   15
Rotts there to propagate some fouler deed.
Still wee Repent and Sin; Sin and Repent;
Wee thaw and freeze, wee harden and relent.
Those Fires which cool'd to day, the Morrowe's heat
Rekindles. Thus fraile Nature does repeat   20
What Shee unlearn't; and still by learning on
Perfitts her Lesson of Confusion.
   Sick Soule! what Cure shall I for thee devise
Whose Leaprous State corrupts all Remedyes?

What Med'cine or what Cordiall can be gott   25
For thee, who poysonst thy best Antidot?
Repentance is thy bane: since thou by it
Only revivst the fault thou didst committ.
Nor grievst thou for the past, but art in paine
For feare thou mayst not act it o're againe.   30
So that thy Teares, like Water spilt on Lime,
Serve not to quench, but to advance the Crime.
  My Blessed Saviour! unto Thee I fly
For help against this home-bred tyranny.
Thou canst true Sorrowes in my Soule imprint,   35
And draw Contrition from a breast of flint.
Thou canst reverse this Labyrinth of Sinne
My wild Affects and Actions wander in.
  O guide my Faith! and by thy Grace's Clew
  Teach mee to hunt that Kingdome at the view   40
  Where true Joyes reigne; which, like their Day, shall last;
  Those never clouded, nor That Overcast.

An Elegy Occasioned by Sicknesse

  Well did the Prophet ask, Lord what is Man?
Emplying by the quæstion none can
But God resolve the doubt, much lesse define
What Elements this Child of Dust combine.
  Man is a straunger to himself, and knowes   5
Nothing so naturally as his Woes.
He loves to travaile Countryes, and confer
The Sides of Heaven's vast diameter:
Delights to sitt in Nile' or Bætis' Lapp
Before he hath sayl'd over his owne Mapp;   10
By which meanes he returnes, his travaile spent,
Lesse knowing of himself then when he went.
Who knowledge hunt kept under forraigne Locks
May bring home witt to hold a Paradoxe,

Yet be Fooles still. Therfore might I advise   15
I would informe the Soule before the Eyes:
Make Man into his proper Opticks look,
And so become the Student and the Book.
   With his Conception, his first Leaf, begin:
What is he there but complicated Sin?   20
When riper Time, and the approaching Birth
Rankes him among the Creatures of the Earth,
His wayling Mother sends him forth to greet
The Light, wrapt in a bloudy winding Sheet,
As if he came into the World to crave   25
No place to dwell in, but bespeak a Grave.
   Thus like a red and Tempest boading Morne
His dawning is: For being newly borne
He hayles th'ensuing Storme with Shriekes and Cryes,
And fines for his Admission with wett Eyes.   30
   How should that Plant whose Leaf is bath'd in Teares
Beare but a bitter fruit in Elder Yeares?
Just such is his: and his maturer age
Teemes with event more sad then the præsage.
For view him higher, when his Childhood's Span   35
Is raised up to Youthe's Meridian;
When he goes proudly laden with the fruit
Which health or strength or beauty contribute;
Yet as the mounted Cannon batters downe
The Towres and goodly Structures of a Towne: 40
So one short Sicknesse will his Force defeat,
And his fraile Cittadell to rubbish beat.
How does a Dropsy melt him to a Flood,
Making each Veine run Water more then Blood?
A Cholick wracks him like a Northerne gust,   45
And raging Feavers crumble him to Dust.
In which unhappy State he is made worse
By his Diseases then his Maker's Curse.
God sayd in toyle and sweat he should earne Bread,
And without Labour not be nourished.   50

Here, though, like ropes of falling Dew, his Sweat
Hangs on his lab'ring Brow, he cannot eat.
    Thus are his Sins scourg'd in opposed themes,
And Luxuryes reveng'd by their Extreames.
He who in health could never be content   55
With Rarityes fetcht from each Element,
Is now much more afflicted to delight
His tastlesse Palate, and lost Appetite.
    Besides though God ordain'd that with the Light
Man should begin his Work; Yet Hee made Night   60
For his repose, in which the weary Sense
Repaires it self by Rest's soft recompence.
But now his watchfull Nights and troubled Dayes
Confused heapes of Feare and Phant'sy raise.
His Chamber seemes a loose and trembling Mine;   65
His Pillow quilted with a Porcupine:
Paine makes his downy Couch sharp thornes appeare,
And ev'ry Feather prick him like a Speare.
Thus when all formes of Death about him keep,
Hee Coppyes Death in any forme but Sleep.   70
    Poore walking Clay! hast thou a mind to know
To what unblest Beginnings thou dost owe
Thy wretched self? Fall sick awhile, and than
Thou wilt conceave the Pedigree of Man.
Learne shalt thou from thine owne Anatomye,   75
That Earth his Mother, Wormes his Sisters bee.
That hee's a short-liv'd Vapour upward wrought,
And by Corruption unto nothing brought.
A Stagg'ring Meteor by crosse Plannets beat,
Which often reeles and falles before his Sett.   80
A Tree which withers faster then it growes;
A Torch puff't out by ev'ry Wind that blowes:
A Web of Fourty Weelkes spun forth in paine,
And in a moment ravell'd out againe.
    This is the Modell of fraile Man. Then say   85
That his duration's only for a Day:

And in that Day more fitts of Changes passe
Then Atomes run in the turn'd Hower-glasse.
  So that th'Incessant Cares which Life invade
Might for strong Truth their Hæresy perswade   90
Who did maintaine that humane Soules are sent
Into the Body for their Punishment:
At least with that Greek Sage still make us cry,
*Not to be Borne, or being Borne, to Dy.   *Non Nasci
  But Faith steares up to a more glorious scope,   95   aùt quàm
Which sweetens our sharp passage: And firme Hope   citissimè
Anchors our torne Barkes on a Blessed Shoare,   Mori.
Beyond the Dead Sea wee here ferry o're.
To this Death is our Pilott, and Disease
The Agent which solicitts our release.   100
  Though Crosses then powre on my restlesse head,
Or lingring Sicknes nayle mee to my bed:
Let this my Thoughte's Eternall Comfort bee,
That my Clos'd Eyes a Better Light shall see.
And when by Fortune's or by Nature's stroak   105
My Bodye's Earthen Pitcher must be broke,
My Soule, Like Gideon's Lamp, from her crack't Urne
Shall Death's black Night to Endlesse Luster turne.

The Dirge

What is th'Existence of Man's Life?
But open Warr, or Slumber'd Strife.
Where Sicknes to his Sense presents
The Combat of the Elements:
And never feeles a perfect Peace   5
Till Death's cold hand signes his release.

It is a Storme, where the hott Bloud
Out-vyes in Rage the boyling Floud:
And each loud Passion of the Mind
Is like a furious gust of Wind,   10

Which beates his Bark with many a Wave
Till Hee casts Anchor in the Grave.

It is a Flow'r, which budds and growes,
And withers as the Leaves disclose:
Whose Spring and Fall faint Seasons keep,   15
Like fitts of Waking before Sleep,
Then shrinkes into that fatall Mold
Where Its first Being was enrolld.

It is a Dreame, whose seeming Truth
Is moraliz'd in Age and Youth: 20
Where all the Comforts he can share
As wandring as his Phant'syes are.
Till in a mist of dark decay
The Dreamer vanish quite away.

It is a Dyall, which pointes out   25
The Sunsett, as it moves about,
And shadowes out in lines of night
The subtile stages of time's flight:
Till all obscuring Earth hath lay'd
The Body in perpetuall Shade.   30

It is a weary Enterlude,
Which doth short Joyes, long Woes include.
The World the Stage, the Prologue Teares,
The Actes vaine Hope and vary'd Feares:
The Scæne shutts up with Losse of breath,   35
And leaves no Epilogue but Death.

To a Lady who sent me a copy of verses at my going to bed

Lady, your art, or wit could nere devise
To shame me more, then in this night's surprise.
Why I am quite unready, and my eye
Now winking like my candle, doth deny

To guide my hand, if it had ought to write;   5
Nor can I make my drowsie sense indite
Which by your verses' musick (as a spell
Sent from the Sybillean Oracle)
Is charm'd and bound in wonder and delight
Faster then all the leaden chains of night.   10
   What pity is it then you should so ill
Employ the bounty of your flowing quill,
As to expend on him your bedward thought
Who can acknowledge that large love in nought
But this lean wish: That Fate soon send you those   15
Who may requite your rhimes with midnight prose?
   Mean time, may all delights and pleasing Theams
Like Masquers revell in your Maiden dreams.
Whil'st dull to write, and to do more unmeet,
I (as the Night invites me) fall asleep.   20

The short Wooing

Like an Oblation set before a Shrine,
Fair One! I offer up this Heart of mine.
Whether the Saint accept my Gift or no,
Ile neither fear nor doubt before I know.
For he whose faint distrust prevents reply,   5
Doth his own Suit's denial prophecy.

   Your will the sentence is; Who free as Fate
Can bid my love proceed, or else retrayt.
And from short views that verdict is decreed
Which seldom doth one audience exceed.   10
Love asks no dull probation, but like light
Conveyes his nimble influence at first sight.

I need not therefore importune or press;
This were t'extort unwilling happiness:
And much against affection might I sin   15
To tire and weary what I seek to win.
Towns which by lingring siege enforced be
Oft make both Sides repent the victorie.

Be Mistriss of yourself, and let me thrive
Or suffer by your own prerogative.   20
Yet stay. Since you are Judge, who in one breath
Bear uncontrolled power of Life and Death,
Remember (Sweet) pity doth best become
Those Lips which must pronounce a Suitor's doome.

If I find that, my spark of chast desire   25
Shall kindle into Hymen's holy fire:
Else like sad flowers will these verses prove,
To stick the Coffin of rejected Love.

Paradox. That it is best for a Young Maid to marry an Old Man

Fair one, why cannot you an old man love?
He may as useful, and more constant prove.
Experience shews you that maturer years
Are a security against those fears
Youth will expose you to; whose wild desire   5
As it is hot, so 'tis as rash as fire.
Marke how the blaze extinct in ashes lies,
Leaving no brand, nor ember when it dies
Which might the flame renew: Thus soon consumes
Youth's wandring heat, and vanishes in fumes.   10
When age's riper love unapt to stray
Through loose and giddy change of objects, may
In your warm bosome like a cynder lie
Quickned, and kindled by your sparkling eie.

'Tis not deni'd, there are extremes in both   15
Which may the phansy move to like or loath;
Yet of the two you better shall endure
To marry with the Cramp, then Calenture.
Who would in wisdom choose the Torrid Zone
Therein to settle a Plantation?   20
Merchants can tell you, those hot Climes were made
But at the longest for a three years' trade:
And though the Indies cast the sweeter smell,
Yet Health, and Plenty do more Northward dwell;
For where the raging Sun-beams burn the Earth   25
Her scorched mantle withers into dearth;
Yet, when that drought becomes the Harvest's curse,
Snow doth the tender Corn most kindly nurse.
Why now then wooe you not some snowy head
To take you in meer pitty to his bed?   30
I doubt the harder task were to perswade
Him to love you: For, if what I have said
In Virgins, as in Vegetals hold true,
Hee'l prove the better Nurse to cherish you.
Some men we know renown'd for wisdom grown   35
By old records and antique Medalls shown;
Why ought not women then be held most wise
Who can produce living antiquities?
Besides if care of that main happiness
Your sex triumphs in, doth your thoughts possess,   40
I mean your beauty from decay to keep,
No wash, nor mask is like an old man's sleep.
Young wives need never to be Sun-burnt fear
Who their old husbands for Umbrellaes wear.
How russet looks an Orchard on the hill   45
To one that's water'd by some neighb'ring Drill?
Are not the floated Medowes ever seen
To flourish soonest, and hold longest green?
You may be sure no moist'ning lacks that Bride
Who lies with Winter thawing by her side.   50

She should be fruitful too, as Fields that joyne
Unto the melting waste of Appenine.
Whil'st the cold morning-drops bedew the Rose
It doth nor leaf, nor smell, nor colour lose.
Then doubt not Sweet! Age hath supplies of wet   55
To keep You like that flow'r in water set.
Dripping Catarrhs and Fontinells are things
Will make You think You grew betwixt Two Springs;
And should You not think so, You scarce allow
The force, or Merit of Your Marriage-Vow;   60
Where Maids a new Creed learn, and must from thence
Believe against their own, or other's sence.
Else Love will nothing differ from neglect,
Which turns not to a Vertue each defect.
  I'le say no more but this: you women make   65
Your Children's reck'ning by the Almanake.
I like it well; So you contented are
To choose their Fathers by that Kalendar.
Turn then old Erra Pater, and there see
According to life's posture and degree   70
What Age, or what Complexion is most fit
To make an English Maid happy by it;
And You shall find, if You will choose a Man
Set justly for Your own Meridian,
Though You perhaps let One and Twenty woo   75
Your Elevation is for Fifty Two.

Paradox. That Fruition destroyes Love

Love is our Reason's Paradox, which still
Against the Judgment doth maintain the Will,
And governs by such arbitrary laws
It onely makes the Act our Liking's cause:
We have no brave revenge, but to forgo   5
Our full desires, and starve the Tyrant so.

They whom the rising blood tempts not to taste
Preserve a stock of Love can never waste;
When easie people who their wish enjoy
Like Prodigalls at once their wealth destroy.   10
Adam till now had stay'd in Paradise
Had his desires been bounded by his eyes:
When he did more then look, that made th'offence,
And forfeited his state of innocence.
Fruition therefore is the bane t'undoe   51
Both our affection, and the subject too.
'Tis Love into worse language to translate
And make it into Lust degenerate:
'Tis to De-throne, and thrust it from the heart,
To seat it grossely in the sensual part.   20
Seek for the Starre that's shot upon the ground
And nought but a dimme gelly there is found:
Thus foul and dark our Female Starres appear
If fall'n or loosned once from Vertue's Sphear.
Glow-worms shine only look't on, and let ly,   25
But handled crawl into deformity:
So beauty is no longer fair and bright
Then whil'st unstained by the appetite:
And then it withers like a blasted flowre
Some poys'nous Worm, or Spider hath crept ore.   30
Pigmaleon's dotage on the carved Stone
Shews Amorists their strong illusion:
Whil'st he to gaze and court it was content,
He serv'd as Priest at Beautie's Monument;
But when by looser fires t'embraces led   35
It prov'd a cold hard Statue in his bed.
Irregular affects, like mad men's dreams
Presented by false lights, and broken beams,
So long content us, as no neer address
Shews the wa'kt sense our painted happiness.   40
But when those pleasing shaddowes us forsake
Or of the substance we a trial make,

Like him, deluded by the phansie's mock,
We ship-wrack 'gainst an Alabaster rock.
What though thy Mistress far from Marble be? 45
Her softness will transform and harden thee.
Lust is a Snake, and Guilt the Gorgon's Head
Which Conscience turns to Stone, and Joyes to Lead.
   Turtles themselves will blush, if put to name
The Act, whereby they quench their am'rous flame; 50
Who then that's wise or vertuous, would not feare
To catch at pleasures which forbidden were,
When those which we count lawful, cannot be
Requir'd without some loss of modestie?
Ev'n in the Marriage-Bed, where soft delights 55
Are customary and authoriz'd Rites,
What are those tributes to the wanton sense
But toleration of Incontinence?
For properly you cannot call that Love
Which does not from the Soul, but Humour move. 60
Thus they who worship't Pan or Isis Shrine
By the fair Front judg'd all within Divine,
Though ent'ring, found 'twas but a Goat or Cow
To which before their ignorance did bow.
Such Temples and such Goddesses are these 65
Which foolish Lovers and Admirers please:
Who, if they chance within the Shrine to prie,
Find that a Beast, they thought a Deity.
Nor makes it onely our opinion less
Of what we lik't before, and now possess, 70
But robbs the Fuel, and corrupts the Spice
Which sweetens and inflames Love's sacrifice.
After Fruition once, what is Desire
But ashes kept warm by a dying fire?
This is (if any) the Philosopher's Stone 75
Which still miscarries at Projection.
For when the Heat ad Octo intermits
It poorly takes us like Third Ague fits;

Or must on Embers as dull Druggs infuse
Which we for Med'cine not for Pleasure use.   80

   Since Lovers' joyes then leave so sick a taste,
And soon as relish'd by the Sense are past;
They are but Riddles sure, lost if possest,
And therefore onely in Reversion best.
For bate them Expectation and Delay,   85
You take the most delightful Scenes away.
These two such rule within the fancie keep,
As banquets apprehended in our sleep;
After which pleasing trance next morn we wake
Empty and angry at the night's mistake.   90
Give me long Dreams and Visions of content,
Rather then pleasures in a minute spent.
And since I know before, the shedding Rose
In that same instant doth her sweetness lose,
Upon the Virgin-stock still let her dwell   95
For me to feast my longings with her smell.
Those are but counterfeits of joy at best,
Which languish soon as brought unto the test.
Nor can I hold it worth his pains who tries
To Inne that Harvest which by reaping dies.   100

   Resolve me now what spirit hath delight,
If by full feed you kill the appetite?
That stomack healthy'st is, that nere was cloy'd,
Why not that Love the best then, Nere enjoy'd?
Since nat'rally the blood, when tam'd or sated,   105
Will cool so fast it leaves the object hated.
Pleasures like wonders quickly loose their price,
When Reason or Experience makes us wise.
   To close my Argument then: I dare say
(And without Paradox) As well we may   110
Enjoy our Love, and yet preserve Desire,
As warm our hands by Putting out the Fire.

[Bishop John King]
The Latine Epitaph hanging over His Grave-stone Translated

Non hic Pyramides, non sculpta panegyris &c.

No Pyramids, nor Panegyrick Verse
Nor costly Heapes of Stone adorne Thy Hearse.
Wee with more thrift Thee to Thyselfe committ
Shouldst Thou lye otherwise, Thould'st loose by it.
For whosoever Lives and Dyes like Thee   5
Shall to Himselfe a Lasting Marble bee.

The Change

Il sabio mude conseio: Il loco persevera.

We lov'd as friends now twenty years and more:
Is't time or reason think you to give o're?
When though two prentiships set Jacob free
I have not held my Rachel dear at three.
   Yet will I not your levitie accuse;   5
Continuance sometimes is the worse abuse.
In judgment I might rather hold it strange
If like the fleeting world, you did not change:
Be it your wisdom therefore to retract
When perseverance oft is Follie's Act.   10
   In pity I can think, that what you do
Hath Justice in't, and some Religion too;
For of all vertues Morall or Divine
We know, but Love, none must in Heaven shine.
Well did You the presumption then foresee   15
Of counterfeiting Immortalitie:
Since had You kept our Loves too long alive
We might invade Heaven's Prerogative,
Or in our progress, like the Jews, comprise
The Legend of an earthly Paradise.   20

Live happy and more prosperous in the next!
You have discharg'd your old friend by the Text.
Farewel fair Shadow of a female faith,
And let this be our friendship's Epitaph:
  Affection shares the frailty of our fate,   25
  When (like our selves) 'tis old and out of date:
  'Tis just all humane Loves their Period have,
  When friends are frail, and dropping to the grave.

St. Valentine's Day

Now that each feather'd Chorister doth sing
The glad approches of the welcome Spring,
Now Phœbus darts forth his more early beam,
And dips it later in the curled stream,
I should to custome prove a retrograde   5
Did I still dote upon my sullen shade.

Oft have the seasons finisht and begun,
Dayes into Months, Those into Years have run,
Since my cross Starres and inauspicious fate
Doom'd me to linger here without my Mate: 10
Whose loss, e're since, befrosting my desire
Left me an Altar without Gift or Fire.

I therefore could have wisht for your own sake
That Fortune had design'd a nobler stake
For you to draw, then one whose fading day   15
Like to a dedicated Taper lay
Within a Tomb, and long burnt out in vain
Since nothing there saw better by the flame.

Yet since you like your Chance, I must not try
To marre it through my incapacity.   20
I here make title to it, and proclaime
How much you honour me to wear my name:
Who can no form of gratitude devise
But offer up my self your Sacrifice.

Hail then my worthy Lot! and may each Morn   25
Successive springs of joy to you be born:
May your content ne're wane, untill my heart
Grow'n Bankrupt, wants good wishes to impart.
   Henceforth I need not make the dust my Shrine
   Nor search the Grave for my lost Valentine.   30

To One demanding why Wine sparkles

So Diamonds sparkle, and thy Mistriss' eyes;
When 'tis not Fire, but Light in either flyes.
Beauty not thaw'd by lustful flames will show
Like a fair mountain of unmelted snow:
Nor can the tasted vine more danger bring   5
Then water taken from the chrystall Spring,
Whose end is to refresh and cool that heat
Which unallayd becomes foul Vice's seat:
Unless thy boyling veins, mad with desire
Of drink, convert the liquor into fire.   10
For then thou quaff'st down feavers, thy full bowles
Carouse the burning draughts of Portia's Coles.
   If it do leap, and sparkle in the cup
Twill sink thy cares, and help Invention up.
There never yet was Muse or Poet known   15
Not dipt or drenched in this Helicon:
But Tom! take heed thou use it with such care
As Witches deal with their Familiar.
For if thy vertue's circle not confine
And guard thee from the Furies rais'd by wine,   20
'Tis ten to one this dancing spirit may
A Devil prove to bear thy wits away;
And make thy glowing Nose a Map of Hell
Where Bacchus purple fumes, like Meteors, dwell.
Now think not these sage moralls thee invite   25
To prove Carthusian or strict Rechabite;

Let fooles be mad, wise people may be free
Though not to License turn their Libertie.
   He that drinks wine for health, not for excess,
Nor drownes his temper in a drunkenness,   30
Shall feel no more the grape's unruly fate,
Then if he took some chilling Opiate.

The Acquittance

Not knowing who should my Acquittance take,
I know as little what discharge to make.
The favour is so great, that it out-goes
All forms of thankfulness I can propose.
Those grateful levies which my pen would raise,   5
Are stricken dumb, or bury'd in amaze.
Therefore, as once in Athens there was shown
An Altar built unto the God unknown,
My ignorant devotions must by guess
This blind return of gratitude address,   10
Till You vouchsafe to shew me where and how
I may to this revealed Goddess bow.

The Forfeiture

My Dearest, To let you or the world know
What Debt of service I do truly ow
To your unpattern'd self, were to require
A language onely form'd in the desire
Of him that writes. It is the common fate,   5
Of greatest duties to evaporate
In silent meaning, as we often see
Fires by their too much fuel smother'd be:
Small Obligations may find vent and speak,
When greater the unable debtor break.   10

And such are mine to you, whose favour's store,
Hath made me poorer then I was before;
For I want words and language to declare
How strict my Bond or large your bounties are.

Since nothing in my desp'rate fortune found,   15
Can payment make, nor yet the summe compound:
You must lose all, or else of force accept
The body of a Bankrupt for your debt.
Then Love, your Bond to Execution sue,
And take my self, as forfeited to you.   20

Psalme CXXX paraphrased for an Antheme

Out of the horrour of the lowest Deep,
Where cares and endlesse fears their station keep,
To thee (O Lord) I send my woful cry:
O heare the accents of my misery.
If Thy enquiry (Lord) should be severe,   5
To mark all sins which have been acted here,
Who may abide? or, when they sifted are,
Stand un-condemned at Thy Judgment's bar?
But there is mercy (O my God) with Thee,
That Thou by it may'st lov'd, and feared be.   10
My Soule waites for the Lord, in Him I trust,
Whose word is faithful, and whose promise just.
On him my longing thoughts are fixt, as they,
Who wait the comforts of the rising day:
Yea more then those that watch the morning light   15
Tir'd with the sorrowes of a rest-less night.
O Israel, trust in that Gratious Lord,
Who plentifull remission doth afford;
And will His people, who past pardon seeme,
By mercyes greater then their sins redeeme.   20

NOTES

ADDITIONAL ABBREVIATIONS USED IN
THE NOTES

A23	British Museum Add. MS. 23229.
A27	B.M. Add. MS. 27408.
Acad. Comp.	*The Academy of Complements*, 1650.
Ash.	Bodl. MS. Ashmole 38.
C	Cambridge University Library Add. MS. 79.
CCC	Corpus Christi College, Oxford, MS. 328.
Clarendon	*History of the Rebellion*, edited by W. D. Macray, 1888.
Corbet	*Certain Elegant Poems by Dr. Corbet*, 1647.
DD	*Deaths Duell*, 1632.
DHK	*A Deepe Groane, Fetch'd At the Funerall of . . . Charles the First*, by D.H.K., 1649.
Don.	Bodl. MS. Don. d. 58.
Eg.	B.M. MS. Egerton 2725.
G	Bodl. MS. Eng. misc. e. 262, compiled by John Gauden.
Gardiner	*History of the Great Civil War*, 2nd edition, 1893.
IB	*A Groane at the Funerall of . . . Charles the First*, by I.B., 1649.
J	St. John's College, Cambridge, MS. 417.
Jones	Bodl. MS. Jones 56.
JV	*Jonsonus Virbius*, edited by Brian Duppa, 1638.
Locke	Bodl. MS. Locke c. 32.
M21	Bodl. MS. Malone 21.
N	Nottingham University Library MS. Pw. V. 37.
Parn. Bic.	*Parnassus Biceps*, edited by Abraham Wright, 1656.
P. d'A.	*Prince d'Amour*, 1660.
PR	*Poems by Pembroke and Ruddier*, edited by the younger John Donne, 1660.
Rawl.	Bodl. MS. Rawl. D. 398.
RP	Bodl. MS. Rawl. poet. 209.
RP26	Bodl. MS. Rawl. poet. 26.
Sandys	*A Paraphrase upon the Divine Poems*, by George Sandys, 1638.
SI	*The Swedish Intelligencer*, Third Part, 1633.
Slo.	B.M. MS. Sloane 1446.
T	Trinity College, Cambridge, MS. R. 3. 12.
Walton	*Life of John Donne*, by Izaak Walton, 1658.
WI	*Wits Interpreter*, edited by John Cotgrave, 1655.
WR	*Wits Recreations*, 1641.
1633	*Poems by J.D. with Elegies on the Authors Death*, 1633.
'1648'	*An Elegy upon the most Incomparable King Charles the First*, dated 11 March 1648.
1654	*The Psalmes of David* [paraphrased by Henry King], 1654.

An Elegy upon Prince Henryes Death (p. 65)

Prince Henry died 6 November 1612. Henry King contributed Latin verses to the Oxford University collection of poems on his death, *Iusta Oxoniensium*, 1612.

Text: H, M, P, *1657*. Printed in *Parnassus Biceps*, 1656 (*Parn. Bic.*), and in *Prince d'Amour*, 1660 (*P. d'A.*), where it was attributed to 'J.D.' Manuscript copies are in *TM*, Bodl. MS. Malone 21 (*M21*), and Bodl. MS. Rawl. poet. 209 (*RP*). There was a gradual process of revision: *Parn. Bic.* and *M21* give different forms of the poem in its first state; *P. d'A.* and *RP* give texts having affinities both with them and with those representing the last state, *MSS*, *TM*, and *1657*. Two final corrections (lines 6 and 18) appear only in *1657*.

Variants:

Title: Upon Prince Henryes Death *H*, *P*.
5 Heark, and feele it read] Death and horror wed *Parn. Bic.*, *M21*, *P.d'A.*   6 Through the astonish't Kingdom, Henry's dead] To vent their teeming mischief: Henry's dead *Parn. Bic.*, *M21*, *P. d'A.*: Through the astonish't world that Henries dead *RP*; Through the astonish't world, Henry is dead *TM*, *MSS*.   7–10 *omitted Parn. Bic.*   11 Oh killing rhetorick] Compendious Eloquence *Parn. Bic.*, *M21*, *P. d'A.*, *TM*: O murthering Eloquence *RP*   13 This were] Why tis *Parn. Bic.*, *M21*: Why twere *P. d'A.*: These were *RP*, *TM*   14 Worthy] Enough *Parn. Bic.*: Able *M21*   15 Or] At *Parn. Bic.*, *M21*: On *P. d'A.*   sad] last *Parn. Bic.*, *M21*   18 Sounds in these fatal accents] Lies in this narrow compas *Parn. Bic.*, *M21*: Throngs in this narrow compasse *P. d'A.*, *RP*, *TM*, *MSS*.   19–28 *omitted Parn. Bic.*, *M21*   19 Cease then unable Poetry; Thy] Here then break off my Muse, thy love and *RP*   20 weak] hoarse *RP*, *TM*   22 To coppy this sad] To write this dismal *P. d'A.*   23 at] on *P. d'A.*   For not] As if *P. d'A.*   24 can write] could paint *P. d'A.*   25–28 *omitted P. d'A.*, *RP*, *which read instead*:

<blockquote>
Suffice! We learn by this Mortality:
The Sun rose but to set, frail man to die.
</blockquote>

11 *Oh* omitted by Manne in *H*; added by King. Manne may have made the mistake because the text he was copying had been corrected and was difficult to read.

14–15 *Hearse Or*: the reading of *MSS.*, *1657*, *TM*, and *RP* is elliptical to the point of obscurity; but the textual evidence is clearly against the adoption of either of the simpler early readings.

28 *His* corrected from *his, M*.

An Elegy Upon S. W. R. (p. 66)

Sir Walter Raleigh was executed 29 Oct. 1618.

The elegy was printed in *The Life of Sir Walter Raleigh*, 1677,[1] pp. 240–1; it was not included when this 'Life' was first printed, before *The History of the World*, 1665.

Text: H, M, P, *1657*; and *TM*, MS. Corpus Christi College, Oxford, 328 (*CCC*), Bodl. MS. Rawl. poet. 209 (*RP*), and many other manuscript miscellanies.

Variants:

Title: An Elegy Upon S.W.R. *1657*: An Elegy. *MSS.*

6 master'd] maistered'st *or* maisterd'st *MSS., TM*   17–18 when they thought . . . Lent thee a] striving how . . . Wing'd thee with *misc. MSS.* 25 worthlesse] poor cheap *misc. MSS.*   27–28 *omitted in some misc. MSS.* 28 must still admire, scarce imitate] may envy, but not imitate *CCC*: may wel envy scarce Imitate *RP*.

4 Compare Raleigh's 'What is our Life? A play of passion'; but King passes immediately to an image of wrestling.   *various* omitted by Manne in *H*; added by King.

5 *of* omitted *P*.

6 *master'd*: the *MSS.* reading, *maistered'st*, is correct, but can hardly be pronounced.

13 *as* written by King in a space left by Manne, *H*.

17 *thee* corrected from *the* by King, *H*.

To his Freinds of Christchurch . . . (p. 67)

Accounts of the occasion of this poem are in Wood's *History and Antiquities of the University of Oxford*, ed. J. Gutch, ii, 1796, pp. 339–40, and in his *Athenae Oxonienses*, ed. P. Bliss, iii, 1817, 522; Wood was quoted by John Nichols in *The Progresses of King James the First*:

It must be known now, that Febr. 13 an. 1617, the Comedy of Barten Holyday, Student of Christ Church, called the 'Marriage of Arts' [or *Technogamia*], had been acted publicly in Christ Church Hall with no great applause, and the wits

---

[1] *The Life of Sir Walter Raleigh* was attributed by Wood to John Shirley (1648–79) of Trinity College, Oxford. *Athenae Oxonienses*, ed. Bliss, iii, 1817, 1220.

now [1621] of the University being minded to shew themselves before the King, were resolved to act the said Comedy at Woodstock; wherefore the Author making some foolish alterations in it, was accordingly performed on a Sunday night 26 Aug. But it beeing too grave for the King, and too Scholarlike for the Auditory (or as some say that the Actors had taken too much wine before) his Majesty after two Acts offered several times to withdraw, but being perswaded by some of those that were near him, to have patience till it was ended, least the young men should be discouraged, adventured it, though much against his will.

Nichols printed contemporary verses in the Appendix to the *Progresses*, pp. 1108–12. He gave the names of the actors, which he found written in a copy of the play then owned by Joseph Haslewood: Henry King's brothers William and Philip both took part.

Text: H, M, P, *1657*. These verses did not go beyond King's own family, and are not found with the satires and defences known to Nichols in manuscript miscellanies, though they are in *Harl.* (cf. p. 57).

Variant:
  20 conster] construe *1657*.

3–4 *Ignoramus* was acted before the King at Cambridge, 8 March 1614/15, and again by his special request in May. It included a hobby-horse named 'Darus Dromo, Musarum Caballus'. See Nichols, op. cit., pp. 49–90.

An Epitaph on . . . Richard Earle of Dorset (p. 67)

Richard Sackville, third Earl, died on his 35th birthday, 28 March 1624. His wife, afterwards Lady Anne Clifford, said of him that he was 'so good a Scholar in all manner of Learning that . . . when he liv'd in the University of Oxford . . . there were none of the young Nobility then Students there that excell'd him'. He matriculated from Christ Church in 1605, soon after Dr. John King became Dean. He was 'so great a lover of Scholars and Souldjers as that with an excessive bounty towards them . . . he did much diminish his Estate, as also with excessive prodigality in housekeeping and other noble ways at Court as Tilting and the like'.[1] A miniature of him by Isaac Oliver, 1616, is reproduced in *Elizabethan Miniatures*, by Carl Winter, King Penguin Books, 1943, plate xv. G. C. Williamson, in *Lady Anne Clifford*, 1922, says that Henry King was Lord Dorset's chaplain, and was allowed £40 a year by his widow, but does not mention the source of his information. Henry King's will mentions his own loss of 'not lesse' than a thousand pounds on Lord Dorset's

---

[1] 'A True Memoriall of the Life of Lady Anne Clifford', ed. E. Hailstone, printed by the Archaeological Institute of Great Britain and Ireland in *Memoirs . . . of the County and City of York*, 1848.

account, of which he was 'hopelesse of repaire, unlesse his Countesse the Dowager in honour or conscience may please to do any thing for her deceased husband's faithfully approved friend'. In *TM* there is a group of four short poems, one of them addressed to Lady Venetia Stanley, ascribed in Henry King's hand to 'R. Dorset'.

A short version of the epitaph was printed in *Certain Elegant Poems by Dr. Corbet*, 1647, p. 51. It was given to Corbet in *The Sixth Part of Miscellany Poems* ('Dryden's Miscellany'), 1716, p. 396. Editors of Corbet, O. Gilchrist in 1807 and J. A. W. Bennett and H. R. Trevor-Roper, 1955, included it as a doubtful poem. Its presence in a better version in all three King manuscripts and in *1657* shows that it is King's.

Text: H, M, P, *1657*. Printed amongst Corbet's poems (*Corbet*) and common in the same version in manuscript miscellanies. *TM* has a version intermediate between *Corbet* and the authoritative manuscripts.

Variants:

3 sad] poor *misc. MSS., Corbet, TM*   7–9 *one line only*, A soul refin'd, No proud forgetting lord *misc. MSS., Corbet*   11 Who lovd men for his honour, not for (*or* his) ends *misc. MSS., Corbet*   13 One that did know] And yet who knew *misc. MSS., Corbet*   17 One] Who *misc. MSS., Corbet*   18 That valew'd not his Fortune] Neither his honour valued *misc. MSS., Corbet*   19 Rich in the Worlds opinion, good (*or* and) mens praise *misc. MSS., Corbet, TM*   20 of] in *misc. MSS., Corbet, TM*   have wish't] desire *misc. MSS., Corbet, TM*   22 lend] spend *misc. MSS.*: shed *Corbet*   23 long and scorn'd, unpitty'd] long scorn'd and unpitied *misc. MSS., Corbet*.

An Exequy to his Matchlesse never to be forgotten Freind (p. 68)

Anne King's burial was entered in the parish register of St. Gregory by St. Paul's, 5 January 1623/4 (see 'The Bodleian Manuscripts of Henry King', by Dr. Percy Simpson, *Bodleian Quarterly Record*, v, 1926–9, p. 333).

Text: H, M, P, *1657*. Manuscript copies are frequent. Thomas Manne wrote out on a single sheet, now British Museum MS. Add. 27408, fol. 70 (*A27*), a version which is shared by Cambridge University Library MS. Add. 79 (*C*) and Bodl. MS. Rawl. poet. 26 (*RP26*), as well as a revised version in *TM*, before he copied the final version in *H*. Other manuscript miscellanies which seem to show traces of early revision are British Museum MS. Egerton 2725 (*Eg.*), Bodl. MS . Don. d. 58 (*Don*), Trinity College, Cambridge, MS. R.3.12 (*T*), Corpus Christi College, Oxford, MS. 328 (*CCC*), and Nottingham University Library MS.

Pw. V. 37 (*N*). The 'Ingenious Poems' added to *A Crew of Kind London Gossips by S[amuel] R[owlands]* for the edition of 1663 were printed from C.U.L. MS. Add. 79, and therefore include the 'Exequy'.

Variants:

Title: The Exequy *1657*.

24 blacknes] darkness *misc. MSS.*   36 The] An *MSS., TM, misc. MSS.*   41–42 *omitted RP26, C, A27*   43 And all that space] Would willingly *RP26, C, A27*   51–57 *omitted Eg., which reads* A glimpse of thee, till we shall rise   53 must] shall *TM, misc. MSS., H before correction*   65–68 *omitted CCC, Don.*   66 Whereof I lately was possest; *N*   67–68 *transposed N;* Most freely though thou see me weep, I gave thee what I could not keep *Eg., T*   70 *omitted, space left, Eg.*   106 Vann] Vaunt *TM, misc. MSS.* (vaunt *corrected to* vanne *Eg.*).

30 *Life P,* in error for *Love.*

34 *is: if M,* probably in error from a long *ſ* in the original.

41 *Were it a Month: a* omitted by Manne, added by King, *H.*

65–70 Manuscript variants and omissions in these lines, and the assonance *grief/keep* in lines 67–68, seem to indicate an imperfect revision.

90 *hollow*] hallow *1657.*

94 *Desire*] Desires *P.*

102 *Compasse*: in spite of the imagery, the meaning *extent* or *limit* (*O.E.D.* 8) is here primarily intended.

106 *Vann, Vaunt*: the last example of the obsolescent *vaunt* recorded in the *O.E.D.* is from Donne's *Devotions,* 1624.

115 *this: which,* probably in error, *P.*

On two Children dying of one Disease . . . (p. 72)

The occasion of this poem was not a real one, because it is impossible that any two of Henry King's children were buried at one time. See Introduction, p. 10.

Text: *H, M, P, 1657*; and in *Harl.* and British Museum MS. Sloane 1446.

The Anniverse (p. 72)

Text: *H, M, P, 1657*. Manuscript copies are in *Harl.* and British Museum MS. Sloane 1446 (*Slo.*).

Variants:

   Title: The Anniverse. An Elegy *1657*: An Elegy *H*, *M*: The Anniversary
An Elegy *P*.

   8 Lamentations] Lamentation *H*, *Slo.*   13 would] might *H*, *Harl.*,
Slo.   14 sharp] sadd *Slo.*   26 tooke] take *H*, *Harl.*, *Slo.*

1 The date of the poem is December or January 1629/30.

22 *availes* misprinted *avail 1657.*

23 The copyists of both *H* and *M* had trouble over *whilst in.*

23, 25 *H* begins the new paragraph at line 25.

By Occasion of the young Prince his happy Birth (p. 73)

   The Oxford collection of poems on the birth of Prince Charles on
29 May 1630, *Britanniæ Natalis*, contains nothing of Henry King's.

Text: *H*, *M*, *P*, *1657*. Manuscript copies are in *TM*, *Harl.*, and British
Museum MS. Sloane 1446 (*Slo.*).

Variants:

   Title: Prince his] Princes *H*. *Dated by King, H: no date, M, P, 1657.*
22 that] who *H*   24 Doth] Does *H*   the] his *Slo.*, *M before correction, P*
47 with Fate wee dallie *Slo.*: wee dally with Fate *Harl.*, *TM*, *H*, *P*, *1657*:
wee with fate dally *M*   49 should] did *TM*   50 were borne] would
live *TM*, *H*   60 long] glad *H*   63 long] forth *H*   70 Vertue]
Vertues *H*.

10 Hannah found that King's choice of metaphor here was particularly
apposite: he quotes from Fuller's account of the day: 'the star *Venus* was
visible all day long, as sometimes it falls out neer her greatest Elongation.
And *two* days after there was an Ecclipse of the *Sun* . . .'[1]

16 *Church-book*: Parish Register.

15–17 *children . . . pledges of . . . Eternity*: cf. the *Zodiake of Life* of Marcellus
Pallingenius, translated by Barnabee Googe, 1565 (sig. Nvii[v]):

> And when the day / wherein thou must be gone
> Is come, thou art not cleane extinct / but shalt alive remayne
> In them who then shall represent / their fathers face agayne—

and Bacon, who says, 'Of Parents and Children' (*Essaies*, 1612), that
children 'increase the Cares of Life; but they mitigate the remembrance
of Death'.

24 *the*: *his M before correction, P*: possibly an earlier reading, not clearly
altered in the original, misled the copyists of *M* (at first) and of *P*.

---

   [1] *The History of the Worthies of England*, 1662, sig. Hhh.

47 The reading of *H*, *P*, and *1657* probably represents a mistake in their original: *M* seems to have attempted an improvement.

52 *Perpetuitye* corrected from *Perpetuity M*.

74 *Posteritye* corrected from *Posterity M*.

Upon the Death of . . . D^r. Donne (p. 76)

Donne died 31 March 1631.

Text: *H*, *M*, *P*, *1657*. King's poem was first printed, with the sermon spoken of in lines 29–34, in *Deaths Duell*, 1632, headed 'An Elegie on Dr. Donne, Deane of Pauls' (*DD*); and again in *Poems by J.D. with Elegies on the Authors Death*, 1633, where it is the first elegy, headed 'To the Memorie of my ever desired friend Dr. Donne', and subscribed 'H.K.' It was also printed with Walton's *Life of John Donne*, in the separate edition of 1658, which was dedicated to King's nephew Sir Robert Holt (see Introduction, p. 13 above). Three different manuscripts, probably all autograph, were the sources of these texts. *1633* agrees very nearly exactly, even in punctuation and capital letters, with *H*. The differences in the other two printed texts look like insignificant alterations made during copying. Two manuscript copies only were found: *TM* and St. John's College, Cambridge, MS. 417 (*J*).

Variants:

   Title: Upon the Death *TM*, *M*, *P*, *1657*: To the Memorie *H*, *1633*, *Walton*   Freind *omitted Walton*   Deane of Paules *omitted H*, *1633*, *Walton*
2 flights] thoughts *Walton*   8 with *1657*: like *MSS.*, *misc. pr.*
14 here] there *DD*, *Walton*   23 of] on *M*   26 may] might *DD*
31 faint] weake *DD*   33 by] of *H before correction*, *J*   38 measure]
measures *Walton*   41 beholden *1657*, *Walton*: beholding *MSS.*, *DD*,
1633   46 once] first *Walton*   49 Unto thy Hearse] Thy memory
Walton   52 which] that *Walton*   thy] thine *1657*, *Walton*   53 Thy]
Thine *H*, *1633*, *Walton*   57 or *H*, *1633*, *1657*, *Walton*: nor *TM*, *M*, *P*, *DD*.
32 *Peece H*, corrected from *peece*.

34 Hannah (p. 181) quotes from Walton's *Life of Donne*: 'Many . . . said that Dr. Donne had preach't his own funerall Sermon'; the title-page of *Deaths Duell* says: 'his last Sermon, and called by his Majesties houshold THE DOCTORS OWNE FUNERALL SERMON'.

An Elegy upon . . . Gustavus Adolphus (p. 77)

Gustavus Adolphus was killed at the battle of Lutzen, 6 Nov. 1632.

Text: *H*, *M*, *P*, *1657*, *TM*. The elegy was printed in *The Swedish Intelligencer*, Third Part, 1633, with nine other poems, all of which are anonymous;

this one alone is subscribed, 'Henry King'. It is also found copied in several manuscript miscellanies, including Bodleian MS. Locke c. 32.

Variants:

8 out] up *H*   10 That] Which *H, TM, misc. MSS.*   11 Aiery] Fiery *SI*   30 Lower . . . then] other . . . but *Locke*   79 Therfore] Wherfore *H*   109 but thy Frailty did] did thy frailtie not *Locke* 133 *O Famâ* &c.] *only in 1657.*

2–3 *is* has to be understood (where in fact it is almost heard) between *Breath* and *Stop't.*

15 Originally punctuated as follows:

> Speak it againe, and lowder, lowder yet;

so in *H* before correction, *P* (yet:), and *1657.* Corrected by King in *H* to what is printed in this text. *M* has an expressive use of punctuation and capitals:

> Speak it againe, and lowder; Lowder Yet.

19 *numerous: P* substitutes *so many.*

26 *faine H, P: feine M: feign 1657.*

37 *Hate: Fate* corrected to *Hate H: Fate P.*

75 *Pointes H,* corrected from *pointes.*

92 *for:* but for.

96 Hannah says that the quotation from Tacitus 'seems to be entirely misapprehended here. King evidently supposes it to refer to Julius Caesar. . . . In reality, it refers to Domitian, and means, that his pretended triumph . . . had not the ordinary warrant of any victory at all.' The mistake is more likely to have arisen from the use of a common-place book and imperfect memory than from inability to construe.

102 *Thy H,* corrected from *thy.*

113 *Spann'd:* quoted amongst examples of the obsolete meaning (I.2.†c) of the verb *span,* 'To set a limit or bound to (life etc.)', *O.E.D.; wee,* omitted from *M,* was added later, perhaps by King.

117–20 The image is of a watch with the fusee escapement.

128 In 1632 was printed *The Learned Tico Brahæ his Astronomicall Coniectur of the new and much Admired [star] Which Appered in the year 1572,* claiming the relation of the star to the career of Gustavus Adolphus. A hundred years later it seemed appropriate to a certain John Lumby to begin his poem commemorating the death of John Hunter of the Queen's College, 'Is Hunter dead & nothing in the Sky?' Bodl. MS. Eng. poet. e. 42, fol. 36.

133 *O Famâ* &c.: adapted from *Aeneid* xi. 124–5; misprinted 'lib. 2' *1657.*

Upon the King's happy Returne from Scotland (p. 81)

The king reached Greenwich 20 July 1633 (*C.S.P.D. 1633–4*, p. 176).
Text: H, M, P, *1657*.

Variant:

43 does] doth H.

5 *You* corrected from *you* H.

12 *Your* corrected from *your* M.

16 *Hopefull* corrected from *hopefull* H.

22 *Reflexe*: cf. 'A Letter', 45 (page 153).

23 *hir* corrected from *her* H; *lonesse* for *lonenesse*, H and P, possibly copying a mistake in the original.

31 *encrease*, semi-colon in H and M.

To . . . Mr Henry Blount upon his Voyage (p. 83)

Henry Blount was at Trinity College, Oxford, 1616–19; Henry King had left Oxford in July 1616 and was living in London. The book which is honoured in this poem is *A Voyage into the Levant*, 1636. Blount was knighted 21 March 1639/40.

Text: H, P, *1657*, and British Museum Add. MS. 33998, which is a very carefully written collection of poems, the majority by Christ Church poets, though this is the only one of King's. The variants in Add. MS. 33998 mostly look like mistakes, but in nine instances (lines 35, 56, 58, 67, 75, 90, 122, 123, and 144) parentheses have been marked by commas or brackets in King's characteristic way.

Variants:

Title: Mr] Sir *1657*.

4 and] or H   63 Next, how fierce] After how H   133 daungers] daunger H.

10 *smoak*: *O.E.D.* I. 2. b. 'The smoke arising from a particular hearth . . . hence, a hearth, fire-place, house', illustrated by a quotation from Sylvester, *Du Bartas*, I. iii. 1097, 'Leading all his life at home in Peace, Alwayes in sight of his own smoak.' In the other examples quoted, 'smoke' is used as the literal equivalent of 'house'.

13 Archbishop Laud described how at Westminster 'after supper (in summer time) they were called to the Mr.'s chamber (spec. those of the 7th forme), and there . . . practised to describe and find out cities and

countries in the mappes'; quoted by T. W. Baldwin, *Shakspere's Small Latine and Lesse Greeke*, 1944, i. 360.

17 Ortelius had been available in English editions since King's childhood: *Abraham Ortelius his Epitome of the Theater of the Worlde* was printed in 1603 and *Theatrum Orbis Terrarum* in 1606. The English *Historia mundi: or Mercator's Atlas* was not printed till 1635.

32 *Tomombee*: Tuman Bey, the last Sultan of Egypt before the Ottoman conquest, 1517.

34 'The whole circuit of the *Citie* seemed to me betweene five and thirtie, or forty *miles*', Blount's *Voyage*, 1636, p. 40.

60 *Opinion*: O.E.D. †6 '. . . the estimation (esp. good estimation) in which one stands . . .'.

63 '*Ottoman* the first *Turkish* Sultan [1300–28] of this Tribe united to his Lordship of *Saguta Bythinia, Cappadocia,* and part of *Pontus*', Peter Heylin, *Microcosmus*, 1621, p. 313.

68–72 *Amurath II*, 1416–50, attacked Serbia in 1437. He 'subdued from the *Constantinople* Empire all *Achaia, Thessaly, Epyrus,* and died before the walls of Croia [Kroja]' (ibid.).

73–76 '*Mahomet II* [1450–81], surnamed the great, and first Emperor of the *Turkes*, ruined the two Empires of *Constantinople* and *Trabezond* 12 Kingdomes and 200 Citties' (ibid.).

102 *lists*: O.E.D., 'List *sb.*³, II. †8, A limit, bound, boundary'.

104 *ingenuous*: an obsolete use, O.E.D. 2: 'Noble in nature . . . (Of persons, of their dispositions, actions, etc.)'; or possibly the nonce-use, representing Latin *ingenuus*, O.E.D. †5.

120 *Levant*: first written *Leuant* P.

To my Dead Friend Ben: Johnson (p. 87)

Jonson died 6 August 1637.

Text: H, P, *1657*. Also printed, probably from King's autograph, in *Jonsonus Virbius, or the Memorie of Ben Johnson Revived by the friends of the Muses*, collected by Brian Duppa, published 1638 (*JV*). From *Jonsonus Virbius* King's elegy, with those of Lord Falkland, Jasper Mayne, and William Cartwright, was printed in *The Second Part of Miscellany Poems . . . publish'd by Mr. Dryden*, 1716. The punctuation of *Jonsonus Virbius* differs from that of the manuscripts, but looks like King's own, and in a few places has been adopted here. Words spelt with capital letters in the manuscripts were usually italicized by the printer.

Variants:

    Title: Vpon Ben. Iohnson *JV*.

    7 who] that *JV*   46 so'unnaturally *P*: so unnaturally *H, 1657*.

1–2 *Wreath . . . Thunder*: 'That Bayes will protect from the mischief of lightning and thunder, is a qualitie ascribed thereto, common with the figtree, Ægle, and skin of a Seale', Sir Thomas Browne, *Pseudodoxia Epidemica*, 1646, II. vi. 6. Francis Douce, in a note on J. Brand's *Popular Antiquities* (Bodl. MS. Douce d. 46, fol. 498), quotes Suetonius as relating 'that Tiberius, who was much afraid of thunder, always wore a laurel crown when the heavens threatened a storm. Cap. LXIX'.

16 *Thine* corrected from *thine H*.

50 *Owne* corrected from *owne H*.

59 *1657* emphasizes the play upon words by giving *thine own sheets* in italics.

To my honourd friend Mr. George Sandys (p. 89)

    King's commendatory verses were printed in the folio edition of *A Paraphrase upon the Divine Poems*, 1638. Amongst the other contributors were Lord Falkland, Godolphin, Carew, Dudley Digges, and Waller. George Sandys was the youngest son of Edwin Sandys, Archbishop of York; he was fourteen years older than Henry King. For the connexion between their families, see Introduction, p. 3.

Text: H, P, *1657*, and *A Paraphrase upon the Divine Poems*, 1638 (*Sandys*). Variations in *Sandys* are probably alterations made by King whilst copying the poem for the printer.

Variants:

    Title: honourd] much honoured *Sandys*.

    25 might] would *Sandys*   54 Pleades] Speaks *Sandys*   57–62 *omitted Sandys*   62 Sternoldes] Other *1657*   64 With] And *Sandys*   65 And . . . skill] Last, . . . Art *Sandys*   81 the] that *H, P*   82 hardly] scarcely *Sandys*   89 not (were it in their] by no meanes (had they *Sandys*   90 Practise] Custome, *Sandys*   96 unstudy'd Stuffes] ill study'd Stuffe *Sandys*   100 t'] to *Sandys*   104 use] adde *Sandys* 109 shall] will *Sandys*   116 Allow] Confesse *Sandys*   123 Writer] Author *Sandys*.

5 *Much less* [is there need] *that* [I] *should*, etc.

6 *License* altered from *Licence H*.

7 *Receav'd* corrected from *receav'd H*.

23 In *H* and *P* the sign for the note is *8o*, evidently a corruption of the original symbol, which may have been ꝗ. The *View or Survey of the State of Religion in the Westerne Parts of the World* was posthumously printed at The Hague, 1629. A pirated edition, 1605, was ordered to be destroyed. The note in *Sandys* calls it 'View of Religion in the Westerne parts'.

24 *The Relation* of George Sandys's 'painfull' and 'Curious' 'Travailes', in Italy, Turkey, Egypt, and Palestine, was printed in 1615.

41 Cf. 24.

44 *Chorography*: *O.E.D.* has a note, 'A term . . . greatly in vogue in 17th c., but now little used, its ancient sphere being covered by *geography* and *topography* jointly'.

53–55 References to Job and Ecclesiastes omitted, *Sandys*.

57–62 *Al the Psalmes of David faithfully reduced into easie meeter by H.D.*, 1620. The metrical version of the act begins:

> Whereas Almightie God hath in all ages shew'd his power
> And mercie in miraculous standing our saviour . . .

King's expression of disapproval was omitted from Sandys's book, and even in the less reticent text of *1657* the name of Sternhold was left out.

64 *Sad* corrected from *sad H.*

71–86 King's own attempt was finished and printed in 1651.

97–106 The punctuation was corrected both in *H* and in *P*: in *H* commas were added after *which*, *skinns*, and *use*, and a full-stop after *comelinesse* was changed to a colon. *P*, with commas added after *Which* and *Cov'ring*, agrees exactly with *H*.

A Salutation of His Majestye's Shipp The Soveraigne (p. 92)

The Sovereign of the Seas was launched on 13 October 1637. Its magnificent appearance and great size (by chance 1,637 tons) aroused interest and pride amongst those who were willing to see in it the justification for the levy of ship-money. A printed account of it by Thomas Heywood, dated 1638, was called *A true Discription of his Majesties royall and most stately Ship*. There were also poems in Latin and English by Sir Richard Fanshawe, afterwards printed in *Il Pastor Fido*, 1647, and in Latin by Alexander Gill (MS. Corpus Christi College, Oxford, 318, fol. 217); and an anonymous ballad, found in Bodl. MS. Rawl. poet. 160, fol. 164, was printed by C. H. H. Firth in *Naval Songs and Ballads*, Navy Records Society, xxxiii, 1908.

Text: H, P, *1657*. There is a good copy on a single sheet in Bodl. MS. Jones 56 (*Jones*), and one in Bodl. MS. Ashmole 38, 141 (see also 139) (*Ash*).

Variants:

24 Sheat] Sheates H, *Jones*   31 amazed] amused H, *Jones*   32 from] to H, *Jones*, *Ash*.

15 *But*, . . . *Meteor*, P and *1657*; the commas are not in H and *M*.

18 *Tires*: obsolete, 'The simultaneous discharge of a battery of ordnance; a volley or broadside', *O.E.D.*

23 *Gales* corrected from *gales* H.

24 *Sheat* corrected from *Sheet* P.

31 *amazed | amused*: in the obsolete sense intended here, *amuse* is practically interchangeable with *amaze*.

An Elegy upon . . . Lady Anne Riche (p. 93)

Anne, Lady Rich, was a daughter of William Cavendish, second Earl of Devonshire. She was married on 9 April 1632 to Robert, Baron Rich, and died 24 August 1638. John Gauden, chaplain to Lord Rich (and later Bishop of Worcester), compiled in memory of her 'The Shadow of the (sometimes) right Faire, Vertuous and Honourable Lady Anne Rich Now an Happy, Glorious and Perfected Saint in Heaven', Bodl. MS. Eng. misc. e. 262 (not printed). Gauden's own prose account is followed by the mourning poems of Dudley, Lord North, his son Dudley, John North, Henry King, Waller, Godolphin, and others.

Text: H, P, *1657*, Gauden (*G*), *TM*. In *G* there are minor textual variants which suggest authentic alterations made in copying; these are therefore recorded here. Characteristic King punctuation is found in lines 39, *Whose, now still, current*, and 70, *Then were, at thy departure, here possess't*.

Variants:

4 Arrow *TM, G, 1657*: Arrowes H, P   9 Griefes] griefe *G*   11 wee] I *G*   26 Only Confusion] Confusion onely *G*   28 thy Rere or] the reare & *G*   36 Hir] there *G*   37 or] & *G*   38 Which] Once H, *G*   45 Dearth] Death H, *TM before correction*   47 must] shall *G* 48 hast'ning] hasting H, *G*   54 Set] ffate *G*   56 point] height *G* 58 Unto] Into *G*   65 vertues] vertue *TM*   66 with] in *TM* 71 thy] the *TM*   72 Thy Losse] our Fate *G*   76 smaller] lesser *G*.

2 Cf. Donne, *Holy Sonnets*, 1633, vi. 7:

And soonest our best men with thee doe goe.

32–33 *Moanes . . . Years*: originally *Mournes . . . Yearns*, in error, H.

45 *Droughtes* corrected from *droughtes* H.

52 *Northumberland*: Anne, Countess of Northumberland, died 6 December 1637.

80 *Thy* corrected from *thy* H.

An Elegy upon Mrs. Kirk unfortunately drowned in Thames (p. 96)

Mrs. Anne Kirke was a lady of the Queen's bedchamber. Her name is in the list of actors who took part with the Queen in Walter Montagu's *The Shepheards Paradise* (printed 1659), 'before the late King Charls'. The accident in which she died was described in letters dated 8 July 1641, printed in *C.S.P.D.*: 'The Court is very sad by reason of a great mishap happened to a barge coming through London Bridge, wherein were divers ladies, and amongst the rest Mrs. Kirke, drowned. The barge fell upon a piece of timber across the lock, and so was cast away'; 'The Queen has taken very heavily the news, and, they say, shed tears for her'. There were verses on the occasion by Robert Heath and Henry Glapthorne, and (written much later) by Mrs. Kirke's niece Anne Killigrew. G. Thorn-Drury's copy of the 1874 edition of Glapthorne's works, now in the Bodleian with shelf-mark Thorn-Drury e. 22–23, contains a list of references to Anne Kirke (ii. 256), to which I am indebted.

Text: P, *1657*. Manuscript copies in *TM* and *Harl.*

Variants:
   Title: Mrs Kirk . . . Thames *1657*: a Lady . . . the Thames P, *TM*, *Harl.*
7 raise] forme *Harl.*   10 the] thy *Harl.*   24 durst] did *Harl.*
29 Current] River *Harl.*   35 far-fam'd pow'r] power for faigned *Harl.*

To the Queen at Oxford (p. 97)

This poem was probably intended for the occasion of the Queen's arrival from the North on 14 July 1643. She was met at Edge Hill by the King, the Prince of Wales, and the Duke of York, to whom King refers in lines 47–48. Anthony Wood's detailed accounts of her reception do not mention Henry King, and it is not in fact likely that he was in Oxford at the time. The verses might have been provided for his brother Philip, who was there between his sequestration, 1642, and the time when he joined Henry at Lady Salter's (*Fasti*, ii. 89, and see Introduction, p. 21, above).

Text: P, *1657.*

Variants:
  Title: at Oxford *omitted* P.
  20 onely] truly P   32 Princesse'] Princesse P: Princes *1657.*
20 *truely* P, perhaps a scribal alteration to avoid the repetition of *onely.*

An Elegy Upon the death of Mr. Edward Holt
(p. 98)

A full account of Edward Holt was given by Hannah, pp. xcviii–c and 205–6; and see Introduction, above, p. 13. He was the son of Sir Thomas Holt, Bart., of Aston, Warwickshire; he matriculated at Hart Hall, 1615, aged 15; he married Henry King's eldest sister, Elizabeth, and had by her two sons and three daughters; he was a groom of the bedchamber to Charles I, and fought on the royalist side; he died of a fever, and was buried in Christ Church Cathedral, 30 August 1643. His son Robert succeeded Sir Thomas as second Baronet, 1654. Henry King's will reveals that he supported Edward and Elizabeth Holt and their children 'when the unnatural usage of an implacable Father denied them competent means wher by they might subsist'.

Text: P, *1657.*

8 The quarrel began in 1624.

10 Edward Holt was about forty-three.

27–28 He was buried 'neere to the head of Bishop [Robert] Kings monument', Bodl. MS. Wood F. 4, p. 60, close to his brother-in-law the younger John King.

Note: The next five poems contain Henry King's impression of events during the Civil War. Much of his information was derived from Royalist newsletters and pamphlets (Hannah printed extracts from some of these). King found it possible to believe almost anything discreditable to the other side. On many matters his point of view agrees exactly with Clarendon's, and it has sometimes seemed best to explain his references by quotation from the *History of the Rebellion* (edited by W. D. Macray, 1888). Other statements and references have been compared with S. R. Gardiner's *History of the Great Civil War*, 2nd ed., 1893, the British Museum's *Catalogue of the Pamphlets . . . collected by George Thomason*, 1908, and the *Journals of the House of Commons*. I refer to these as *Clarendon, Gardiner, Thomason Tracts*, and *Commons' Journals.*

On the Earl of Essex (p. 99)

Robert Devereux, third Earl, died 14 September 1646. King's rather majestic statement of the royalist view seems to show an undercurrent of respect for the 'Dead General'.

Text: P, *1664*.

Variants:
  Title: An Epitaph Upon the Earle of Essex P.
  18 Tide] Side *1664*   38 Sware] Swear *1664*.

1 Bishop John King, alone with Archbishop Abbot, had opposed the divorce from Frances Howard in 1613. The second wife was Elizabeth Paulet, 1631.

8 He resigned his commission on 2 April 1645.

18 *Tide | Side*: *fury* and *falshood* could (for Henry King) be only on one side; the line is metaphorical, *Side* a misprint.

36–38 The words of the resolution of Parliament were: 'That they will live and die with the Earl of *Essex*, whom they have nominated General in this Cause', *Journals* of both Houses, 12 July 1642.

Epigram: Hammond (p. 101)

Colonel Robert Hammond, nephew of Dr. Henry Hammond, was Charles I's custodian on the Isle of Wight from November 1647 to November 1648. The incident to which the epigram alludes is probably the one of which a 'flying report' reached Sir Edward Nicholas on 21/31 March 1647/8: 'that Hammond came in to the King at two of the clock in the night; . . . and . . . went readily to his cabinet, and searched it' (*Papers collected by Edward Earl of Clarendon*, ii, 1773, Appendix, xlvi). There may be a connexion between the rope in the epigram (apparently not mentioned elsewhere) and the King's attempted escape through a window 'by a Cord' (*Memoirs of the Two last Years of the Reign of King Charles I*, by Sir Thomas Herbert, &c., 1702, p. 190).

Text: P; first printed in *Sparrow*.

12 *Hamans tall Gallowes*: Esther iii–vii, and especially vii. 9–10.

An Elegy on Sir Charls Lucas, and Sir George Lisle (p. 101)

Fairfax ordered these two to be shot 'for some satisfaction to Military Justice, and in part of avenge for the innocent blood they have caused to be spilt' at Colchester, 26 August 1648, the day on which the royalist defence of the city was relinquished (*A Letter from . . . Lord Fairfax . . . concerning the surrender of Colchester, the Grounds and Reasons of putting to death Sir Charles Lucas and Sir George Lysle*, &c., dated 29 August, published 2 September 1648). The reference to Thomas Rainsborough's death, 249–50, dates the poem after 29 October 1648. 255–8 show King in fear, if not in expectation, of Charles I's death.

Text: 1664.

57 *improve*: the adverse sense was normal in seventeenth-century use: see *O.E.D.*; and cf. King's Elegy on Lady Stanhope, 33 (p. 133), and the Elegy on Charles I, 180 (p. 122).

66 *the faithless Bashaw*: Hannah quoted George Sandys's *Relation of a Journey*, 1615, p. 219; King might also have discussed the story with James Howell, though his account in the *Survay of the Signorie of Venice* was not published till 1651.

78 *By Syllae's . . . red proscription's Line*: by the example of Sulla: whose history was probably familiar to King in Plutarch, read in the fifth form at Westminster.

83 *by which* understood before *the world*.

92 *renders*: probably derived from the verb, *O.E.D.* 13, 'refl. To present (oneself), take steps to be *at . . .* a certain place. Hence *intr.* to be present; to hold, obtain (rare)'.

105 marg. *1643*: King seems to have been uncertain of the date and *1664* has *164 . .* Charles was negotiating for Danish troops, which 'were to have been purchased by the cession of Orkney and Shetland', when war broke out between Denmark and Sweden and the troops were needed at home (*Gardiner*, i. 270).

115 Matthew Hopkins procured the death of an appalling number of 'witches' before he was himself hanged as a sorcerer, 1647; see *D.N.B.*

117 *Cad*: King's use is quoted in *O.E.D.* with one other passage, from Francis Osborne's *Advice to a Son*, 1658: 'these Cadds or Familiars'; and cf. 134 (p. 105).

122 *Darby-house*: the Committee of Derby House succeeded the Committee of Both Kingdoms at the beginning of 1648.

142 *from*: Hannah's emendation from *for*, 1664.

179–80 Of Alexander Rigby, Dugdale in *A Short View of the Late Troubles in England*, 1681, p. 577, says: 'did not Mr. *Rigby* . . . move twice, *that those Lords and Gentlemen which were Prisoners . . . should be sold as Slaves to* Argiere, *or sent to the new Plantations in the* West-Indies . . .?' King later gave £200 'towards the redemption of Captives from Algiers': Bodl. MS. Tanner 45, fol. 73.

183 Three thousand prisoners taken at Naseby were brought to London, *Gardiner*, ii. 256–7.

183 St. Fagan's, 8 May 1648.

210 I Kings xii. 31: Jeroboam 'made priests of the lowest of the people, which were not of the sons of Levi'.

222–4 Fairfax served under Horace, Baron Vere of Tilbury, in the Low Countries, 1629, and married his daughter Anne.

231, 240, 250 Whalley and Rainsborough were appointed to see the sentence carried out. Rainsborough was murdered at Pontefract, 29 October 1648.

250 *at Pomfret: from Pomfret 1664*, apparently in error.

253, 255 *Knowledge . . . add . . . are ours: Knowledge* is treated as a plural noun.

284 *Caput Algol: Algol* signifies *the demon*; Algol is a variable star in the constellation of Perseus.

292–4 2 Samuel xx. 9–10.

A Deepe Groane, fetch'd at the Funerall of . . . Charles the First (p. 110)

Charles I was buried in St. George's Chapel, Windsor, 9 February 1648/9. Clarendon describes how 'the King's body was laid, without any words, or other ceremony than the tears and sighs of the few beholders. Upon the coffin was a plate of silver fixed with these words only, "*King Charles. 1648*" ' (xi. 244). The 'Deepe Groane' was probably written for publication soon after the funeral.

Text: Two editions were published in 1649, the first attributed to 'I.B.', the other to 'D.H.K.' Thomason's copy was 'D.H.K.', and he dated it 16 May (*Thomason Tracts*, i. 744). *DHK* has substantial errors in nineteen places where *IB* gives the correct reading, but on four occasions errors in *IB* were corrected in *DHK*; these, particularly 54, *Gourney* for *Goury*, are unlikely to have been put right by the careless printer of *DHK* on his own initiative, and John Sparrow decided that he worked from a corrected copy of *IB* (*Sparrow*, pp. 175–6, 187). On the title-page of *DHK*, Latin verses were added, and *A Groane* (*IB*) was altered to *A Deepe Groane*.

DHK was reproduced, with all its errors, but without King's initials, in the two editions of *Monumentum Regale*, 1649 (106–7 in *A New Bibliography of the Eikon Basilike*, by F. F. Madan, Oxford Bibliographical Society Publications, N.S. iii, 1950). The Bodleian copy of Madan 106,

Pamph. C. 88 (4), was used and marked by someone concerned with the compilation of *Reliquæ Sacræ Carolinæ*, 1650 (Madan 61). On the title-page of Pamph. C. 88 (4) is a note, 'pr[int] Bp. K[ing's] verses p[ost] Montrosses', and other marks are on pp. 1 and 31–46: K[ing]'s poem was numbered '4', later altered to '7', and in the *Reliquæ* it is the seventh, following verses subscribed 'Montrosse'; lines marked and numbered in Pamph. C. 88 (4) are the first on each page of the *Reliquæ*, the numbers being those of the pages within the quire Ee; the initials 'D.H.K.' were added at the end of the poem, and were reproduced in the *Reliquæ*.

The text printed here is *IB*, with the additions and corrections from *DHK*, all of which are mentioned in the notes. There are seven places where *IB* and *DHK* agree in punctuation which is misleading to a modern reader, and these have been altered; in 211 John Sparrow's emendation *last* for *least* has been adopted, against the evidence of *IB* and *DHK*.

6 *weep*. DHK: *weep*, IB.

18 *Totall* DHK: *totall* IB; *Charles is Murthered*: cf. Elegy upon Prince Henry, 6 (p. 65).

21 Caligula's wish, that all the Romans should have shared one head, to be beheaded in a single execution.

24 *fourth Division of the world*: the population was four, Adam, Eve, Cain, and Abel.

27 *epidemicke*: O.E.D. †2 includes the obsolete meaning 'universal'.

29 *mine's* DHK: *min's* IB.

31 *November's plots*: The Army's *Remonstrance*, dated St. Albans, 16 November 1648, was presented to the House of Commons on 20 November. It demanded 'That the capital and grand author of our troubles, the person of the king . . . may be speedily brought to justice for the treason, blood, and mischief he is therein guilty of' (quoted *Gardiner*, iv. 235) with, according to Clarendon, 'many other unpractical particulars, which troubled the Parliament the less for their incoherence, and impossibility to be reduced into practice' (xi. 202).

35 *Light* DHK: *light* IB.

40 *Villanie*. DHK: *Villanie*, IB.

43 *Brand*: DHK and IB both have semi-colon. The colon is needed to introduce the 'rubrick'.

53 *Raviliack*: the assassin of Henry IV of France, 14 May 1610.

54 *Goury*: IB reads *Gourney*. The failure of the Earl of Gowrie's plot on the life of King James was commemorated by thanksgiving services on the anniversary, 5 August, throughout the reign in England.

64–70 John Wilde, made by Parliament Chief Baron of the Exchequer, was the judge who condemned Captain Burly to be hanged, drawn, and quartered for treason: his offence was an attempt to raise a force to rescue the King from his custodians on the Isle of Wight (*Clarendon*, x. 145).

75 Cf. 'An Elegy upon . . . Charles the First', 445 (p. 129).

86 *Innocence*, *DHK*: no comma *IB*.

94 *Median . . . Basilick*: the *median* vein in the upper arm divides into the *median basilic*, which was commonly opened for blood-letting, and the *median cephalic*. King was more concerned with the etymology than with the anatomical situation.

99 *leading IB*: *deading DHK*, whose reading Mason and John Sparrow adopted, because King uses *dead* as a transitive verb in his sermon on Duppa; but the pillar of fire and cloud in Exodus xiii. 21, to which a reference is here intended, *led* the children of Israel.

119 *inroule*: perhaps the obsolete sense, *O.E.D.* †4, 'To write . . . to engross . . .', is meant; or perhaps a figurative sense. 115–20 are reminiscent of 'The Woes of Esay'. Cf. 'An Elegy upon . . . King Charles', 232 (p. 124).

121 *That John-à-Leyden King*: Cromwell. Johann Buckholdt, of Leyden, Anabaptist 'King' of Münster, 1534, was executed 22 January 1536, and his quarters were hung on the tower of St. Lambert's church. An account of him is in the second edition of *Pansebeia*, by Alexander Ross, 1655. Cf. 'An Elegy upon . . . Charles the First', 195 (p. 123).

128 *bequeath'd*, *DHK*: *IB* has no comma.

134 *blast*: *blayne DHK* and modern editions; but a *plague-sore* was a *blayne*; *blast*, meaning (*O.E.D.* 6) 'A sudden infection (formerly attributed to the blowing or breath of some malignant power, foul air, etc.)' balances the other half of the line.

147 *coffin'd DHK*: *conffin'd IB*.

148 Cf. 'To A.R. upon [Overbury's *Wife*]', 3 (p. 155).

171 *Honour*, *DHK*: *IB* has no comma.

173–4 *Cynegirus*: Justin (read in the fifth form at Westminster) tells that after the battle of Marathon, Cynegirus tried to hold an enemy ship, first with his right hand, then with his left, and at last with his teeth (II. ix. 16).

176 *Foyles*: an obsolete wrestling term, 'a throw not resulting in a flat fall', *O.E.D.*, appropriate in this reference to what happened when Antaeus, thrown by his enemies, recovered strength from contact with the earth.

179–80 *Horatius Cocles*: the opponent of Lars Porsenna of Clusium.

183 *The Gantlet thus upheld*: the King's acceptance of the challenge.

201–4 *Codrus*: the last king of Athens, 'who in the warres against the *Pelopennesians*, having intelligence by an oracle that his enimies should have the victory, if they did not kill the *Athenian* King: attired himselfe like a beggar, and forced the *Pelopennesians* to kill him', Peter Heylin, *Microcosmus*, 1621, p. 210.

211 *last* John Sparrow's emendation: *at least IB, art least DHK*; Clarendon (xi. 245) says that 'Upon the return of [Charles II] . . . it was generally expected that the body should be removed from that obscure burial and . . . should be solemnly deposited with his royal ancestors in King Harry the Seventh's chapel in the church of Westminster'.

214 *Nephews*: cf. 'To my honourd friend Mr. George Sandys', 32 (p. 89). *Teares and wonder*, the reaction of the next generation to their fathers' crime.

216 *Tyrant, on DHK: Tyrant upon IB*.

218 *Olibian*: obsolete; *olibanum* is frankincense.

219 *times DHK: time IB*.

235 *Reigne, DHK: Reigne. IB*.

An Elegy upon the most Incomparable King Charls the First (p. 117)

Printed anonymously as a quarto pamphlet, which was not included in Thomason's collection. It was dated 'From my sad Retirement March 11. 1648'; but it cannot have been finished and printed before 1659, for at line 301 is a reference to p. 320 of *The History of the English and Scotch Presbytery*. The title-page of this work states that it was 'written in French, by an eminent Divine of the Reformed Chuch, and now Englished. 1659'.[1] The first draft of the poem was probably finished on 11 March 1648/9; but it was prepared for publication only when the Restoration was in sight.

Text: '*1648*' (see above), *1664*. The texts differ very slightly: in both sometimes, but not often, spelling was modernized, or King's punctuation and use of capital letters were disregarded. The text here is printed from *1664*, but in a few places capital letters or punctuation have been taken from '*1648*', by which are corrected also three misprints of *1664*, i.e. 12, *our* omitted; 100, *Husband* for *Husband's*; 312, *Resolving* for *Resolved*.

---

[1] It has been attributed both to Isaac Basire and to Pierre du Moulin, and Wood noted on his copy 'said to be written by Dr. Jo. Bramhall'. A note on p. 316 states that 'this book in the French was printed in the year 1650', but King certainly referred to the English translation. See note to line 301 (p. 217 below).

Variants:

Title: '*1648*' *adds* Persecuted by two Implacable Factions, Imprisoned by the One, And Murthered by the Other, January 30th 1648.

14–15 *Hadadrimmon:* Zechariah xii. 11, 'as the mourning of Hadadrimmon in the valley of Megiddon'. Josiah was slain at Megiddo, 2 Chronicles xxxv. 22–24.

33–34 *Jehosaphat:* 2 Chronicles xviii. 3, 29–31.

39–41 *Hezekiah:* 2 Kings xx. 13.

43–44 2 Chronicles xxiv. 4–13.

62 *Reformation* '*1648*': *Reformations 1664.*

63 *Alva's Counsels:* the Duke of Alva presided over the Spanish court which was given the name 'Council of Blood' for its ruthless activities in the Netherlands, autumn 1569.

73 'A sacred vow and covenant taken by the Lords and Commons assembled in Parliament upon the discovery of the late horrid and treacherous design for the destruction of this Parliament and the kingdom', i.e. Waller's plot, cf. *Clarendon*, vii. 67–70. Taken by the Commons, 6 June, by the Lords, 9 June, and published 27 June (*Commons' Journals* and *Thomason Tracts*, and cf. line 283).

86–94 Clarendon, writing in 1646, commented on nine Acts passed during 1641, 'These Acts of Parliament . . . (. . . besides that fatal bill for the continuance of this Parliament) will be hereafter acknowledged by an incorrupted posterity to be everlasting monuments of a princely and fatherly affection [of the king] to his people', iii. 271. The Act for a triennial Parliament was passed 16 February 1641, the Act for the perpetual Parliament 10 May 1641 (*Clarendon*, iii. 79–80, 256; iii. 206–10, 271).

107 2 Samuel xv. 2–6.

129–34 'An Ordinance of both Houses of Parliament for the ordering of the militia . . .', *Clarendon*, iv. 307, 350. The king's message to Parliament, withholding his assent from the bill, was received and debated on 29 February; on 15 March it was resolved 'that in this Case of extreme Danger, and of his Majesty's Refusal, the Ordinance . . . doth oblige the People, and ought to be obeyed, by the fundamental Laws of this Kingdom' (*Commons Journals*). 134 *each Militia:* cf. *Clarendon*, v. 36, 'Whilst they were so eager in pursuit of the militia . . . they had their eye upon another militia, the royal navy'.

138 *Watkins, Pennington, and Ven:* at the time of the king's attempt to arrest the Five Members, John Venn and Isaac Penington, members for London and Middlesex, took the order for a guard from the House of Lords to the Lord Mayor (*C.S.P.D., 1641–3*, 235, 237). *Watkins*, who was conspicuous

with them on 10 January, when the Trained Bands were brought out to protect the Five Members on their return to Westminster, may have been William Watkins, member for Monmouth.

159–60 *Clarendon*, iv. 313: 'Then [the House of Commons] fell to raising of moneys under pretence of the relief of Ireland, and for that purpose prepared one Act for the payment of four hundred thousand pounds to such persons as were nominated by themselves', March 1641/2. *Stale*: a hawking word, meaning 'decoy', applied inexactly.

175 Cf. *Mercurius Rusticus*, by Bruno Ryves, 1646, pp. 210–11.

181 *Lactantius*: *Divinæ Institutiones*, II. iv. 16.

185 *Theodoret*: *Ecclesiastical History*, III. xi. A reference to the same story is in Bruno Ryves's *Mercurius Rusticus*, 1646, p. 206, in connexion with sacrilege at Chichester.

192 *Gaguin*, misprinted *Ganguin*: *Compendium de origine et gestis Francorum*, first printed 1495: '[Iudæi] et cum pignoris loco vestes, & sacrosancta ecclesiæ vasa a creditoribus suscepissent, ea in sordidos usus admouebant.'

195 *John of Leyden*: see note on 'A Deepe Groane', 121, p. 213.

203–4 Daniel v. 1–3.

224 2 Kings x. 27.

230 *Copronimus*: the Emperor Constantine V.

239 *Athaliah*: 2 Chronicles xxiv. 7, 'For the sons of Athaliah, that wicked woman, had broken up the house of God.'

241 *Commons' Journals*, 5 February 1643/4. Misprinted *Feb. 3*, '*1648*' and *1664*.

246, 251 *Bell* . . . *Strew'd Ashes*: in the apocryphal *Bel and the Dragon*, Daniel exposed the fraud of the priests of Bel, who claimed that their god devoured offerings of food. He spread ashes, on which were seen the footprints of those who removed the offerings by night.

250 *Pantagruel*: King probably read Rabelais in French; Sir Thomas Urquhart's translation was printed in 1653.

275 The standard was set up 22 August, and the king's message to the two houses of Parliament was sent on 25 August. Clarendon (v. 449; cf. vi. 1 n. 2) also dated the setting up of the standard 25 August.

283 Cf. 73 (p. 119).

286 Both houses voted 'That this House doth Declare, That . . . for the Safety of the King's Person, the Defence of both Houses of Parliament . . . for the Preservation of the true Religion, of the Laws, Liberties, and Peace of the Kingdom, they will live and die with the Earl of *Essex*, whom they

have nominated General in this Cause', *Journals* of both Houses, 12 July 1642.

287–90 1 Kings xii. 26–30.

291 Judges xii. 5–6.

293 *Trains*: 'pieces of carrion or the like laid in a line or trail for luring certain wild beasts . . . into a trap . . . *Obs.*' *O.E.D.* †7.

301 'They commanded the people to take up Armes under the penalty of being hanged', *History of the English and Scotch Presbytery*, 1659, p. 320.

320 *The 19 Propositions*: published 2 June 1642 (*Gardiner*, iii. 127).

333–8 *His Country-men*: the Scots. *April 27. 1646*: the date of the king's leaving Oxford, disguised as a servant. *May 5*: the king became the Scots' prisoner.

338 *Achish*: a Philistine; 1 Samuel xxvii. 2–7.

356–8, 365, 374 The two questions, of payment of the English debt to the Scots army, and of what was to be done with the king when the Scots left England, arose at the same time. The security for the payment of £200,000 was raised on the bishops' lands (*Gardiner*, iii. 145, and C. V. Wedgwood, *The King's War*, 1958, pp. 603 ff.).

387–8 The king arrived at Holmby House 16 February 1647, and was abducted from there by Cornet Joyce, 4 June.

390 *the Fatal Isle*: the Isle of Wight; Gardiner (iv. 7) quotes Marvell's lines on Cromwell:

> . . . twining subtile fears with hope,
> He wove a Net of such a scope
> That *Charles* himself might chase,
> To *Caresbrooke*'s narrow case.
> That thence the *Royal Actor* born
> The *Tragic Scaffold* might adorn,

which are 'too absurd to need refutation'.

391–4 For Hammond, see p. 209. Major Edmund Rolph was his second in command. In June 1648 Rolph was accused of an attempt on the king's life. There was an inquiry in Parliament, and Rolph was sent down to be tried at the Winchester Assize, from where the answer came back, *Ignoramus* (*Commons' Journals*, 31 August). In the Thomason collection are publications about the affair, some of which associate Hammond with Rolph's supposed plot.

403 *A Declaration from Sir Thomas Fairfax and the General Councel of the Army of their Resolutions to the Parliament in their Proceedings concerning the King*, 9 January 1647/8, in favour of the Vote of No Addresses. *thundering*: *thundring* '1648' and *1664*.

432 *hand-wolves*: *O.E.D.* quotes Beaumont and Fletcher, *Maid's Tragedy*, IV. i, 'Though I am tame . . . I may leap, Like a hand-wolf [i.e. a wolf brought up by hand] into my natural wildness'.

436 *these '1648'*: *those 1664*.

437–8 Judges xv. 4–5.

450 *Toil*: *O.E.D.* '*sb.*² . . . 1. A net . . . set so as to enclose a space into which the quarry is driven . . . .'

485–6 Cf. 14–15 and note.

490–506 F. F. Madan, in *A New Bibliography of the Eikon Basilike* (Oxford Bibliographical Society Publications, N.S. iii, 1950), Appendix I, on the authorship of the *Eikon Basilike*, says: 'Doubts as to the authenticity of the *Eikon* followed closely on its first publication. . . . The Royalists were inclined to regard doubt as sacrilege.' The question was not seriously presented to royalist minds until Gauden made his claim to be the author in 1660, but King's parenthesis, 499–502, may seem to 'protest too much'. *the Best of Thine Alive*: Charles II.

519–20 1 Kings xvi. 9–10; and 2 Kings ix. 30–31, 'Jezebel . . . said Had Zimri peace, who slew his master?'

An Elegy occasioned by the losse of the . . . Lady Stanhope (p. 132)

Anne, Lady Stanhope, was the third daughter of Algernon Percy, tenth Earl of Northumberland and King's patron at Petworth (pp. 18, 20). She died 29 November 1654, within a few days of her twenty-first birthday, and was buried at Petworth. The 'bright Northumberland', whose death King had spoken of earlier in his Elegy on Lady Rich, was her mother; she is mentioned again here, 33.

Text: *1657*.

2 *trace*: *O.E.D. v.*¹, III. 9, 'To mark, make marks upon'.

29, 35 *Of these part . . . The rest*: our tears, 25.

30 *fail*: *O.E.D.* gives 'Death. *Obs. rare*', and quotes *Henry VIII*, I. ii. 145.

37–38 The same image of the mourner as a following traveller is in 'The Exequy', 89–104 (p. 71); there by sea, in this poem by road. *O.E.D.* gives an obsolete transitive verb *post*: 'II. †4 . . . To . . . hasten, hurry (a person)'.

An Elegy Upon . . . L[ady] K[atherine]
C[holmondeley] (p. 133)

She died at Cholmondeley, 15 June 1657, and was buried at Malpas, 3 July.

Text: *1664*, and *H*, where it was added by a third hand; see Introduction, p. 49.

Variants:

Title: An Elegy on the right Honourable and my Worthyest Freind the Lady Katherine Countesse of Leinst'r. *H.*

15–18 *omitted H*　　40 your] the *H*　　43 Crosses] Sorrowes *H.*

1–8 This was the eighteenth poem of its kind that King had written.

23 *long wish'd End*: cf. 'An Exequy' (1624), loc. cit.

32–33 *Rest) . . . mischance, 1664: Rest, . . . mischance)* *H.*

35 *And flinging from mee my, now loathed Pen H*: Dr. Simpson drew attention to this 'delicate example of seventeenth-century punctuation', *Bodleian Quarterly Record,* v, 1926–9, p. 326.

The Woes of Esay (p. 136)

An expanded paraphrase of Isaiah v. 8–30; in particular, the fourteen lines on 'pretended Witt' (61–74) represent a single verse of the original. There are changes in order, so that the defiance in verse 19, 'Let him make speed, and hasten his work, that we may see it', is in King's poem immediately followed by the prophecy of retribution, verse 26, 'He will lift up an ensign to the nations from far, and will hiss unto them from the end of the earth.' In l. 99, King's version calls attention to Signs as already present. There may here be an allusion to such portents of dissolution as were generally noticed by his contemporaries, among them Donne ('The first Anniversary', 1612, ll. 377–98), King's friend Henry Reynolds[1] (who in *Mythomystes* [1632] wrote that the world 'seemes bed-rid, as upon her deathbed, and neere the time of her dissolution'), and Bishop Godfrey Goodman (*The Fall of Man*, 1616; cf. Hope Mirrlees, *A Fly in Amber*, 1962, pp. 132–5). Or, if particular 'signs' were intended, they may have been those exceptionally numerous portents observed by J. B. Ricciolus in 1618, when 'praeter Trabes igneas, & Dracones volantes', there had appeared 'Cometae tres aut quatuor' (*Almagestum Novum*, 1653, VIII. i. 3).

Associated in *MSS.* with occasional poems of 1612–24.

Text: H, M, P, *1657*, TM.

Variants:

11 Countryes] cities *TM*   16 a Tombe] their Tombe *MSS*.   19 that] who *TM*   32 sad] harsh *TM*   33 which] that *MSS*. 83 must] might *TM*   98 too] so *TM*   99 like] his *TM*   110 upp, on] upon *TM*, H *before correction*, M, P *before correction*.

43 *Good*: the scribe of *M* started to write *good* and corrected himself to *Good*: *P* reads *good*.

60 Deuteronomy xxxii. 32, 'their grapes are grapes of gall, their clusters are bitter'.

69 *imp*: the *O.E.D.* quotes the use of 'imp' here as a 'misunderstanding of the hawking term'. King wrongly uses it for 'clip'.

90 *It* corrected from *it TM* and *H*.

97 *revolting*: Mr. Sparrow emended to *revolving*, 'the "hand" is the revolving hand of a clock'; *revolting* is possible, as recorded from Golding's Ovid

---

[1] Cf. 'A Blackmore Mayd' and note.

in *O.E.D.* I. †4, 'Shee . . . then reuolted too the place in which he had her found', *Met.* x. 68.

98 *TM*'s reading *so* for *too* is probably an error.

107 *rapt*: *O.E.D.* gives, I. 1, 'As *p.pple.* passive. Taken and carried up *to* or *into* heaven . . .' e.g. 1610 Guillim, *Heraldry*, III. ii (1660), 99, 'To this place . . . were Enoch, Elias and Paul rapt up before their deaths'.

110 *upp, on*: see Introduction, p. 51.

An Essay on Death and a Prison (p. 139)

Associated in *MSS.* with occasional poems of 1612–24.

Text: H, M, P, *1657*; also in *TM*, and again copied by Thomas Manne on a single sheet which is now fol. 160 of British Museum Add. MS. 27408.

Variants:

   5 shee] it th' *TM*   33 if they were like] were they like to *TM*
67 seduction] seducing *TM*.

4 *shee' was*: so written in all three *MSS.* H has also, at 30 of this poem, *to' afflict*; in 'The Woes of Esay', 113, *the' affrighted*; and in 'To his unconstant Freind', 51, *the' enamour'd*. This probably reflects King's own practice in marking elision.

50 Monarchy? *1657*: *MSS.* have full stop.

65–68 A much compressed reference to the story of the Fall. Cf. the opening of *Paradise Lost*:

the Fruit
Of that Forbidd'n Tree, whose mortal tast
Brought Death into the World, and all our woe.

King's lines are made obscure by the possibly misleading juxtaposition of the separate persons, the Mother (Sin) and the Wife (Eve), and by his construction in 66, where the two phrases are parallel, referring to *Grief*, though the second looks like an appendage (qualifying *tast*) of the first.

70 *revert*] returne P.

76 *Th'Assurance* corrected from *The Assurance* M; cf. note on line 4 above. The word is used in its legal sense, *O.E.D.* '4, The securing of a title to property', here, a title to sorrow.

To his unconstant Freind (p. 142)

Associated in *MSS.* with occasional poems of 1612–24.

Text: H, M, P, *1657*, and *TM*.

Variants:

16 do perish *1657*: had perish't *MSS.*   44 or] nor *TM*   59 wild]
some *TM.*

5 line omitted Malone's copy of *1664.*

7 *Bannes H*: *Bañes M*: *Banes P, 1657.* The sign for omitted *n* was interpreted
in *H*, copied in *M*, and disregarded, not being understood, in *P* and *1657.*

35 No new paragraph, *MSS.* and *1657.*

50 *wearing*: *O.E.D.* gives for the verb *wear*, used transitively, a meaning
(10) 'to fatigue, weary'; the nearest to King's intransitive use is (13) 'Of
persons . . . To lose strength, vitality . . . by the decay of time'.

55 *silent shades, and Myrtle walkes*: cf. *Aeneid* vi. 440 et seq.

60 *the*] *thy P.*

73 *One* corrected from *one M.*

Madam Gabrina, Or the Ill-favourd Choice
(p. 144)

Saintsbury translated the motto:

> If a bad woman once has fix'd you,
> Put a mile of ground betwixt you.

Associated in *MSS.* with occasional poems of 1612–24.

Text: *H, M, P, 1657.* A different version in Bodleian MS. Ashmole 38 was
probably written down from an imperfect memory.

Variants:

Title: *motto only, H, M*: Madam Gabrina, Or the Ill-favour'd Choice
added, P.

18 on] in *H before correction, M before correction*   21 a] the *H*
25 their *M corrected*: the *H, M before correction, P, 1657*   33 drawst]
drawes *H*   41 this] thy *H before correction, M before correction.*

3 *the*: *his P.*

4 *slumbering*: *slumb'ring M, slumbring P.*

8 *Canidia,* the witch, subject of Horace's lampoons, Epodes xv and xvii.

18 Stow's *Survay of London,* 1598, mentions 'Bridgestreete, commonly
called (of the Fishmarket) New Fishstreete' (p. 167). During times
appointed for fasting there had to be more fish.

19 Dekker has the same pun on the Rose Theatre in *Satiromastix* (1601):
'th'ast a breath as sweet as the Rose, that growes by the Beare-garden',
Dramatic Works of T. Dekker, ed. Fredson Bowers, i, 1953, p. 343.

21 *A Fox*: Mason quotes William Bullein, who in *Bulleins Bulwarke of Defence against all Sicknesse*, 1579, says 'All the parts of the Foxe . . . are good . . . agaynste the Palsey' (fol. 76ᵛ).

25 *their*: the correction in *M* looks like King's own.

37–38 Capitals of *H*, where Manne has corrected *rest* to *Rest*.

The Defence (p. 145)

Saintsbury translated the motto:

> For it is still the lover's mind
> That all, except himself, are blind.

Associated in *MSS.* with occasional poems of 1612–24.

Text: *H*, *M*, *P*, *1657*; also printed in *The Academy of Complements*, 1650[1] (*Acad. Comp.*), *Parnassus Biceps*, 1656 (*Parn. Bic.*), and in *Poems by Pembroke and Ruddier*, edited by the younger John Donne, 1660 (*PR*). It is in many manuscript miscellanies; and in John Gamble's book of songs, New York Public Library MS. Drexel 4257, there is an anonymous setting of 24 lines (three verses, 1–8, 11–18, and, including an extra phrase, 19–28 omitting 25).[2] This poem was more often copied than the lines it is supposed to answer. The three printed versions may show a process of development: *Acad. Comp.* lacks the opening lines to connect it to 'Madam Gabrina'; *PR* has a connecting paragraph, but not the usual one, and shares readings with *Acad. Comp.*; *Parn. Bic.* has the same opening as the authoritative *MSS.* and *1657*, but still retains some readings of *Acad. Comp.* and *PR*. The manuscript miscellanies usually agree with *PR* or *Parn. Bic.*

Variants:

Title: motto only, *H*, *M*: The Defence *added P*.

1–10 *omitted Acad. Comp.*   6 African] Indian *PR*   7–8 *omitted PR*
9 For] Yet *PR*   11 But 'tis not . . . or] It is not . . . nor *Acad. Comp.*, *PR*: 'Tis not the . . . *Parn. Bic.*   13 is my liking] are my passions *Acad. Comp.*: is my fancy *PR*, *Parn. Bic.*   15 grow on] be of *Acad. Comp.*, *PR*   17 stalk] stock *Acad. Comp.*, *PR*   19 look] search *Acad. Comp.*, *PR*   20 A richer Beauty] Far richer treasure *Acad. Comp.*: A richer treasure *PR*   22 As Time, or Age cannot] That age nor art can it *Acad. Comp.*: That Art nor Age can it *PR*: As time and

---

[1] But not in the 'seventh edition', 1646, which had three of King's poems, all of which were again printed (with minor corrections) in 1650.

[2] The same setting is in MS. Drexel 4041 subscribed 'A'. Professor Vincent Duckles in his doctoral dissertation on Gamble's book suggested that the composer might be John Atkins, who died in 1673.

age cannot *Parn. Bic.*   24 Thou couldst behold] That thou couldst view *Acad. Comp.*, PR, *Parn. Bic.*   26 They'ld force thee to] Thouldst (or Thoult) wonder, and *Acad. Comp.*, *Parn. Bic.*: Then wonder and *PR*.

3 *forme*: *O.E.D.* gives *form* (I. I. †e), 'Beauty, comeliness', in use 1632; or there may here be a claim that the lover perceives the philosophical *form*, *O.E.D.* I. 4. a, 'The essential determinant principle . . . the essential creative quality'.

23 *Perspective*: Spy-glass.

The Surrender (p. 146)

Associated in *MSS.* with occasional poems of 1612–24.

Text: H, M, P, *1657*; other manuscript copies in *TM*, *Add.*, and British Museum MS. Sloane 1446 (*Slo.*).

Variants:

   Title: An Elegy. H, M: The Surrender. An Elegy. P.

   12 and] in *Slo.*, *Add.*   13 Yet *1657*: But *MSS.*: *omitted Add.*   cleere] strict *Slo.*   which] that *Slo.*, *Add.*, *TM*, H   18 Mayden-faith] virgin faith *Slo.*   23 Since then] But since *Slo.*   29 take] send *Slo.*, *Add.* 30 That] Wee *Slo.*   32 Unwinde . . . knitt] Unweave . . . wound *Add.*: Unwinde . . . made *TM*   a Love] our Loves *TM*, *Slo.*, *Add.* 33 here] must *TM*.

14 *that*: altered in P to *which*.

34 *Thyself. Lo*] *thyself, so 1657*, probably a mistake due to confusion of long *ʃ* and L.

Sonnet 'Dry those faire, those Christall eyes' (p. 147)

Set to music by John Wilson in Bodleian MS. Mus. b. I. Associated in *MSS.* with occasional poems of 1612–24.

Text: H, M, P, *1657*; printed in *Poems by Pembroke and Ruddier, 1660* (*PR*).

Variants:

   4 in] from *PR*   6 Shoare] Seat *PR*   8 Which] That *MSS.*, *PR* 11 the] thy *PR*.

Sonnet 'When I entreat' (p. 148)

Set to music by John Wilson in Bodleian MS. Mus. b. I. Associated in *MSS.* with occasional poems of 1612–24.

Text: H, M, P, *1657*, and B.M. MS. Sloane 1446 (*Slo.*).

Variants:

6 tis eavening still with me though't be but noone. *Slo.*   12 by sor-
rowe wilt or age be soone benighted. *Slo.*

Sic Vita (p. 148)

Associated in *MSS*. with occasional poems of 1612–24.

Text: H, M, P, *1657*; also in *TM* and B.M. MS. Sloane 1446 (*Slo.*), and
printed in *Poems by Francis Beaumont*, 1640 (see Appendix III, p. 254).

Variants:

11 Dew dryes *M corrected, P corrected, 1657*: Dew Dry'd *TM, Slo.*, H,
P *before correction*: Dew's dry'd *M before correction, Beaumont*.

Sonnet. 'I prethee turne that face away' (p. 149)

Set to music by John Wilson and printed in *Select Ayres and Dialogues*,
1659.
Associated in *MSS*. with occasional poems of 1612–24.

Text: H, M, P, *1657*; and printed in *Wits Recreations*, 1641 (*WR*).

Variants:

9 Whome thy feirce] For your bright *WR*   10 Sooty Indian]
Indian sootie *WR*.

Sonnet. 'Tell me you Starrs that our affections move' (p. 149)

Set by John Wilson, in Bodleian MS. Mus. b. 1; and more elaborately
by Walter Porter, to music for two voices and bass, with an introductory
'sinfonia' (printed in his *Madrigales and Ayres*, 1632). Walter Porter was
Wilson's kinsman: he addressed him, in a dedicatory letter in *Mottets of
Two Voyces*, 1657 (Bodl. Mus. Sch. D. 349), as 'my loveing Cous'.
Associated in *MSS*. with occasional poems of 1612–24.

Text: H, M, P, *1657*, and *Slo.*; printed in John Cotgrave's *Wits Interpreter*,
1655 (*WI*).

Variants:

2 yee] you *Slo., WI*   that] this *Slo.*   4 breast is] breasts as *Slo., WI*
5 Desire] desires *Slo.*   7 for] of *Slo.*   9 or give] give to *Slo., WI*
10 yet unthaw'd, does on] I suppose doth in *Slo., WI*.

The Farwell (p. 150)

John Sparrow in his note on this poem (pp. 159–60) says that 'the Sapphic line which serves as a motto is also appended to Sidney's sonnet "Leave me O love" and does not seem to occur elsewhere'. The line is not of classical origin. He explains the likeness between King's poem and one of uncertain authorship, 'Farewell ye gilded Follies', by supposing both to be in part translations of a lost Latin poem, of which this was the first line. The last verse of King's poem occurs, quite inappropriately, appended to 'Hence all you vain delights', from Fletcher's *Nice Valour*, in two copies by different hands in Bodl. MS. Rawl. poet. 84, fols. 40 rev. and 66 rev.

Associated in *MSS.* with occasional poems of 1612–24.

Text: H, M, P, *1657*; the last four lines only remain of the copy that was in *TM*.

Variants:

Title: *motto only*, H.

4–6　　　　To dote on those that lov'd not, and to fly
　　　　　　Love that woo'd me. Go bane of my content,
　　　　　　And practise *MSS.*

21 My lasting *1657*: And for an *TM, MSS.*　　　22 Thus when sad Lovers *1657*: Eternally: if any *TM, MSS.*　　the weeping Stone *1657*: the Stone *TM, MSS.*　　23 Center *1657*: compasse *TM, MSS.*　　24 will *MSS., 1657*: shall *TM*.

8 *had: hath* P, in error.

A Blackmore Mayd wooing a faire Boy . . . by Mr. Hen. Rainolds and The Boy's answere (p. 151)

The originator of these poems was George Herbert: Rainolds's poem is a translation of his verses 'Aethiopissa ambit Cestum Diversi Coloris Virum', printed by F. E. Hutchinson in his edition of *The Works of Herbert*, 1941, p. 437, from *Ecclesiastes Solomonis. Auctore Joan. Viviano . . .*, &c., printed at Cambridge, 1662. Mason suggested that this Henry Rainolds was the same one to whom Drayton addressed an epistle; a discussion of the most likely Henry Reynolds is in *The Works of Michael Drayton*, edited by J. W. Hebel, K. Tillotson, and B. H. Newdigate, v, 1941, p. 216. The poems were set to music by Wilson and were printed in *Select Ayres and Dialogues*, 1669.

Associated in *MSS.* with occasional poems of 1612–24.

Text: H, M, P, *1657*; *Academy of Complements*, 1646 and 1650 (*Acad. Comp.*), *Parnassus Biceps*, 1656 (*Parn. Bic.*), and numerous manuscript miscellanies including B.M. MS. Sloane 1446 (*Slo.*); amongst these there is much variation, but also some agreement. In three readings *M* agrees with the miscellanies against H, P, and *1657*. Possibly King altered his friend's poem and his own before H was copied, and *M* here preserves an earlier text.

Variants:

Title: sent to . . . Hen. Rainolds *omitted MSS.*; *subscribed* Mr. Hen. Rainolds *MSS.*

1 Stay] Why *M, misc. MSS., Acad. Comp.*   4 does] doth *1657*   5 The whole World, doe] Nay [*or* Yea] do thou once *Acad. Comp., Slo.*   6 Will seeme to thee] The world will seem *Acad. Comp., Slo.*   7 see] view *M, misc. MSS., Parn. Bic.*   14 When] Since *M, misc. MSS., Parn. Bic., Acad. Comp.*: some *Slo.*   15 might] must *misc. MSS., Parn. Bic.*: would *Acad. Comp., Slo.*   21 Yet if my Shadow Thou wilt] But if thou wilt my shadow *Acad. Comp., Slo.*   23 take] keep *misc. MSS., Parn. Bic., Acad. Comp.*   24 That hasts] And flee *some misc. MSS., Parn. Bic.*: That flies *other misc. MSS. including Slo., Acad. Comp.*   26 And then I will] And I'll *misc. MSS., Parn. Bic.*: Then I'le *Acad. Comp.*

5 *doe* added above the line in both H and P (probably by King in H).

A Letter (p. 152)

Associated in *MSS.* with occasional poems of 1612–24.

Text: H, M, P, *1657*; also in *Harl.* and B.M. MS. Sloane 1446.

8 *my owne Fate*: P substitutes *of my Fate*.

18 *can* omitted by Manne, written in by King, H.

20–21 The *MSS.* and *1657* disagree over punctuation, giving full stop or colon after *Acquaintance*, full stop (H and P), semi-colon (*1657*), or comma (*M*), after *smiles*. The difficulty was to isolate the parenthesis *Like such . . . smiles*, without breaking the continuity of the main sentence.

23 *Test*: O.E.D. 2b, *proof*; the worth of King's friendship being proved by his reticence and independence.

45 *by Reflexe*, i.e. by reflection of his Friend, King is *to appear . . .* , &c.

49 *opinion*: cf. 'Epitaph on Richard Earle of Dorset', 19, 'One high in faire opinion'.

71 *Observer*: O.E.D. gives an obsolete meaning, 'One who shows respect, deference . . .'.

Presentation Poems: 'Upon a Table-book . . .', '. . . Upon Overburye's Wife', '. . . Upon Mr. Burton's Melancholy', 'To a Freind . . .', 'To A.R. . . .' (pp. 154–5)

These short poems, with an early version of the verse on 'why Wine sparkles' (cf. p. 243 below), the 'Epitaph on Niobe turn'd to stone', and the verses on 'a Braid of Haire in a Heart', are placed in the manuscripts next after the distinct group of twenty early poems (see p. 52 above).

There was confusion over the titles of these verses. *H* and *1657* agree that the Table-book and *The Anatomy of Melancholy* were given to one person, who in *H* is called 'a Noble Lady'. In *M* the two-line epigram on *A Wife* is for the same lady as the Table-book; in *P* it is for the same lady as the *Anatomy*.

Text: *H, M, P, 1657.*

Variants:

Upon a Table-book . . . a Lady] *Title*: Upon a Table-book . . . a Noble Lady *H*.

To the same Lady Upon Overburye's Wife] *Not in H. Title*: Upon the same *1657, where it follows* To a Freind upon Overburie's Wife.

To the same Lady Upon Mr. Burton's Melancholy] *Title*: To a Lady Upon . . . *M, P*.   6 Then e're] Before *H*.

To A.R. upon the same] To A.R. in eandem *MSS*.

'Upon a Table-book': cf. a commendatory poem by Richard West on Randolph's poems, 1638:

> Their Braines lye all in Notes; Lord! how they'd looke
> If they should chance to loose their Table-book!

Jasper Mayne wrote a poem on 'Mrs. Anne King's Table Book of Pictures'.

Overburye's Wife: *A Wife Now The Widdow*, by Thomas Overbury, 1614.

'To the same Lady Upon . . . Melancholy', 6, *Then*: *There P*, a misreading which could have been due to an indistinct correction from *Before* to *Then ere* in the original.

To A.R. upon the same: Hannah suggested that *A.R.* was Lady Anne Rich, later the subject of an elegy by King. If so, these lines were written after 9 April 1632, the date of her marriage.

Upon a Braid of Haire in a Heart sent by Mris. E. H. (p. 155)

Saintsbury suggested that Mris. E. H. was possibly King's sister,

Mrs. Elizabeth Holt (see Introduction, p. 13, and 'An Elegy upon the death of Mr. Edward Holt' and note). Elizabeth was probably married about 1624. For the date of these lines cf. note on Presentation Poems, p. 228.

Text: H, M, P, *1657*.

Variant:

5 Think] know *M*, *probably in error* (cf. 3).

An Epitaph on Niobe turn'd to Stone (p. 156)

See note on Presentation Poems, p. 228.

Text: H, M, P, *1657*, British Museum MS. Sloane 1446.

Epigrams (pp. 156–7)

Text: H, M, P.

Quid faciant Leges ubi sola pecunia regnat? . . . Petronius Arbiter, *Saturæ*, xiv. 2.

Casta suo gladium cum traderet Arria Pæto. . . . Martial, I. xiii.

Pro captu lectoris habent sua fata libelli. . . . Terentianus Maurus, 1286. *Not in H.*

Qui Pelago credit, magno se fænore tollit. . . . Petronius, op. cit. lxxxiii. 10.

Nolo quod cupio statim tenere. . . . Petronius, op. cit. xv. 9.

My Midd-night Meditation (p. 157)

This poem was sometimes ascribed to Henry King's brother John. In British Museum Add. MS. 25303 a copy of it is followed by a monogram of the initials *H* and *K*, written with a flourish on the left stroke of the *H* capable of causing the misreading *I* or *J*. British Museum Add. MS. 21433 is a contemporary transcript of Add. 25303, and here the monogram is expanded to 'J:K:'; but sometimes the mistake may have been due merely to confusion between the two brothers. This was one of the best-liked of King's poems in his own time; and it appeared in print, with the 'Penitentiall Hymne', as late as 1705, in *Miscellanea Sacra*, headed (as it often was in manuscript miscellanies) 'Man's Misery, written by Bp. King'. (I owe this reference to Mr. D. G. Neill.)

Inserted amongst the 1612–24 group in *M*; copied after Presentation Poems, *H* and *P*.

Text: H, M, P, *1657*; printed in *The Harmony of the Muses*, 1654, and *Parnassus Biceps*, 1656.

Variant:

11 which *1657*: that *MSS*.

3 *e'ry*: spelt so in *MSS.*, *1657*, and *Miscellanea Sacra*, 1705.

Sonnet. '*Tell mee no more how faire shee is*' (p. 158)

Set to music by John Wilson in Bodleian MS. Mus. b. 1. In Bodl. MS. Rawl. poet. 65 the poem occurs with the name of the composer 'Jer. Savill', but I have not found his setting. Inserted amongst the 1612–24 group in *M*; copied after Presentation Poems, *H* and *P*.

Text: H, M, P, *1657*: and in *Add.* and B.M. MS. Sloane 1446.

Variants:

2 have no minde] doe not care *Add.*   7 mee not] not mee *Add.*

Sonnet. '*Were thy heart soft*' (p. 158)

Set to music by John Wilson in Bodleian MS. Mus. b. 1.

This sonnet is not in *H*, but after a group of twenty poems at the beginning (see Introduction, p. 52), Manne left one blank page, which might have been intended to divide a collection of early verse from the rest, but is more likely to have been kept for this poem. If it had been copied on the blank page, it would have been next to the verses 'To his Freinds of Christchurch', as it is in *P*, and close to some of the same poems that are near it in *M*. This seems to be its proper place in the chronological sequence.

Text: M, P, *1657*.

Variant:

9 O Heavens,] You Gods *M, P*.

Silence. A Sonnet (p. 159)

Copied near the 'Anniversary' (1629/30) *H*; amongst occasional poems of 1630–33 *M* and *P*.

Text: H, M, P, *1657*.

Variants:

Title: Sonnet H, M: A Sonnet P; Silence *added above*.

11 *I'le* corrected from *I'de* by Manne, H.

Sonnet. To Patience (p. 160)

Associated with occasional poems of 1630–3 in *MSS*.

Text: H, M, P, *1657*, and *Harl.*

Variants:
  Title: Sonnet H: To Patience M.
  6 or] and *Harl.*

The Vow-Breaker (p. 160)

Associated in *MSS*. with occasional poems of 1630–3.

Text: H, M, P, *1657*; printed in *Parnassus Biceps, 1656.*

Variant:
  Title: Sonnet H; The Vow-Breaker *added by King.*
  23 (*I feare*) *1657*:, I feare, H; (I feare *M, P, both omitting closing bracket.*

A Penitentiall Hymne (p. 161)

The 'Hymne' was set to music by John Wilson, and appears to have been sung as an anthem in the Chapel Royal: it is a contemporary addition in Bodl. MS. Rawl. poet. 23, a royal anthem book of which British Museum MS. Harl. 6346 is a Restoration copy. MS. Rawl. poet. 23 is dated by a list at the end headed 'The King's Chaplains in ordinarie attendance. 1635', revised in 1636. The name of Dr. King appears for January. John Wilson became one of the King's musicians in 1635.[1] The 'Hymne' was included with the other anthems from this collection in James Clifford's *The Divine Services and Anthems*, 1663, and again in *Miscellanea Sacra*, 1705.[2] Only the words are given, and Wilson's music seems not to have survived.

Associated in *MSS*. with occasional poems of 1630–3; cf. Introduction, p. 52 n.

Text: H, M, P, *1657*; printed, after a little revision, by King in *The Psalmes of David*, second ed., 1654 (*1654*). Manne wrote the 'Hymne' on a blank unnumbered page at the beginning of *H*, at a time later than the copies with which he first began, as the comparative shakiness of his hand shows.

Variants:
  7 Justice *1654*: rigour *MSS.*, *1657*   24 grow . . . in *1654*: turne . . . with *MSS.*, *1657*   27 thine *1654*: thy *MSS.*, *1657*.

---

[1] *Grove's Dictionary of Music and Musicians*, 5th ed., 1954, article on Wilson by G. E. P. Arkwright; and H. C. de Lafontaine, *The King's Musick*, 1909, p. 91.
[2] I owe this reference to Mr. D. G. Neill.

8 *can nor* H, P, corrected in both from *can not*; *cannot Miscellanea Sacra*.

14 *lav'd* corrected from *lov'd* H; *lov'd Miscellanea Sacra*.

15 *Side* M, corrected from *side*.

19 *lather*: James Clifford reads *Laver*, which is better: *O.E.D.* 2 '*trans.* and *fig.* . . . any spiritually cleansing agency'.

21 *Gilead's balme*: Jeremiah viii. 22: 'Is there no balm in Gilead; is there no physician there? why then is not . . . health . . . recovered?'

23 *His* H, corrected from *his*.

24 Cf. Isaiah i. 18 and Donne, *Holy Sonnets*, 1633, ii, 'Oh my blacke Soule', 13–14:

> Or wash thee in Christs blood, which hath this might
> That being red, it dyes red soules to white.

Sonnet. 'Goe Thou, that vainly dost mine eyes invite' (p. 162)

Set to music by John Wilson in Bodl. MS. Mus. b. 1.
Associated in *MSS.* with occasional poems of 1630–3.

Text: H, M, P, *1657*.

Variants:
  1 mine] my H   8 that] my H   9 which] that *MSS.*

The Departure (p. 163)

The occasion of this poem and 'An Acknowledgement' was the departure to the west country ('Departure', 35, 'Acknowledgement', 36) of some 'best of Friends'. Associated in *MSS.* with occasional poems of 1630–3.

Text: H, M, P, *1657*, and *Harl.*

Variants:
  Title: An Elegy. H, M, *Harl.*, P *originally*: The Departure *added in P.*
  6 largest] larger H   42 on] in H *before correction*   45 your] the M
53 this] the H.

47 John Sparrow and Saintsbury felt that this irregular line had to be emended, but the extra syllables are light and may be absorbed into the first and fifth 'feet':

> Tis the last / service / I would / do You / and the best.

An Acknowledgment (p. 164)

Text: H, M, P, *1657*, and *Harl*.

15 *skoare*: figurative, from the obsolete 'A notch cut in a stick or tally, used to mark numbers in keeping accounts, also the tally itself', *O.E.D.*

20 *wrott*: a normal form, recorded in *O.E.D.*

23 *cleare*: misread by the scribe of *P* as *deare*. The open bow and looped ascender of King's *d* were particularly liable to confusion with *cl*.

28 *makes* for *wakes P*, in error.

34–36 *Ecliptick Line ... Westerne Tropick*: the *Ecliptick line* is 'The great circle of the celestial sphere which is the apparent orbit of the sun. So called because eclipses can happen only when the moon is on or very near this line', *O.E.D.*; *Tropick*: 'Each of two solstitial points, the most northerly and southerly points of the ecliptic, at which the sun reaches his greatest distance north or south of the equator, and "turns" or begins to move towards it again' (*O.E.D.* I. 1 †a), or 'Each of two circles of the celestial sphere ... touching the ecliptic at the solstitial points' (I. 1b). King's treatment of astronomical imagery here is inexact, or of partial application only, but though to *move* on the *Ecliptick line* would in reality be to regain light, and the *Tropicks* are those parts of the sky in which the sun is never seen, there is given a perfectly clear picture of this universe whose poles are east and west, and in which he is enduring the winter solstice. The simplicity with which the inappropriate aspects of the comparison have been ignored by the poet makes it a bad example of wit of Donne's kind, for which George Williamson praised it (*The Donne Tradition*, 1930, p. 144; cf. R. Tuve, *Elizabethan and Metaphysical Imagery*, 1947, p. 363).

42 *Road*: a continuation of the sea-image.

To my Sister Anne King ... (p. 166)

This is copied in *MSS.* near 'Upon the King's happy Returne', 1633, and with the six poems which follow. For Anne, Henry King's youngest sister, see Introduction, pp. 20–23. She was not married until 1648 or 1649.

Text: H, M, P, *1657*.

4 In *H* and *P* a stop was erased after *bought*.

8 *Weare* corrected from *were M*, possibly by King. *misperfection* for *imperfection*, *1657*.

The Pink (p. 167)

In the list of *errata* in *1657* is the statement 'The Pink never wrote by the Author of these Poems'; but its presence in *MSS.*, with King's added title in *H*, shows that this was a mistake. Associated in *MSS.* with the poem on the king's return, 1633.

Text: *H*, *M*, *P*, *1657*, and in *Harl.* amongst King's poems, subscribed 'H. King'.

Variant:
   Title: Sonnet *H*; The Pink *added by King above*.

4 *durst*: *P* reads *should*, a correction over an erasure.

7 Punctuation of *H*, corrected, and *1657*: no commas before correction in *H*, none in *M* and *P*.

19 *Aire*: *she*, *1657*, corrected in Errata.

Sonnet. The Double Rock (p. 167)

Set to music by John Wilson in MS. Mus. b. 1.
Associated in *MSS.* with the poem on the king's return, 1633.

Text: *H*, *M*, *P*, *1657*.

Variant:
   Title: Sonnet *H*; The Double Rock *added by King above*: The Double Rock *M*.

5 *may*: written by King over erasure, *H*, formerly *will* (?).

6 *Chimistry*: *Chymestry* altered by King to *Chymistry H*.

8 Colon added, probably by King, *H*: full stop *M*: semi-colon *1657*: comma *P*.

9 *soe*: written by King over erasure, *H*, formerly *then* (?).

The Retreit (p. 168)

Associated in *MSS.* with the poem on the king's return, 1633.

Text: *H*, *M*, *P*, *1657*; manuscript copies in *Add.* and British Museum Add. MS. 23229 (*A23*) have different versions of lines 9 and 10; in these places King himself made erasures and corrections in *H*. Printed in *The Academy of Complements*, 1646 and 1650.

Variants:

Title: Sonnet *H*; The Retreit *added above by King.*

8 which] that *A23*   your] the *Add.*   9 Loe! ⟨th⟩us] *written by King over erasure H*: Here then *H before correction, Add., A23*   10 False to Thy Vowe, and Traitour to] Thy Vowe and Traitour to *written by King over erasure, H*: as false to (dearer then thy bedd) *Add.*: False to what's dearer then thy bed *A23, probably H before correction*   13 shalt thou ever] ever shalt thou *MSS., Add., A23.*

9 *Divorce* corrected from *divorce H.*

The Forlorne Hope (p. 168)

Associated in *MSS.* with the poem on the king's return, 1633.

Text: *H, M, P, 1657.*

Variants:

9 They] Those *H*   10 illusion] Illusions *H*   14 can] will *H.*
1 Brackets added, *H.*
8 *Bury* corrected from *bury H*, possibly by King: *M* reads *bury.*

Love's Harvest (p. 169)

Associated in *MSS.* with the poem on the king's return, 1633.

Text: *H, M, P, 1657*; an early form is in British Museum MS. Add. 23229 (*A23*). Printed in *The Academy of Complements*, 1646 and 1650 (*Acad. Comp.*). King's own corrections in *H* leave this earlier version visible in line 12. The final version of lines 11–12 was not decided upon until after *P* was copied, and is found only in *1657.*

Variants:

2 is] bee *A23*   9 He that Abortive Corne cutts off his] Whoe cutts abortive Corne, from of yᵉ ground *A23*   11 So those . . . reap their Love . . . they] So he . . . Reapes his Love . . . he *MSS., A23*   12 Do in effect but Cuckold their] Whores a chaste wife, and Cuckolds his *H before correction, A23, Acad. Comp.*: Doth in effect but Cuckold his *H corrected*: Does in effect but Cuckold his *M, P.*

3 *use*: usury.

10 *Husband*, punctuation of *P* and *1657.*

12 *effect*: the copyist of *M* made a mistake in this word, perhaps because he was following a corrected, and no longer clear, copy.

Being waked out of my Sleep by a Snuff of Candle ...
(p. 169)

Associated in *MSS.* with the poem on the king's return, 1633.

Text: H, M, P, *1657.*

11–13 *Lamps* ... *sickly 'gin to wink*: John Sparrow noted the echo of Donne, 'The Apparition', 6, 'thy sicke taper will begin to winke'.

The Legacy (p. 170)

'The Legacy', with four other poems, the Elegy on Bishop John King, 'The Labyrinth', the Elegy 'occasioned by Sicknesse', and 'The Dirge', was copied near occasional poems of 1636–8 in *MSS.* For the biographical implications of this poem, see Appendix I, p. 247.

Text: H, M, P, *1657.* This was the first poem copied by the scribe of *M* at the end of *H* (see Introduction, p. 49). The differences between *H* and *M* after this are very few.

7 *Thine,*] *Thine*; H and *M*.

19 *Mortalitye*: final *e* added, H.

42 *Shouldst*: *Should M*.

50 *Moniment*: the *i* is a correction in H.

58 *Alive*: corrected from *alive* H.

An Elegy upon the Bishopp of London John King
(p. 172)

Bishop John King died on Good Friday, 30 March 1621. There is nothing to contradict the impression given by the position of the Elegy in the manuscripts that it belongs to a later date. It was printed by Fuller in *The History of the Worthies of England,* 1662, sig. T2ᵛ (p. 132).

Associated in *MSS.* with occasional poems of 1636–8.

Text: H, M, P, *1657*, TM, *Add.*

Variants:
Title: the Bishopp] the Lord Bishop *1657.*

6 Thou] once H *before correction*, TM *before correction, Add.*   23 when] where *TM before correction.*

Note: in *M Thy* is spelt with a capital *T* throughout, but this tidiness is probably the scribe's; the less consistent readings of *H* give a variety of emphasis which was probably intended by King, and is reproduced here.

6 *Thou*: written over *once* erased, by Manne in *TM*, and probably by King in *H*.

8 *Resurgam*: 'He commanded in his Will, his body to be buried in the Cathedrall Church of S. Paul, without any Pompe or solemnities, onely with a Tombestone with this Inscription, Resurgam', note in Henry King's *Sermon* . . . *touching the supposed Apostasie of* . . . *Iohn King*, 1621, p. 71. Cf. Wren's *Parentalia*, 1750, p. 292, on an encouraging omen during the rebuilding of St. Paul's after the great fire: 'when the *Surveyor* [Christopher Wren] in Person had set out, upon the Place, the Dimensions of the great Dome, and fixed upon the Centre; a common Labourer was ordered to bring a flat Stone from the Heaps of Rubbish (such as should first come to Hand) to be laid for a Mark and Direction to the Masons'; on the stone was 'this single Word in large Capitals, *RESURGAM*'.

14 A reference to the descent claimed by the Bishop's children from the Saxon kings of Devonshire (see *Hannah*, pp. i–ii, xcii–xcvii, 176–7).

19 *Errata 1657*: 'Pag. 100. lin. 3. *for* Mattox *read* Mattocks.'

The Labyrinth (p. 173)

Associated in *MSS.* with occasional poems of 1636–8.

Text: H, M, P, *1657*, Harl.

Variants:

14 Wee scarce think what wee doe] We scarce think what to do *1657*: wee thinke not what to doe *Harl.*   39 O guide] guide thou *Harl.*

12 *her*: M reads *our*, in error.

14 *to do*, *1657* and *Harl.*, perhaps an error from *to advise*, *to act*, in the preceding line.

26 *thy*: P reads *the*, in error.

41 *which*, . . . *Day*, punctuation of *P*, where the commas were added.

An Elegy Occasioned by Sicknesse (p. 174)

Associated in *MSS.* with occasional poems of 1636–8.

Text: H, M, P, *1657*, *TM*, and Bodl. MS. Rawl. D. 398, fols. 168–9ᵛ (*Rawl.*), corrected by King. Most of the corrections in *Rawl.* deal with mistakes of the copyist, and are not recorded here. MS. Rawl. D. 398, with D. 317

and D. 399, are part of a miscellaneous collection of Hearne's which included papers formerly owned by Dr. John Fell. His father, Samuel Fell, was an intimate friend of Philip King, Henry's uncle, as appears from letters exchanged by them, now Bodl. MSS. Rawl. D. 397, fol. 260c, and Tanner 69, fol. 178. John Fell kept a number of King family papers, amongst which are drafts and copies of verses in Latin and English, including a sheet of Latin verses on a feversent from Henry whilst at Christ Church to his father. Also pr. *The Harmony of the Muses*, 1654 (*HM*).

Variants:
    81 which] that *TM, MSS., Rawl.*   95–108 *omitted HM.*

1 Psalms viii. 4 and cxliv. 3. In 'To . . . Mr. George Sandys', 67, King calls the psalmist 'the Prophet'.

9 *Bætis*: now Guadalquivir. The names of the same great rivers were brought together by Sir Richard Fanshawe in his poem 'On his Majesties Great Shippe . . . The Soveraigne of the Seas':

> For which the French Garoon, Nyle's sev'nfold streames
> The Spanish Betis, doe envy the Thames.

19–26 Cf. (for example) Godfrey Goodman, *The Fall of Man*, 1616, p. 72. 'Speaking of mans miseries, I will begin with mans first beginning or birth . . . conceived in sinne, and death is the wages of sinne . . . borne with the effusion of blood'; and *Purchas his Pilgrim*, 1619 (dedicated to Bishop John King), pp. 156, 161, 164, 'And what else is Generation, but from and to Corruption?' 'The Mother cryes with painefull Passion . . . and the Infant . . . he cryes too.' 'But proceed in further view of this new-come Guests welcome and entertainment into the World.' 'Man onely laments and salutes the World with Teares', &c.

33 *is his*: *is this 1657.*

36 *up to*: *unto P.*

51 *though*, . . . *Dew*, Commas were added in *H*, probably by King, and in *Rawl.* as well they look like his additions. John Sparrow emended *ropes* to *dropes*; but there is an acceptable figurative meaning of *ropes* quoted in *O.E.D.* 6 †c, 'A long series. *Obs.*' (cf. 'ropes of pearls').

53 *themes*: *O.E.D.* on *theme*: '1†b. A subject treated by action (instead of by discourse, etc.); hence, that which is the cause *of* or *for* specified action, circumstance, or feeling . . . *Obs.*'

62 *Repaires* corrected from *Repairs* by King, *Rawl.* Similarly in line 91 *maintain* was corrected to *maintaine*, and in *H*, line 75, *Anatomy* to *Anatomye*.

83 *Weelkes*: the spelling of all three *MSS.* An *l*, never pronounced, was in early Scotch forms, *O.E.D.*

84 Omitted by the copyist of *Rawl*. King wrote it in; his spelling is exactly reproduced in *H* and *M* except that he has *u* for *v* in *ravell'd*.

90 *Might*: *May P*.

94 The last line of a translation, most probably by Bacon, of an epigram in the Greek Anthology attributed to Posidippus. The English was printed in Thomas Farnaby's *Florilegium Epigrammatum Graecorum*, 1629, and in *Reliquiae Wottonianae*, 1651. Cf. Sir Herbert Grierson in *M.L.R.* vi, 1911, p. 145; the copy he describes among Wotton papers in MS. C.C.C. Oxford 318 is in the hand of the antiquary William Fulman (1632–88), but the connexion with Wotton is certainly genuine.

94/95 A line drawn across the page of *Rawl*. divides the poem at this place. A sense of falling here into serenity is partly due to echoes in 97 of phrases familiar to King from Donne's 'Hymne . . . at . . . going into Germany', 'In what torne ship soever I embarke', and the 'Hymne to God the Father':

> I have a sinne of feare, that when I have spunne
> My last thred, I shall perish on the shore.

106–7 The relevant part of the story of Gideon begins at Judges vii. 16.

The Dirge (p. 177)

Associated in *H* and *P* with occasional poems of 1636–8.

Text: H, P, *1657*, TM.

Variants:

8 Out-vyes in Rage] Vyes Rages with *H*   12 casts] cast *H*
26 The] His *H*

27–28   Whilst it demonstrates Times swift flight
             In the black Lines of Shady night *H*

28 stages] Motions *TM*   30 The] His *H*   35 with] in *H*, *TM*.

19–24 *moraliz'd*: cf. *O.E.D.*'s quotation from Drummond of Hawthornden, of an obsolete use of *Morality*: 'She presented . . . a fair Face, . . . but on the other Side . . . was the Image of Death; by which Morality he surpassed the others [other painters of the same subject], more then they did him by Art.' *Fam. Ep., Works* (1711), 140. *Age and Youth* (signifying the transience of youth) are a 'morality' of the elusive nature of happiness.

To a Lady who sent me a copy of verses at my going to bed (p. 178)

Text: P, *1657*; H and M have an earlier version of the first paragraph:

> Doubtlesse the Thespian Spring doth overflow
> His Learned bank: Else how should Ladyes grow
> Such Poëts? as to court th'unknowing time
> In verse, and entertaine their friends in Rhime.
> Or you some Sybill are, sent to unty
> The knotty Riddles of all Poetry;
> Whilst your smooth Numbers such perfections tell,
> As prove your self a Moderne Oracle.

Variants:
  Title: who] that H, M.
  11 is it then] then it is H, M.

The early version is among poems of the early sixteen-thirties in H and M. The second version seems to have superseded it before P was copied, but not till after H was finished; that is to say, it was probably rewritten during the early sixteen-forties.

The punctuation of lines 1, 2, 15, 18, and 20 is that of P.

The short Wooing (p. 179)

This poem and those following, with two possible exceptions (see p. 243), were written too late to be included in H and M.

Text: P, *1657*.

Variants:
  Title: The Wooing. P.
  8 retrayt, P: retreat. *1657*   24 must pronounce] comprehend P.

Paradox. That it is best for a Young Maid to marry an Old Man (p. 180)

The last line seems to date this poem 1644.

Text: P, *1657*.

Variants:
  8 brand, nor ember] brond, nor ember P: brand nor embers *1657*
  35–38 *omitted* P   47 Are not the floated Medowes ever] The floated Meadowes commonly are P   48 green?] greene: P   73 will] would P.

The punctuation of *P* has been preferred in lines 8, 14, 18, 24, 33, 42, 51, 60, 62, 67, and 71 to the conventional punctuation of *1657*.

33 *hold*: holds *1657*.

57 *Fontinells*: an obsolete medical term including 'a natural issue for the discharge of humours from the body', *O.E.D.* †2.

64 *Which* relates to *Love*.

69 *Erra Pater*: perhaps a specific reference to *A Prognostication for ever . . . by Erra Pater . . . very profitable to keepe the body in health*; but if so King had not himself 'turned' its pages.

Paradox. That Fruition destroyes Love (p. 182)

See note on 'The short Wooing' (p. 240) for date.

Text: P, *1657*, TM.

Variants:
  Title: Paradox.] The Paradoxe. *P*.

27 and] or *P*   67 the] this *P*   70 what] that *P, TM*   79 as] like *P, TM*   80 not for] more then *P, TM*   81–100 *omitted P, TM*
101 What tast is left, or Spirit to delight *P, TM*   103 that] which *P, TM*.

22 *dimme gelly*: cf. Donne, Epithalamion for the Earl of Somerset, 1613, 204–5:

> As he that sees a starre fall, runs apace,
> And findes a gellie in the place.

40 *wak't*: weak *1657*, in error; cf. 37.

81–100 These lines are found only in *1657*. A note in *P* after 80 reads 'Vid: Paper', but the loose sheet to which this must refer is lost. The lines were probably composed after the poem in its original state had been copied in *P*, and had therefore to be added on a separate sheet.

The Latine Epitaph . . . Translated (p. 186)

This translation, with 'The Change', 'St. Valentines Day', the revised 'To one demanding why Wine sparkles', and the Epigram on Hammond (1647/8), was copied in *P* after the change of hand (see Introduction, p. 50). The translation was added in a space after the Elegy on Bishop John King.

The Latin epitaph was hung near the tomb in St. Paul's, on a tablet with other verses, all of which are printed in Dugdale's *History of*

St. Paul's Cathedral, 1658, p. 73 (cf. Introduction, p. 19). There is a copy of the Latin epitaph in Henry King's hand in Bodl. MS. Rawl. D. 398, fol. 195; he may have composed it, but this can hardly be taken as evidence that he did. Dugdale's text is this:

> Non hic Pyramides; non sculpta Panegyris ambit
>   Hos cineres; lapidum nec pretiosa strues.
> Quod frugale magis, tibi te committimus unum:
>   Si jaceas aliter, vilior umbra fores.
> Nam tibi qui similis vivit, moriturque Sepulcrum
>   Ille sibi vivax, et sibi Marmor erit.
>
> SeqVntVr qVI nonDVM præCessere.

There is another English version, scribbled by the younger John King on a letter-cover addressed to himself 'at his chamber in Christes Church', in Bodl. MS. Rawl. D. 317, fol. 171:

> No Pyramis, nor carv'd toomb-complement
> Circles these ashes, noe nor preceous pile
> Thou art thine owne best toomb & lesse is spent.
> Hadst thou lyen deerer, thou hadst lyen more vile;
> For hee whose course & periode is like thine,
> Is to himself a long liv'd marble shrine.

For MSS. Rawl. D. 317 and 398, see note to 'An Elegy Occasioned by Sicknesse', pp. 237–8.

Text: *P*. First printed by John Sparrow.

The Change (p. 186)

Saintsbury translated the motto: 'The wise man changes consciously: the fool [or rather, madman] perseveres.' For date see note on 'The Latine Epitaph' (p. 241).

Text: *P, 1657*.

Variants:

21 the] your *P*   23 female] firme-vowd *P*   25–26 *omitted P*.

3–4 Genesis xxix. 20, 27, 30.

19–20 There was current among the Jews a belief in an eternal Earthly Paradise, where the Messiah awaited his coming. Dr. Cecil Roth refers me to O. S. Rankin, *Jewish Religious Polemic*, 1956, pp. 188–9.

22 *the Text*: the motto of these verses.

St. Valentine's Day (p. 187)

For the biographical implications of this poem see note to 'The Legacy' and Appendix I, p. 247. For date see note on 'The Latine Epitaph' (p. 241).

Text: P, *1657*.

Variant:
    24 your] as *P*.

To One demanding why *Wine sparkles* (p. 188)

The revised version was copied after the change of hand, that is, in any case after March 1647/8, in *P* (see Introduction, p. 50). The revision had not been made when the copying of *P* began.

Text: *P, 1657*; in *H, M*, and nearer the beginning of *P*, there is the following earlier version, copied with the presentation poems after the earliest collection of 1612–24:

> 'To one that demanded why the Wine sparkles'
> Wee doe not give the Wine a sparkling name
> As if wee meant those sparkes emply'd a Flame;
> The flame lyes in our bloud: And 'tis desire
> Fed by loose appetite setts us on fire.
> Hee that drinkes Wine for health, not for excesse,
> Nor drownes his temper in a drunkennesse,
> Shall feele no more the Wine's unruly fate
> Then if he dranke some chilling Opiate.

Variants:
    16 or] and *P*   21 'Tis] Then *P*.

12 *Portia's Coles*: the story is in Plutarch's life of Brutus.

17 *Tom*: possibly, but not necessarily, May.

26 *Rechabite*: Jeremiah xxxv. 6.

The *Acquittance* (p. 189)

This poem and 'The Forfeiture' have the appearance of private poems, too closely dependent on their occasion to stand alone. They are found only in *1657*, but they may have been already among King's papers when the *MSS*. were copied and deliberately omitted from them.

Text: *1657*.

The *Forfeiture* (p. 189)

Text: *1657*.

Psalme *CXXX paraphrased for an Antheme* (p. 190)

This is the psalm to which Samuel Woodforde refers in *A Paraphrase upon the Psalms of David*, 1667, Preface, sig. c1ᵛ: 'The Bishop's is close, exactly answering the Text, and for that kind of measure, which himself has truly observ'd to be the least graceful of any, very smooth, and roundly expressed; though that Essay of his on the CXXX *Psalm* in Heroick verse, paraphrased for an Anthem, make it to be wish't, he had us'd a like freedom in the rest.' A setting is in MS. Christ Church music 440, fol. 37.

Text: *Psalmes of David* 1651, &c.

APPENDIXES

APPENDIX

ON THE QUESTION OF HENRY KING'S
SECOND MARRIAGE

THE poem 'On two Children dying of one Disease' showed that
there is no need to take as fact in King's biography each situation
implicit in the poems.[1] Amongst those written after 'The Exequy'
are some which, taken literally, provide a story of a second mar-
riage: in 'The Forlorne Hope' (p. 168) he has loved in vain for
ten years; in 'The Change' (p. 186) for twenty; then come the
'Paradox: That it is best for a Young Maid to marry an Old Man'
(p. 180), for which the last line, with its reference to the age fifty-
two, seems to indicate the date 1644, and 'The Short Wooing'
(p. 179), more or less to the same purpose; at last in 'St. Valen-
tine's Day' (p. 187) she has consented to marry him; and in 'The
Legacy' (p. 170) she has become his wife, and he writes for her
of his own death. The dates suggested by the positions of these
poems in the manuscripts are very nearly compatible with such
a sequence: 'The Forlorne Hope', 1633–8; 'St. Valentine's Day',
after March 1647/8. The exception is 'The Legacy', which should
be the last, but which belongs in the manuscripts to the 1636–8
group. If, outside the poems, there were evidence of a second
marriage this discrepancy would argue against the dating which
I have thought the manuscripts indicated. But no such evidence
has been produced. The poems are more likely (as Saintsbury,[2]
disagreeing with Mason,[3] thought) to rest on a foundation of
possibility, but not of fact: their concern is the imagined outcome
of existing circumstance. Even the consideration of marriage with
a woman younger than himself must for King have raised the
question of her early widowhood; and this imagined 'cross' was
rather extravagantly 'beguiled' in the fifth verse of 'The Legacy':

> If now to my cold Hearse Thou deigne to bring
> Some melting Sighes as thy last Offering,

[1] Cf. p. 10 above.

[2] *Minor Poets of the Caroline Period*, iii, 1921, pp. 180–1.

[3] 'Life and Works of Henry King', *Transactions of the Connecticut Academy of Arts and Sciences*, xviii, 1913, pp. 238–9.

My peacefull Exequyes are crown'd. Nor shall
I ask more honour at my Funerall.
  Thou wilt more richly balme mee with thy Teares
  Then all the Narde fragrant Arabia beares.

Mason's argument for a second marriage was partly based on
his attribution to Henry King of the poem 'Wishes to my sonne
John, for this new, and all succeeding yeares: Jan. 1. 1630[/1]':
'if one or two details be emended, this piece may be unhesitatingly
assigned to King'.[1] A detail on which Mason did not comment was
in the lines

> As 'twas thy Grandsires choice, and mine
> maist thou attaine John the divine
> chief of thy Titles:

the point of this is surely that the writer's name was John. From
a reference in this poem to a wife then alive,

> A Wife
> I wish thee, such as is thy Sires,

Mason dated the second marriage of Henry King early in 1630.[2]
But no emendation of detail is needed if the poem is attributed
to John, whose eldest son was given the name of his father and
grandfather, and whose younger children (see p. 250) were born
1620–3.

---

[1] *Poems*, 1914, p. 223; 'Life', 1913 (see previous note), p. 286.
[2] 'Life', p. 239; cf. *Sparrow*, pp. 165 and 178.

APPENDIX II

FURTHER NOTES ON THE CANON

(i) *English Poems of John King* (*1595–1639*)

MASON's ascription of poems in Bodl. MS. Rawl. D. 317 to Henry King was based on his failure to distinguish between the hands of Henry King and his brother John, and the unfounded belief that B.M. MS. Harl. 6917, where the same poems are found again, was 'chiefly devoted to Henry King's own work'. The poems in question are:

'Upon the untimely death of J.K. first borne of H.K.', fol. 175.
'The Complaint', 'Fond hapless man . . .', fol. 161.
'On his Shadow', fol. 173.

With these belong
'I love and am not lov'd again', MS. Rawl. D. 398, fol. 160.
'An Epitaph upon Dr. Don', MS. Rawl. D. 317, fol. 158.
'Great Moderator of the starry sky', MS. Rawl. D. 317, fol. 147.

Of these six, the first, erroneously said to be 'signed' in the manuscripts, was printed by Mason as certainly Henry King's; the second and third were printed among 'Doubtful Poems'; Dr. Simpson added the others in 'The Bodleian Manuscripts of Henry King' (*B.Q.R.* v, 1926–9, pp. 324–40), on which he later commented in 'John and Henry King: A Correction' (*B.L.R.* iv, 1952–3, pp. 208–9), where all six were given to John. All of them are in his hand, and some have the appearance of author's drafts. Mason had also printed as Henry King's, 'Wishes to my sonne John, for this new, and all succeeding yeares: Jan. 1. 1630' from MS. Harl. 6917. Reason to think that this last is John King's was mentioned in Appendix I. In 'I love and am not lov'd again' there are lines to connect the verses with John King's courtship of the widow Mary Barron (her will is printed in J. J. Muskett, *Suffolk Manorial Families*, ii, 1908, p. 299):

> My Fortune's ample: and Content
> A Joynture never can bee spent.
> But did I graspe the Indian Ore;
> Or all the wealthy Ormus store;

Or what between the Center lyes,
And the vast Circle of the Skyes;
I should not count my Purchase deer,
To make a Baron a King's Peer.

All these poems are found in Thomas Manne's notebook (cf. p. 56 above) and in B.M. MS. Harl. 6917–18 (p. 57 above), with others which should probably be ascribed to John King. In *Harl.* three poems on the death of Henry's wife are ascribed to 'Dr. John King':

'A Letter to his most loving Brother H.K. upon the death of his Late Wife',

'Upon a Ringe bequeathed as a Legacy from my loved sister Mrs. A:K:',

'Upon the Candle-Stick she gave mee'.

Probably an appended 'Epitaph', not ascribed, belongs with these:

'Reade, 'twas a Berkley . . .'.

These poems were copied at the beginning of *TM*, with Henry King's 'Exequy'.

Later in *TM*, towards the end of Manne's own writing, comes an 'Epitaph upon Dorothee King', also in *Harl.* (6918, fol. 8ᵛ); to which was added by a different hand an 'Epitaph upon William King', not found in *Harl.* Both these epitaphs were on brasses at Windsor, of which rubbings are in the British Museum, MSS. Add. AAA and CCC: from these it appears that Dorothy, daughter of John and Mary King, died 18 October 1630, aged eight months; and William, their second son, 22 November 1633, aged ten weeks. John King was a canon of Windsor from 1625 till his death early in 1639.

With these poems, which are probably, but not certainly, John King's work, are found in *TM* and in *Harl.* three on the death of Bishop John:

'Here lyes (unless some dare belye . . .',

'Upon the Day of his Death', 'That sacred Friday . . .',

'Epitaph': 'No pyramis, nor guilded Elogie . . .'.

The 'Epitaph' differs from the one in the younger John's hand in

MS. Rawl. D. 317, quoted in the notes to Henry's verses, p. 242, and the authorship of all these unascribed poems is uncertain.

A poem on the death of Mrs. Anne Isles, wife of Thomas Isles, Canon of Christ Church 1622–48, is plausibly subscribed 'J.K.', but is not in John's hand, in MS. Rawl. D. 398, fol. 177:

> Wee envy not thy Triumph cruell Death.

I have not found the date of Mrs. Isles's death, and I do not know to which brother first belonged the idea of the line which Henry used on the death of Lady Anne Rich, 24 August 1638, 'I envy not thy mortall triumphes, Death'.

(ii) *Other Poems attributed to Henry King*

'A Contemplation on Flowers': 'Brave flowers, that I could gallant it like you', attributed to H. Kinge, perhaps by confusion with 'The Pink', in MS. Harl. 6917, fol. 105ᵛ; cf. pp. 57–58 above.

'Elegy on Gustavus Adolphus': 'Brave Prince! although thy fate seeme yet too strange', attributed to 'Dr. Hen: King', Bodl. MS. Malone 21, fol. 7, printed without ascription in the third part of *The Swedish Intelligencer*, 1633. Probably confused with 'Like a cold fatall sweat'.

Translation from Posidippus, 'The world's a bubble', attributed in Bodl. MS. Don. d. 58 to 'Dr. King before his death'. In 'An Elegy Occasioned by Sicknesse', l. 94, King had quoted from this poem the last line, 'Not to be Borne, or being Borne, to Dy'. Cf. Introduction, p. 11, and note.

'Farewell ye gilded follies', doubtfully attributed by Izaak Walton to Sir Henry Wotton in *The Compleat Angler*, 1661; in manuscripts it is given sometimes to Donne, sometimes to Sir Kenelm Digby, and in British Museum MSS. Harl. 6057 and Egerton 2725 it is attributed to Dr. King. Cf. *Sparrow*, p. 160.

In the *Bodleian Quarterly Record*, i, 1914–16, p. 233, Imogen Guiney suggested King as a possible author of a poem written in a copy of *Eikon Basilike*, 1648, beginning 'Couldst thou before thy death have giv'n what we . . .', but one line, 'Our Bodley's shelves will now be full', seems to show that the writer was still at Oxford; and though it is typical of Oxford verses of the time, it has no particular likeness to the poems of Henry King.

The author of the first poem in *Obsequies to the memorie of Mr. Edward King*, 1638, was the dead man's brother, another Henry King.

Amongst the funeral prose and verse on the death of the Countess of Leinster at the end of *H* (cf. p. 49 above), is an epitaph printed in *Hannah* as King's, p. 102. Dr. Simpson also was inclined to accept it as his (*B.Q.R.* v, 1926-9, pp. 325-6); but it is in-expert in a way that King, by this date, was not: it is abrupt in its transitions, and over-ingenious; and it contains, what he hardly ever used even in less formal pieces, a double rhyme (rather/father):

> Sleepe Pretious Ashes, in thy sacred Urne
> From Death and Grave til'th last Trump sounds Returne
> Meane while imbalm'd in Vertues. Joseph's Tombe
> Were fitter for Thee, then the Earth's darke womb.
> Cease Frends to weepe shee's but asleep not Dead
> Chang'd from her Husband's, to her Mother's Bed
> Or from his Bosome, into Abram's rather
> Where now shee rests. Blest Soule in such a Father
> Thus Death hath donne his Best, and worst. His Best
> In sending vertue to her place of Rest
> His worst in leaving Him, as Dead. In Life
> Whose cheefest Joyes were in his dearest Wife.

(iii) *Poems of King's attributed to others*

'To his unconstant Freind' and 'The Surrender' were attributed in British Museum MS. Harl. 6057 to 'Th: Ca:' and 'T.Car', and were printed by W. Carew Hazlitt in *Poems of Thomas Carew*, 1870.

'My Midd-night Meditation' was often attributed in manuscript miscellanies to Dr. John King; see note, p. 229.

'Sic Vita' was printed in *Poems of Francis Beaumont*, 1640, and second edition 1653; see Appendix III.

'An Epitaph on . . . Richard Earle of Dorset' was printed in *Certain Elegant Poems by Dr. Corbet*, 1647; see note, p. 197.

'The Defence' and 'Dry those fair . . .' were included by the younger John Donne in *Poems of Pembroke and Ruddier*, 1660.

'Tell me you stars' was copied next to Sir Simeon Steward's 'Fairy King' in British Museum Add. MS. 11511, and attributed to him.

'The Pink' was denied in their *corrigenda* by the printers of 1657; see note, p. 234.

The Elegy on Gustavus Adolphus was printed in *Works of William Drummond of Hawthornden* 'from the Author's Original Copies', 1711 ('Poems', p. 54), presumably from a copy found amongst Drummond's papers.

The 'Blackmore' poems were printed by A. B. Grosart in *Works of Sir John Davies*, 1869, i. 469.

(iv) *Fragments*

Among the King papers in Bodl. MSS. Rawl. D. 317 and 397–9 are the following scraps, copied in Henry King's hand, and possibly his own composition:

> Let Faux his Powder-plot amaze nomore;
> Since one Breath blew the Howse out of the Doore.
> I need not bid you wonder (Times to come!)
> A Souldier spake, A Parlament was Dumbe.
> Silenc'd It was Brave Generall by Thee:
> Well may'st Thou boast of Christian Libertye;
> For sure Christ's Pow'er did never more Increase,
> Then when He made the Devills hold their Peace.
>   (Rawl. D. 398, fol. 176*.)

> A Battaile amongst the ᵃBees
> Shall happen betwixt Two ᵇTrees:
> The Loss shall be full ᶜThree
> But ᵈSixe shall give the Remedye.
>   When all This is come and gone
>   Then Lyon and Dragon set up agen.
>   (Rawl. D. 397, fol. 317; Rawl. D. 317, fol. 211ᵛ.)

ᵃ Nasebe, Buckbe, Rugbe, Coldashbe, Holdenbe, Kilsbe, Berbe, Thornbe with other Parishes of that termination in those parts [Rawl. D. 397 adds 'Ashbee']
ᵇ Coventree and Daventree
ᶜ Three Kingdomes
ᵈ Suppos'd to be 1656
Time employ'd in turning from sin may fulfill it.

APPENDIX III

'SIC VITA'

'SIC VITA' was printed in *Poems by Francis Beaumont*, 1640, with a parody, 'Like a ring without a finger' on sig. [K3]. The parody is part of a ballad called 'Pretty Comparisons wittily grounded... To the tune of *Like to the Damask Rose*', printed as a broadsheet by Francis Coules, Old-bayly (working 1626–81; cf. H. R. Plomer, *A Dictionary of Booksellers and Printers 1641–1667*, 1907, p. 49), and reprinted in *Roxburghe Ballads*, edited by William Chappell, ii, 1874, p. 12. A setting of 'Like to the damask rose' is found in MS. Christ Church music 87, and was printed in *New Ayres and Dialogues composed for voices and viols*, 1678; in the manuscript a modern pencil note ascribes the tune to Henry Lawes. The words are those printed in Francis Quarles's *Argalus and Parthenia*, 1629, where the first verse is followed by one other, with the subscription (probably applying only to the second verse) 'Hos ego versiculos F. Quarles'. The same first verse is in Simon Wastell's *Microbiblion*, also 1629, in which four verses follow the first. Again in 1629 the tenth edition of *The Crums of Comfort*, printed for Michael Spark, included the same verses as Wastell's, with an answer, 'of Mans Resurrection': 'Like to the Seed put in Earths Wombe'. William Browne of Tavistock made one verse, 'Like to a silkworm of one year', from the same images as he used in *Britannia's Pastorals*, iii, song 1, which was dated by F. W. Moorman (*Quellen und Forschungen zur Sprach- und Culturgeschichte*, lxxxi, 1897, p. 15) 1624–8. Strode wrote a pair of stanzas on the same model called 'Song of Death and the Resurrection': 'Like to the rowling of an Eye' (autograph MS. Corpus Christi College, Oxford, 325, fol. 64ᵛ). Another parody, often attributed to Corbet in manuscripts, began 'Like to the silent tone of unspoke speeches', and was first printed in *Wits Recreations*, 1641, sig. Y4ᵛ.

A much earlier poem of the kind was printed by H. Huth in *Inedited Poetical Miscellanies*, 1870, from a manuscript which he said 'seems to have formed at one time the common-place book of the celebrated Gabriel Harvey'. The poem is headed 'A View or Spectacle of Vanity. 1584', and includes these lines:

> Muse well on Caesar, and Behould him Dust: his Lyfe a Glasse:
> A glas, that breaks: A stream, that runnes: A breath, that straight
>   doth passe:
> His lively breath is spent: his flowing stream is ebd away:
> His brittel glas is broken quyte: his flower did soon decay.[1]

In the second edition of *Poems by Francis Beaumont*, 1653, there was added 'A Description of Love', earlier printed in *Bosworth-field with other poems by Sir John Beaumont*, 1629, p. 99, which seems to contain in its last verse an allusion to poems of the 'Sic Vita' kind:

> These lines I write not, to remove
> United soules from serious love:
> The best attempts by mortals made
> Reflect on things which quickly fade;
> Yet never will I men perswade
> To leave affections, where may shine
> Impressions of the Love divine.

The model for the seventeenth-century attempts seems to have been the one verse, 'Like to the damask rose', the best known of the kind, whoever wrote it. It is recorded as having been found on a tombstone 'In Wandsworth Burying Ground Surry' (Bodl. MS. Top. gen. e. 32, fol. 74). King's poem (my reason for not doubting it to be his comes in the note on text, p. 53 above) is probably original in detail only: his orderly progress of pairs of images, from air, from earth, and from water, is unique.

---

[1] Huth appears to have printed poems from a collection of transcripts owned by F. W. Cosens, now Bodl. MS. Firth d. 7, from fol. 54 of which (to escape Huth's modernization) the quotation above is taken.

INDEXES

INDEX OF FIRST LINES OF POEMS

INDEX OF FIRST LINES

INDEX OF FIRST LINES

INDEX TO INTRODUCTION AND NOTES